Prescription for an Ailing World

Prescription for an Ailing World

WAYNE ALLEN

WIPF & STOCK · Eugene, Oregon

PRESCRIPTION FOR AN AILING WORLD

Copyright © 2017 Wayne Allen. All rights reserved. Except for brief quotations in critical publications or reviews, no part of this book may be reproduced in any manner without prior written permission from the publisher. Write: Permissions, Wipf and Stock Publishers, 199 W. 8th Ave., Suite 3, Eugene, OR 97401.

Wipf & Stock
An Imprint of Wipf and Stock Publishers
199 W. 8th Ave., Suite 3
Eugene, OR 97401

www.wipfandstock.com

PAPERBACK ISBN: 978-1-5326-1566-5
HARDCOVER ISBN: 978-1-5326-1568-9
EBOOK ISBN: 978-1-5326-1567-2

Manufactured in the U.S.A.   NOVEMBER 16, 2017

All biblical quotations unless otherwise indicated are taken from Tanakh: The Holy Scriptures: The New JPS Translation According to the Traditional Hebrew Text

To Patricia Claire,
whose life and conduct exemplifies
compassion, kindness, and generosity

Contents

Preface | ix
Acknowledgments | xi

Introduction   Is the World Getting Better? | 1
Chapter One   The Human Condition | 10
Chapter Two   The Four R's | 40
Chapter Three   The Three H's | 87
Chapter Four   The Two A's | 113
Chapter Five   The Big "I" | 127
Chapter Six   Unfinished Business—How to Read the Bible | 146
Chapter Seven   The Prescription | 164

Bibliography | 171
Author Index | 177
Subject Index | 181
Ancient Document Index | 187

Preface

AN OLD JEWISH FOLK story tells of the legendary Wise Men of Chelm—a mythical town whose residents are far from wise—who send a delegation to the big city with a princely sum of money in order to purchase justice. The emissaries were quickly identified as easy marks and were taken for all their money in exchange for a barrel, reputed to contain justice. Gleefully they return to Chelm eager to report on the outcome of their mission. Upon their arrival they proudly announce that secured in the barrel was the world's justice. After prying open the lid, they discovered that the contents were merely so much rotten fish. The Wise Men concluded that they had seen the justice of the world . . . and it stinks!

There is much that stinks in the world. Rudeness and incivility are the least of it. Injustice, deception, selfishness, violence, indifference are no mere exceptions. They are the rule. But all is not lost. I have seen goodness prevail. And as I have tried to account for these countercultural acts of nobility, I began to ask what conditions were necessary to allow their proliferation and what values would lead to their predominance? I concluded that the very same values that characterize what the ancient Greeks called "arete" (moral excellence) are embedded in the Jewish tradition that I have been teaching for more than forty years. However, this is not a religious tract. I am not advocating any religious belief. I am advocating good conduct. Serendipitously, the good conduct I advocate seems to be well entrenched in the patterns of Jewish behavior to which I refer.

This book is the outcome of a lifetime of observation and study. My hope is that readers are convinced that the world in which we live could be improved if people in this world improve. And that people can improve through a training regimen based on ten essential values.

Acknowledgments

I have learned much from my teachers and more from my colleagues
but I have learned more than both from my students.

B. TA'ANIT 7A

WITH SPECIAL APPRECIATION OF Harvey and Heather Shapero whose encouragement and support have been essential to the publication of this book.

Introduction

Is the World Getting Better?

ON FRIDAY, JUNE 11, 1897, a certain Reverend Doctor Clifford spoke to a reportedly large congregation in Melbourne, Australia. His lecture topic—"Is the World Getting Better?"—surely struck a chord since a review of his lecture was published on the front page of the local Hobart, Tasmania, newspaper, the *Mercury*, the very next day.[1] He was reported to have affirmed "with a clear conscience" that the world is indeed getting better, citing as proof the spread of education, a decrease in public drunkenness, better working conditions for the masses, better nutrition, better housing, and an increased civility in political discourse.

Almost twenty-seven years later, a newspaper panel consisting of a cross section of Melbourne's elite came to the opposite conclusion. Answering the editorial question "Is the World Getting Better?"[2] an experienced pedagogue fulminated against the deficiencies of public education. A respected jurist bemoaned the statistical increase in the number of marriages ending in divorce and "the alarming disregard of law by bootleggers, yegg-men, robbers, and murderers; the shocking violence committed continually against persons and property in the best organised governments of the world, prove the failure of civilisation entirely to suppress crime and to establish an ideal citizenship." A medical doctor, while acknowledging the increase in life expectancy and decrease in infant mortality primarily as a result of better hygiene, advances in medicine and surgical techniques, points to a 250 percent increase in arteriosclerosis and a 500 percent

---

1. Clifford, "Is the World Getting Better?," 1.
2. *The Age*, "Is the World Getting Better?," November 22, 1924.

increase in cancer over the last fifty years. Worse still, "physically degenerating habits" including the use of coffee and tea, the overuse of tobacco and the abuse of alcohol and narcotics were, in his opinion, leading the human race to its ultimate ruin.

It is hard to imagine that Melbourne had deteriorated so precipitously in a single generation . . . and for good reason. Although there were several years of economic depression, the general trend during the first three decades of the twentieth century was toward growth, expansion, and civic improvements. In fact, the answer to the question "Is the world getting better?" had nothing to do with Melbourne specifically but what factors might be adduced to determine the answer.

A century later and a hemisphere away, the same debate continues. American pundits who see the world getting better point to statistics. Extreme poverty is falling. In 1981, 53 percent of the world lived on less than $1.25 per day. In 2011, a mere 17 percent must do so. Hunger rates all over the world are falling. Child labor is declining. Life expectancy is rising. Neonatal mortality has declined by 50 percent since 1990. War is on the decline. Political scientist Dr. John Mueller confidently proclaimed in 2004: "War is merely an idea. Unlike breathing, eating, or sex, war is not something that is somehow required by the human condition or by forces of history. Accordingly, war can shrivel up and disappear, and it seems to be in the process of doing so."[3] Homicide rates are falling. More people are living under democracy than at any time in human history. Literacy rates are up. And infant mortality has declined by 50 percent since 1990. Indeed, measured by health and wealth, the last two hundred years have been marked by extraordinary progress.

Yet the statistics do not go without challenge. For example, while fewer people are living on less than $1.25 per day, the World Bank reports that in 2011 two billion people are still living on less than $2.00 per day. War is not really in decline (see chapter 1) and to the victims of the ongoing wars in Syria, Iraq, the Congo, Nigeria, Ukraine war is not "merely an idea." In general, homicide rates are falling in the United States and in Europe but are increasing dramatically in Africa and in South America. While more people are living in countries where elections are held, this does not mean that democracy is spreading. In fact, the percentage of people in the world living under full democracy—including freedom of the press, free speech, freedom of religion, and an independent judiciary—is relatively small and

---

3. Mueller, *Remnants of War*, 2. See also pp. 24–38 and 161–82.

static. The International Human Suffering Index created in 1987 by the Washington, DC–based Population Crisis Committee shows a worldwide decline in suffering over time. Yet the Human Misery Index shows that the 2011 rate in the United States is the highest it has been since 1983. In trying to resolve the statistical contradictions, University of Minnesota sociologist and professor Dr. Ronald E. Anderson studied the physical, mental, and social aspects of human suffering. In his 2013 book, entitled *Human Suffering and Quality of Life*, he writes: "Global inequality is a major cause of suffering and widens the gap in care. Despite some progress in reduction of suffering, global inequality has been growing steadily for at least two centuries." In other words, the widening gap in global inequality has outpaced the benefits of technological advances so the result is a net increase—not decrease—in human suffering.

The statistics are—at best—ambiguous. But the fact that a substantial number of people believe that the statistics make the case for optimism is attributable to two factors: confirmation bias and the fallacy of equivocation.

First consider the phenomenon of "confirmation bias." When reflecting on a question, psychologists have noted, people tend to look only for evidence that supports their answer and is consistent with their point of view while failing to ensure that there is no contradictory evidence that is inconsistent with their perspective. This tendency is called "confirmation bias" and it is quite common. For example, hockey players (and fans) are notoriously superstitious, particularly in the playoffs. If their team goes on to win a series while they remained unshaven, they will not shave thereafter. They claim that their victory was contingent on the condition of being unshaven. Of course, they fail to consider a host of other factors that might have been at work like additional practice, better scouting, injuries to the opposition's key players, or that other beardless teams might have won their series, too.

In addressing the question "Is the world getting better?" those who are hopeful and optimistic tend to look at the statistics that support their inclination without looking carefully at what the statistics really show. This is not to say that those who do think the world is getting better are a deceptive bunch who selectively filter the sources and cite only those that confirm their thinking (although this can be the case as well). Rather, they fail to fully consider what the evidence actually shows. Thus, in the case of decreasing poverty, trumpeting the decline in the number of people living on less than $1.25 per day as proof that the world is getting better should be vitiated by considering whether living on less than $2.00 per day—the "improvement"—is a fair standard of living.

Second, asking the question "Is the world getting better?" requires answering the prior question "What do you mean by better?" The question may very well be one of socioeconomic progress. Alternatively, the question may be one of moral advancement. Thus the question itself is ambiguous. Logicians refer to using a term with more than one sense in a single argument as an error in clarity of expression. The specific name for this error is the fallacy of equivocation. The word "better" means "improved." But "improved" how? From the standpoint of health and wealth the world does indeed seem to be getting better. But are people actually behaving better, that is, more nobly, more sympathetically, more virtuously? On the first meaning of "better" the answer may be "Yes!" But on the second meaning of "better" the answer is most certainly "No."

Thus the Melbourne jurist interpreted the 1924 crime statistics as a societal and moral failure. Or, as the Reverend Carlyle B. Haynes observes in his ensuing written contribution: "There is a seething, restless discontent working in human hearts the world around today, which seeks to throw off these safeguards of civilisation. Lawlessness, as wide as the world, is in evidence, revealing the working of the natural heart under the veneer of civilisation . . . Take away the veneer of civilisation in any community, take away the incentives to virtue and the restraints against vice which civilisation has established, and there would instantly be a demonstration that the world is not better, but far worse than ever before." He concludes: "The world may be getting better off, but it is *not* getting better."[4]

The error in applying socioeconomic statistics and examples of technological progress to the question of global improvement leads to the fallacious conclusion that the world is getting better. Actually, while people may be living more comfortably, it is not the case that people are living any more decently. People alive today are largely "better off" but certainly not "better."

That people are not "better" does not mean that it must remain so. Aristotle argued that people could be trained to become virtuous. In the first chapter of book 2 of his *Nichomachean Ethics*, Aristotle writes:

> Excellence of character results from habit [ethos], which is in fact the name it has acquired [ethics], the word for "character-trait" being a slight variation of that for habit. This makes it quite clear that

---

4. *The Age*, "Is the World Getting Better?"

> none of the excellences of character comes about in us by nature
> for no natural way of being is changed through habituation.

No one is naturally ethical, says Aristotle, because were this the case, nothing could ever change that fact. The opposite is also true. No one is naturally unethical because if this were the case, all criminals would be incorrigible, rehabilitation would be impossible, and there is no possibility that bad people could ever change. But our experience tells us otherwise. The evidence shows that many people jailed for their crimes become model citizens. The ineluctable conclusion to draw is that some procedure exists than can change a person's conduct. Aristotle identifies this procedure as habit, or, more precisely, habituation. He does not mean habit as a kind of irrepressible vice. He means conditioning. People are conditioned to be good. Aristotle notes the linguistic similarity between the Greek word for "habit" and the Greek word for "excellence of character." Excellence of character can be acquired through following a pattern of good behavior over time.

Conditioning people to become better in the Aristotelian sense, that is, inculcating people with excellence of character, ought to be the single-most important global task. Without a dramatic transformation in human behavior, life as we know it—despite the advances in technology—is at risk of becoming, as philosopher Thomas Hobbes once characterized it, "solitary, poor, nasty, brutish, and short."

As an ordained rabbi and a trained philosopher, I have come to appreciate more and more how the regimen of Judaism serves as the habituation for excellence in character. In fact, in the ensuing chapters I will show how developing excellence of character is the underlying goal of all of Jewish thought and practice. In a world where people are "better off," people still need a treatment program to make them better. Judaism is that treatment program.

Do not misunderstand. I am not saying that human beings are innately and irredeemably evil or congenitally maladjusted. I am saying that were all of humanity a physician's patient, the objective physician could only conclude that the patient is profoundly sick. In fact, the patient continues to worsen. But the patient can be helped. The world—meaning the people who inhabit the world—is ailing. But there is a prescription that, if followed, would offer more than treatment. It would offer a cure. That prescription is Judaism.

Prescription for an Ailing World

I will argue that Judaism is the prescription for an ailing world. This is not to say that everyone needs to convert to Judaism if the world is to recover. To the contrary, Judaism maintains that the ideal is not for all people to become Jewish but for all people to become good. Judaism does not demand sameness but goodness. Accordingly, this book is not a missionizing tract designed to win converts for Judaism. Rather, it offers insights into the principles of Judaism that, if followed, will make the world a morally better and emotionally healthier place.

Arguing that Judaism is the prescription for an ailing world should not be misconstrued as a defense of the ethical conduct of all Jews. To claim that all Jews live by the principles of Judaism is empirically false and patently absurd. Rabbi Bernard Bergman, owner of a chain of New York nursing homes reputed to have provided inadequate care, spent one year in jail and was compelled to repay almost two million dollars following his conviction of Medicaid fraud in 1976. In 1987 Ivan Boesky was convicted of insider trading. The Jewish Theological Seminary of America removed his name from the library he endowed—but kept the money! One of Bill Clinton's last acts as president in 2001 was to pardon financier Marc Rich who fled the United States for Israel after being charged with fifty-one counts of tax evasion totaling $48 million. Lobbyist Jack Abramoff, a professed Orthodox Jew, served forty-three months of a six-year sentence following his 2006 conviction for mail fraud, conspiracy to bribe public officials, and tax evasion. Rabbi Gilles Bernheim, the former Chief Rabbi of France who resigned under pressure, was exposed as a plagiarist in 2013 after having been exposed as fudging his academic credential two years earlier. And Bernie Madoff is still serving a 150-year prison sentence for cheating gullible investors of $65 billion in his pyramid scheme. All that these—and other—malfeasants prove is that there are Jews who fail to follow what Judaism teaches. This is an indictment of human fallibility, not Judaism. That the Bible includes prescribed punishments for wrongdoers assumes that people will err. That the Bible and its interpretations include principles by which to live presumes that people can improve. The objective of the chapters that follow is to convince the reader to appreciate the principles on which Judaism stands rather than focus on the vices for which individual Jews may succumb. And by embracing these principles life can be better.

Further, arguing that Judaism is the prescription for an ailing world should not be misconstrued as a claim that Jews are morally superior to non-Jews. There is no compelling evidence to support such an extravagant claim.⁵

To be sure, Judaism is not very popular these days. In promoting the positive impact of Christianity on Western civilization in his 2006 book *Victory of Reason*, sociologist Rodney Stark effectively denies any contribution of Judaism. Thomas Lackmann's fanciful 2003 book, *Jewrassic Park*, has American Jews returning to Germany as Hollywood monsters to exact their revenge. Portuguese Nobel Laureate Jose Saramago caused a furor in 2003 when he said, among other things, "The Jews endlessly scratch their own wound to keep it bleeding, to make it incurable, and they show it to the world as if it is a banner."⁶ British philosopher and television personality Bryan Magee, in his memoirs, *Confessions of a Philosopher*, published in 1997, writes: "Of all the religions I studied, the one I found least worthy of intellectual respect was Judaism."⁷ Even Jews have been less than enthusiastic about Judaism. In his 1998 book entitled *Naked Pictures of Famous People*, charismatic satirist John Stewart bemoaned Judaism's lack

---

5. Even statistics are indecisive. The *Jerusalem Post* reported on June 26, 2008, that according to a University of Haifa Center for the Study of Crime, Law, and Society, the murder rate has remained low and relatively unchanged in Israel since 1980, registering at 2.37 per 100,000 people in 1980 and declining to 2.29 per 100,000 people in 2006. This is one of the lowest rates in the world. Yet the murder rate alone does not paint a complete picture of morality. The number of Jews in prison populations is also indecisive. A 2011 survey of all inmates in US prisons as reported by chaplains shows the mean religious affiliation as 66% Christian, 9% Muslim, and a mere 1.7% Jewish. But the Jewish population is the same as the pagan population in prisons and both are more than the Buddhist population at 1%. Other surveys show that by far the fewest number of prisoners identify as atheists. Other surveys in Canada and the United Kingdom (*Jewish Chronicle*, May 1, 2017) reveal that the Jewish prison population is increasing. Critics claim that self-reported figures are unreliable. Some prisoners identify as Jewish thinking they will get better food or more privileges. Some identify as Jews to challenge the prison system. Yet, on the other hand, there are Jewish prisoners who do not identify as Jews out of shame. Lee Ellis visited fifty research studies on the religious affiliations of the prison population in the United States and concluded that rather than self-identification, the more reliable correlation is between church attendance and crime rates with the more frequent attendees representing the fewest prisoners. Ellis further concluded that "among the main Western religions, membership in the Jewish religion is associated with lower crime rates" (Ellis, "Religiosity and Criminality," 215, 232). However, this study is more than thirty years old.

6. His remarks were originally published in Spanish in the Madrid daily *El País*, translated by Paul Berman in *The Forward*, and cited by Martin Levin in the *Globe and Mail*, July 6, 2002.

7. Magee, *Confessions of a Philosopher*, 347. He goes on to say that even his Jewish friends claimed there is nothing intellectually worthwhile in Judaism.

of "pizzazz." As a result: "Judaism is no longer able to compete in a free market religious environment." Professor Douglas Rushkoff, in his 2003 book, *Nothing Sacred*, claims that "now, just as humanity finds itself on the brink . . . Judaism has contracted and retreated, rendering itself one of the last places Jews, or anyone, would turn for guidance and support."[8] And in 2009 Professor Trond Adresen of Trondheim University in Norway wrote: "There is something immensely self-satisfied and self-centered at the tribal mentality that is so prevalent among Jews . . . [They] as a whole, are characterized by this mentality . . . It is no less legitimate to say such a thing about Jews in 2008–2009 than it was to make the same point about the Germans around 1938." Collectively, these authors say that Judaism is unimportant, irrelevant, vengeful, self-loathing, intellectually deficient, uninspiring, useless, and woefully tribal.[9] But I will argue that those who hold these unsympathetic views are simply uninformed.[10]

My intention is not to promote Judaism at the expense of any other religion or belief system. It is my view that any religion or system of beliefs that teaches compassion and tolerance and advocates goodness is a worthy religion. To undermine them would be senseless and counterproductive to my project. So I will avoid disparaging comparisons. I will present what I believe to be a fair and accurate depiction of Judaism and let the reader draw his or her own conclusions.

To properly cover every principle that inheres in Judaism would be an immense—and on my view, unnecessary—task. The principles on which I

---

8. Rushkoff, *Nothing Sacred*, 3. He goes on to condemn traditional Judaism (72) as "racist" and "sexist." He further contends that the only way to save Judaism is to radically reinvent it.

9. There is no need for me to include the ranting of those whose views have been given new currency with the recent rise in virulent anti-Semitism. See Efraim Karsh's article, "War against the Jews," in the July 2012 issue of *Israel Affairs*, 319–43, in which he recalls some of the earlier attacks against Judaism, including British Arabist Freya Stark's 1943 comment: "I really can't see that there is any kind of way of dealing with the Zionist question except by a massacre now and then . . . What can we do? It is the ruthless last penny that they [meaning 'Jews'] squeeze out of you that does it . . . the world has chosen to massacre them at intervals, and whose fault is it?" Charles de Gaulle's 1967 claim that Jews are "an elite people, self-assured and domineering," and US General George S. Brown's 1974 claim that Jews "own, you know, the banks in this country, the newspapers, you just look at where the Jewish money is in this country."

10. Alan Wolfe scathingly reviewed Rodney Stark's book in the February 2, 2006, edition of the *New Republic*. For a contrary assessment than that of Stark, see Thomas Cahill's *The Gift of the Jews*. Saramago's comments were widely aired in the media and were roundly—but not universally—condemned.

shall focus are the ones that I believe would make the biggest difference in the improvement of the human condition. Of course, any number of the principles I shall present can be claimed by other religions as ones they would endorse as well. But my contention is not that no other religion except Judaism advocates any of these principles but that no other religion but Judaism inculcates all of these principles and to the same degree. It is to that task that I now turn.

After assessing the nature of the human condition from ancient times to this day (chapter 1), I will proceed to show how ten principles inherent in Judaism aim toward promoting excellence of character. Chapter 2 will focus on four principles beginning with the letter "R." Chapters 3 and 4 respectively will focus on three principles beginning with the letter "H" and two beginning with the letter "A." Chapter 5 has but one principle—integrity—as its exclusive concern. Since I cite a number of biblical passages throughout, I am compelled to defend the use of a religious text that some consider either fictitious or offensive. Therefore, I devote chapter 6 to a consideration of "How to Read the Bible" and show that the Bible is not the bugaboo its critics hold it to be. Finally, I succinctly present the prescription for an ailing world in the last chapter.

Chapter One

The Human Condition

> What is a human being that You should care about him or people that You should take account of them? Yet You have made him a little lower than the angels and crowned him with honor and glory.
>
> PSALM 8:5–6[1]

HUMAN BEINGS ARE LIVING contradictions. We can rise to the heights of the heavens. We can also sink to the depths of depravity that, according to the psalmist's theology, means being unworthy of God's attention. We can distinguish ourselves through great deeds of nobility or through despicable deeds of infamy. And while there are notable examples of the former, it is the profusion and persistence of the latter that calls the goodness of human character into question.

Human beings have always killed. Despite the various attempts by some poets, philosophers, and anthropologists to promote the notion that our earliest human ancestors were peaceful, caring, and cooperative,[2] the

---

1. My translation.

2. The idealized state of nature finds its expression in Plato. In book 3 of his dialogue *Laws*, Plato claims that before civilization "men's isolation prompted them to cherish and love one another." In this natural state "tendencies to violence and crime and feelings of jealousy and envy simply do not arise." But Plato does not claim that these early men were "good," meaning "moral." Rather, by "good" Plato means naïve and artless. Nevertheless, this state of nature is characterized by cooperation and consideration rather than violence.

THE HUMAN CONDITION

evidence is quite the contrary. In 1972, anthropologist W. T. Divale investigated ninety-nine groups of hunter-gatherers from thirty-seven cultures and found that sixty-eight were at war at the time. Twenty more had been at war in the more recent past (five to twenty-five years previously) and all others reported they were engaged in warfare in the distant past. In 1978, anthropologist Carol Ember in her book *Cultural Anthropology* calculated that 90 percent of hunter-gatherer societies are known to engage in warfare and 64 percent wage war at least every two years. Professor Lawrence Keeley, an archaeologist, assembled the data that showed that 60 percent of all male deaths of the indigenous people of South America and New Guinea were the result of intertribal warfare.[3] In fact, the warriors make weapons as damaging as their technology allowed. Attempted genocide, torture, amputations for trophies, and occasional cannibalism of enemy flesh were also part of the culture of war. Harvard archaeologist Steven A. Leblanc presents the evidence from a 10,000-year-old Paleolithic graveyard in Africa that held the remains of 59 people, "at least twenty four of whom showed direct

---

Thomas Hobbes takes a different view. In his *Leviathan*, Hobbes proposes that human nature is characterized by the incessant struggle to gain power over others and to avoid death. In chapter 13 he introduces a hypothetical condition that would exist were there no laws and no law enforcement. Given men's proclivity to domination and self-preservation at all costs, civilized life would be impossible. It would be a war of each man against the other with "continuall feare, and danger of violent death; And the life of man, solitary, poore, nasty, brutish, and short."

Around the same time as Hobbes, the British poet John Dryden proposed a contrasting view, that of the "noble savage" which later finds expression in the works of Rousseau. In his *Social Contract*, Jean-Jacques Rousseau depicts early Man as a "stupid and unimaginative animal." Yet in his *Discourse on Inequality* he puts forward the idea that in the state of nature men are essentially happy. But happy does not mean good. Virtue comes with morality and morality is a function of civilization. Only by leaving the state of nature and becoming a social being with all it entails can a person become truly virtuous. Between that period of savagery and civilization lies a "primitive state" where human beings are "placed by nature at an equal distance from the stupidity of brutes and the pernicious good sense of civilized man." "Nothing can be more gentle than him," writes Rousseau about Man in that transitional state.

3. Keeley, *War Before Civilization*. He explodes what Michael Shermer, *Science of Good and Evil*, calls the "myth of the beautiful people." Jeffrey Moussaieff Masson, *Beasts: What Animals Can Teach Us about Good and Evil*, 45, is inclined to believe that human beings were not always killers and misanthropes. Jared Diamond lends some support to Masson, claiming that human cruelty arose after human beings transitioned from hunter-gatherers to farmers, cf. "Worst Mistake in the Human Race," *Discover*, May, 1987, 64–66. Even if Masson and Diamond are correct in their assessment of human history, there is no going back to this pre-civilized state. It is now in our culture to kill members of our own species.

evidence of violent death."[4] From a site in Utah, LeBlanc discovered the remains of ninety-seven men, women, and children killed violently, shot with darts, stabbed, and bludgeoned. In his book *Before the Dawn*, Nicholas Wade cites the work of Keeley and others and notes that contrary to the anthropologists of the postwar [sic] period, who had artificially and without warrant "pacified the past," the truth is that our prehistoric predecessors and the primitive cultures that survive them were cruel, brutal, and violent. As Leblanc, in his book *Constant Battles*, quips, "anthropologists have searched for peaceful societies much like Diogenes looked for an honest man" and with the same lack of success.

The stories of isolated tribes who never knew of violence are myths: the product of wishful thinking rather than hard evidence. Contrary to Margaret Mead's description of peaceful New Guineans and Samoans, Derek Freeman[5] documented case after case of Samoans who beat and kill their daughters who are found to have engaged in premarital sexual relations and instance after instance of rape and revenge killings. The !Kung San people of the Kalahari desert who Elizabeth Marshall Thomas described as the "harmless people" actually have a murder rate higher than that of American inner cities. Anthropologists learned that sneaking into the murderer's group and executing everybody—men, women, and children—while they slept avenged murder. The so-called "gentle Tasaday" tribe of the Philippines—once reported in the media to have no words for conflict, violence, or weapons—were actually the subject of a hoax to procure them a "homeland" so that Ferdinand Marcos and his corrupt cronies could enjoy exclusive mineral and logging rights.[6]

Civilization has not made human beings any more peaceful. Global Security reports that as of 2015, thirty-seven wars or conflicts resulting in

---

4. Cited by Shermer, "Ignoble Savage," 33.

5. Derek Freeman exposed the perfunctory research and the attitudes that shaped Mead's thinking in his 1983 work, *Margaret Mead and Samoa: The Making and Unmaking of an Anthropological Myth*, well discussed by Michael Shermer in his article "Paradigms in Collison: Margaret Mead's Mistake and What It Has Done to Anthropology."

6. Elizabeth M. Thomas's book *The Harmless People*, describing the !Kung San tribe of the Kalahari desert, first published in 1960, is still available, revised in 1989. Her first visit to the area was in the 1950s. Later researchers came to very different conclusions. See Keeley, *War Before Civilization*. The Tasaday reports first surfaced in 1970 with a National Geographic Society television special and a *New York Times Magazine* article. In 1977, John Nance published a book about the tribe called *The Gentle Tasaday*. Even after information came to light that it was all a hoax, people continued to believe the initial reports. That belief persisted for more than a decade.

167,000 deaths were being fought around the world, some continuing since the 1960s. According to Project Ploughshares, these wars involve about one-third of the world's population. The United Nations defines "major wars" as military conflicts inflicting one thousand battlefield deaths or more per year. In 1965 there were ten such wars. In 2000, there were fifteen, with at least twenty other lesser conflicts ongoing. Warfare has not become the scourge of humanity but its preoccupation.[7]

The World Federalist Association notes that more people have died in violent conflict and wars in the twentieth century than in any previous century and even more have been killed by genocide. A new breed of historian has emerged as a result: "atrocitologists." And their statistics are mind-boggling. Zbigniew Brzezinski counts a "modest" 167–175 million victims of twentieth-century warfare and genocide. In his 2001 *Historical Atlas of the Twentieth Century*, Matthew White counts 188 million victims. M. Cherif Bassonni counts 203 million, with 86 million of the total occurring after the end of the Second World War. Milton Leitenberg counts between 214 and 226 million victims. And in his *Death by Government*, Rudolph J. Rummel counts an astounding 258,327,000 victims. If anything, the advancement of civilization has not reduced the number of humans killed by humans but simply made the killing of humans more efficient. As best as I

---

7. Global Security, the United Nations, and the World Federalist Association all have accessible websites. Bassonni's statistics were reported in the *Chicago Times*, October 25, 1998. Although there seems to be a downward trend in the number of armed conflicts around the world since 1995—Project Ploughshares counts 28 in 2009 and 24 in 2010—most of the world's current conflicts have persisted for at least a decade and few have been finally resolved. That suggests that while there are fewer actual wars, the enmities that caused them are merely momentarily dormant. Violence and warfare are not disappearing any time soon. In his 2014 book entitled *War! What Is It Good For?* Ian Morris argues that on his estimation Stone Age humans had a 10%–20% chance of dying violently compared with 1%–2% in the twentieth century even with two world wars, nuclear weapons, and genocides. He further argues that war is the engine that drives societies to organize into bigger groups with stronger governments which, in turn, raises the costs of using violence to settle problems. Morris also argues that while all animal species—including humans—have a penchant for violence, human beings can transcend biology and figure out ways to rein in violent behavior. Even assuming his statistical analysis is reliable, Morris does not account for extremist ideologies—religious and political—that often trump reason. Anthropologist Yuval Harari, in *Homo Deus: A Brief History of Tomorrow*, shares Morris's optimism. He argues that war—just as famine and plague—is now under control, "transformed from incomprehensible and uncontrollable forces of nature into manageable challenges" (6–7, 19). If there are any compelling grounds for Harari's optimism—and this is disputable—it is only because human beings have begun to accept the teachings of the ancient prophets of Israel.

can tell, there have been only ten days in all of human history without war, violence, and atrocities. Those were the ten days in 1582—from October 4 to October 15—that Pope Gregory XIII deleted from the calendar in order to synchronize the Julian calendar with the solar calendar.

Human beings have always been killers and human beings remain potential killers. Stanley Milgram, a Yale University social psychologist conducted his now famous "shock" experiments in an attempt to determine how an otherwise, intelligent, educated, cultured person could—like the Nazis—torture and even kill other human beings all the while remaining insensitive to their suffering. The experiment he set up was purportedly to test the effect of punishment on memory. In fact, it was an experiment designed to test how far ordinary people might go in harming others. Working in league with Milgram were confederates who posed as "learners" while the test subjects were "teachers." The latter would read a list of paired words to the "learners" and then read only the first word of each pair with the "learner" then supposed to remember the second. If the "learners" made a mistake or couldn't recall, the "teachers"—and the real test subjects—had to administer an electric shock. No actual shock was felt. The "learners" merely pretended to be shocked, with more violent reactions to higher levels. But to the "teachers" it was all real. The degree of electrical shock that could be administered ranged from slight to severe. Milgram's confederates were instructed to intentionally give wrong answers. And Milgram's test subjects were told to increase the level of electric shock for each wrong answer. What Milgram discovered was that 65 percent of his test subjects administered the strongest shock possible; shocks indicated to be dangerous. And all of his subjects administered at least a strong shock. Despite the fact that the "learners" pretended to be in extreme pain and pleaded for the "teachers" to stop, a substantial proportion continued to raise the shock level even to the end.

Stanford University's Philip Zimbardo tested Milgram's results by creating what he called the "Stanford County Jail." In a mock prison set up in the basement of his psychology building, Zimbardo randomly selected students to be either "prisoners" or "guards." Realism demanded that the guards were given sunglasses, whistles, clubs, and cell keys with prisoners in uniforms kept in small cells. Although the experiment was designed to last for two weeks, Zimbardo terminated it after six days. Disturbingly, otherwise normal American undergraduate students in the role of guards manifested cruel and violent behavior.[8] Building on the extant research, social psychologist Roy F. Baumeister, in his 1997 book *Evil: Inside Human Violence and Cruelty*, concludes that all human beings have the potential to be cruel and violent. Alexander Solzhenitsyn expresses that same thought in *The Gulag Archipelago* where he writes:

> If only it were all so simple! If only there were evil people somewhere insidiously committing evil deeds, and it were necessary only to separate them from the rest of us and destroy them. But the line dividing good and evil cuts through the heart of every human being . . . it is after all only because of the ways things worked out that they were executioners and we weren't.

Indeed, Solzhenitsyn's thought was anticipated by an earlier and equally keen observer of human behavior, Mark Twain, who noted: "Of all the animals, man is the only one that is cruel. He is the only one that inflicts pain for the pleasure of doing it. It is a trait that is unknown in the higher animals."

In 2008 Jerry Burger at the University of California–Santa Clara largely reproduced the original Milgram experiment and got the same results. Burger found that twenty-eight of the forty "teachers" were willing to temporarily continue "shocking" an actor who was begging them to stop, complaining that his heart was hurting. Burger also included female "teachers." He discovered that there was no statistical difference between men and women in their willingness to administer "shocks." In fact, women were slightly more compliant.

Two years later, on March 17, 2010, French television broadcast "Le jeu de la mort" (*The Game of Death*) in which contestants were told they were participants in a game-show pilot. During the game, contestants would be expected to administer electric shocks to other contestants who answered questions incorrectly. Of the eighty contestants, sixty-four were

---

8. Stanley Milgram's results were published in his book *Obedience to Authority: An Experimental View*. Zimbardo's description of his confirmation of Milgram appears in two sources: the 1969 edition of the *Nebraska Symposium on Motivation* and in his 1991 book, *The Psychology of Attitude Change and Social Influence*. The Burger experiment was reported in the journal *American Psychologist* (2008). French anthropologist Rene Girard examined the evolution of torture in his 1977 study entitled *Violence and the Sacred*. He contended that administering pain to a designated scapegoat is a unifying factor in society that also allows it to appease otherwise internecine violent instincts. See also Maggie Nelson, *The Art of Cruelty: A Reckoning*, in which she exposes how cruelty suffuses all aspects of society and all echelons, including the cultural elite.

willing to administer what would have been fatal shocks had there been any live electrical connection.

Given this information, it is not surprising to hear that when human beings are not killing one another, they are torturing each other. Amnesty International estimates that between 1998 and 2000 more than 150 governments allowed torture to be carried out in their countries.[9] But it is not merely the pervasiveness of torture that is troubling. It is the fact that cruelty to others has become a source of entertainment. In 1974, Serbian performance artists Marina Abramović gave one performance of her "Rhythm 0" in Naples, Italy. She stood motionless for six hours with a variety of objects set out on a table for audience members to use on her body any way they saw fit. It did not take too long before her clothes were cut off, her body burned, sliced, and mutilated. Only when a man held a loaded gun to her head did some audience members intervene. In the United Kingdom, reality television was taken to new levels of depravity in the 2004 program "Shattered" in which contestants were sleep-deprived for many days and in the 2008 program "Unbreakable" in which contestants underwent various forms of torture. The motto of the show tells it all: "Pain Is Glory, Pain Is Pride, Pain Is Great to Watch." As eighteenth-century François de La Rochefoucauld once cynically said: "Man has an infinite capacity for enduring the suffering of others."

And when human beings are not torturing each other, they exploit one another. People exploit one another for material gain and for sexual favors. In 2001, there were an estimated 27 million slaves in the world: more than at any time in human history. By 2016, that number had grown to 45.8 million according to the Walk Free Foundation's annual global slavery index. In Albania, young girls are lured into the sex trade and trafficked by organized crime rings. Sex slaves are kept in many places throughout the world. In Mauritania Arab-Berbers buy and sell black Africans as inheritable property. (Even though it became illegal to own another person in Mauritania in 2007.) In Brazil, Burma, the Ivory Coast, and the Dominican Republic, young and old are forced into slave labor by the government or by corporations. Even in India—a democratic state—the government estimates that some five million adults and ten million children are bonded in servitude with some children forced to work fourteen hours a day. The

---

9. Information on slavery, forced labor, and indentured servitude are available through www.iabolish.com. The *New York Times*, June 4, 1992, reported on indentured servitude in India.

United Nations International Labor Organization puts the figures considerably higher, estimating between 44 million and 100 million child workers.

Crime in the United States accounts for more death, injuries, and loss of property than all natural disasters combined. According to the Bureau of Justice Statistics of the United States Department of Justice, in 2005, 23 million people were victims of crime. Twenty-two percent of that total—almost five million people—were victims of violent crime. Though the crime rate has been showing significant declines since 1991, some perspective is helpful. In 1991, the US crime rate was 313 percent higher than the 1960 rate. In 1996, a US resident was almost five times more likely to be a victim of crime than in 1960 and almost twice as likely to be a victim of violent crime. According to the US Department of Justice, over half the increase in the prison population since 1995 is due to an increase in the prisoners convicted of violent offenses. More troubling in Canada is that the crime rate among young people aged 12–17, as measured by the total number accused by the police, increased 5 percent in 2003. It was the third gain in the four previous years. And violent crime among youth increased 3 percent, with notable increases in homicide, attempted murder, and assault. Further, while the overall crime rate in Canada has declined from 1998 to 2007, assault with a weapon or causing bodily harm has climbed steadily year after year, posting more than a 32 percent rise over the decade. The FBI estimates that in the year 2009 an estimated 1,318,398 violent crimes occurred in the United States alone. If the same number holds true today, by the time you finish reading this sentence another five Americans will have been murdered, raped, assaulted, or robbed by an armed assailant.[10] And,

---

10. www.disastercenter.com, the US Department of Justice, Bureau of Justice Statistics, and Statistics Canada all publish up-to-date crime statistics. *Maclean's* magazine featured a story on the climbing assault rate in Canada in its August 18, 2008, edition under the title "Less Crime, More Fear." Vigorous debate persists on whether or not crime rates are increasing. Edward Greenspoon and Anthony Doob (*Globe and Mail*, February 22, 2011) insist they are decreasing. This view was shared by Ted Robert Gurr in his "Historical Trends in Violent Crime: A Critical Review of the Evidence," published in *Crime and Justice*. Gurr acknowledges the surges in violent crime in 1850, 1900, and 1960 but argues that these are "historically temporary deviations from the downward trend." In reaction, John Moore (*National Post*, February 23, 2011) contends that any measurable decrease is the result of either selectively interpreting the data or an increase in unreported crime. Much of the argument depends on the period studied. Looking at crime statistics from year to year or over a few years will yield a different result than looking at the statistics over a period of decades. Besides, the statistics are uneven. As *Time* magazine reports on June 15, 2015, after a forty-year decline, homicide rates in New York City are up 15% from 2014 to 2015. Over the same period homicide rates are up 48% in Atlanta, 18% in

perhaps, even more unsettling is the fact that homicide is the third leading cause of death of American children five to fourteen years of age.[11]

Reflecting on the changes he has observed in Canadian society over the last fifty years, Toronto homicide detective Mark Mendelson concludes: "there has been a dramatic decline in the perceived value of a human life."[12]

Chicago, and a phenomenal 82% in St. Louis. In 2016, homicides are up in roughly thirty American cities, with Chicago experiencing a 70% increase in the first quarter alone.

Prior to the recent upswing, the decline in gun violence, according to the *New York Times* (December 12, 20015), has been attributed to the increase of the number of police officers patrolling American streets since 1994, the use of technology in determining high-risk areas and assigning police accordingly, a reduction in alcohol consumption, the elimination of lead in the environment (lead poisoning affects the control areas in the brain), and a thriving economy.

Even accepting as proof the questionable statistics that show a decline in violent crime, what is undeniable is that people continue to harm other people. Helmut Schoeck, *Envy: A Theory of Social Behaviour*, attributes this phenomenon to envy, which he claims lies at the heart of all violence. In the Jewish tradition, the noted Spanish philosopher Rabbi Joseph Albo (1380–1444) suggests that human beings are genetically predisposed to violence. Thus animal sacrifices were required not to placate or feed God, but to redirect human violence from people to animals.

In 1999, former US Secretary of Education William J. Bennett assembled *The Index of Leading Cultural Indicators*, intended to provide an empirical assessment of the social condition of American society. It included a statistical portrait of crime rates over a thirty-year period beginning in 1963. The results showed a 500% increase in violent crime! This study disputes the contention of German sociologist Norbert Elias who, in his 1978 book *The Civilizing Process*, claimed that humanity is evolving into a more pacific species, as well as the contention of Steven Pinker, *The Better Angels of Our Nature*, that violence has, in fact, declined over the centuries. See also anthropologist Neil Whitehead's *Terror and Violence: Anthropological Approaches* and *Violence* that take issue with Pinker's claims. The controversy is certain to persist simply because of the often-conflicting data. For example, according to a June 2012 FBI report, US crime statistics—including violent crimes—are at their lowest point in decades. At the same time, the murder rate in American towns with populations less than ten thousand increased by 18%. And while the overall murder rate declines, the pace of spree-killings is increasing dramatically as Donna Cooper shows in her July 24, 2012, report for the Center for American Progress. And while in December 2014 Statistics Canada reported that the national rate of murder "marks the lowest homicide rate since 1966," the homicide rate in the Caribbean and Latin American has quadrupled since the beginning of the twenty-first century! In 2016 alone, killings in Venezuela have risen to 28,479 (*New York Times*, January 14, 2017). The Tribune News Service notes that the 6 million total homicide victims worldwide from 2000 to 2012 makes it "a more frequent cause of death than all wars combined." What should not be lost in the competing statistical analyses is the fact that human beings have yet to be weaned away from violence and crime.

11. See Susan Hatters Friedman et al., "Child Murder by Mothers: A Critical Analysis of the Current State of Knowledge and a Research Agenda."

12. Detective Mark Mendelson's observation on the decline in the perceived value

The Human Condition

Human beings are callous. By Jessica Williams's accounting in her 2004 book *50 Facts that Should Change the World*, one in five of the world's people live on less that $1.00 per day. According to World Bank Statistics, the total number of people worldwide living on less than $2.00 per day has increased from 2.45 billion to 2.74 billion from 1981–2001 at the same time that collective wealth has grown geometrically. In the year 2004 alone 8.2 million US households showed a net worth of more than one million dollars. This represents a 33 percent increase over the previous year, the highest jump ever. Yet at the same time and for the same year, nearly 35 million Americans live in hungry or "food insecure" households. A survey of twenty-nine major cities found that emergency food requests are up 16 percent and one in five requests for food cannot be filled. An estimated 1.1 million senior adults skip meals because they have no food in the house. The Canadian Council on Social Development reports that 15 percent of all persons in Canada were living in poverty in 1990. By 1999, the proportion increased to 16.2 percent, with 1.3 million children under age 18 living in poverty. Concomitantly, food has never been more available. In July 2015 the United Nations proudly announced that 72 or 129 countries achieved the millennium goal of halving the percentage of hungry citizens. At the same time, however, twenty-four African countries are facing food crises—twice as many as in 1990. In effect, hunger is less a problem of food production and more a problem of food distribution. It seems that while there is much food available, it simply isn't being shared with those who are in need.[13]

Increasing poverty despite increasing wealth can be explained by the simple fact that people are taking more interest in themselves rather than

---

of human life appeared in the December 17, 2012, issue of *Maclean's*, 16, in the article entitled "Getting Away With Murder."

13. Statistics on hunger are published by www.convoyofhope.org and the Canadian Council on Social Development. The increase in US household net worth was reported by TNS and *Time* magazine.

Writing in *Science* magazine, vol. 236, 1987, P. H. Abelson notes that due to improved agricultural techniques, fertilizers, and pesticides, there is "a substantial world surplus of food." Yet, in a paper published by the Worldwatch Institute, no. 64, 1985, W. Chandler in "Investing in Children" notes that "more people than ever before are malnourished." In his recently published book *Three Famines: Starvation and Politics*, Thomas Keneally concludes that in each of the cases of the Irish famine of 1845, the Bengali famine of 1942 and the Ethiopian famine of the 1970s, governmental mismanagement, stereotyping, and ideological constraints were more responsible for the loss of five million lives than the effects of disease or drought.

in others. In their 2009 book, *The Narcissism Epidemic*, W. Keith Campbell and Jean M. Twenge argued that narcissism is on the increase over the last thirty years, especially among young people. Aside from the usual types of surveys that are conducted that prove the point, the lyrics to popular songs seems to support the scientific evidence. Professor Twenge of San Diego State University notes that in the early 1980s love songs were positive and featured two people with shared interests and yearnings (John Lennon's ["Just Like] Staring Over"). Recent songs, however, are about individual desires and personal focus (Fergie's "It's Personal, Myself, and I"; Keri Hilson's "All Eyes on Me when I Walk In").[14] The rise of public sex in England, called "dogging," may also be attributable to narcissism, in this case, this sense that no one else matters but the entangled couple. After all, one's sexual desires need to be satisfied wherever and whenever those desires erupt. Orgies are frequent at highway rest stops, in random yards, in wooded areas, under roadways as well as in public restrooms, and is now a subject of concern to many locals offended by what they see as public displays of what ought to be a private act. And in reflecting on the summer 2011 riots in England, Kelley McParland argues that a society dedicated to equality and social justice has only engendered a sense of entitlement. And when people do not get what they think they deserve, society itself becomes the target. McParland concludes: "If you can be given so much, and still want to destroy things, the fault doesn't lie anywhere but within."[15]

The Vancouver riot of 2011 is instructive. Vancouver is consistently voted one of the most "livable" cities in the world. It enjoys a temperate climate, spectacular scenic views, and boasts a high median income. As in all urban areas, there are pockets of poverty but the average cost of homes in Vancouver approaches $1.2 million. When the Vancouver Canucks lost the seventh and deciding game of the Stanley Cup Hockey Finals to the Boston Bruins, people went wild. Police cars were set afire. Stores were looted. People were hurt. After three hours the police moved in. When the riot ended, it was time to reflect. The first reaction was shock and disbelief. After all, this is Canada: a country where people wait patiently on queues, where everyone is polite, and violence is what happens elsewhere, or so it was thought. The second reaction was to blame a hard core of outside

---

14. The *New York Times* reported on three decades of computer analysis of popular music lyrics in an article by John Tierney, May 8, 2011.

15. Kelly McParland's comment on the riots was published in the *National Post*, August 11, 2011, under the heading: "The welfare state's illegitimate rebels."

anarchists or drunken teens. But journalists ultimately took a different view. Writing for the *Toronto Star* (June 17, 2011), Christopher Hume concludes that the riot "which had no purpose save destruction" is a sign of "malevolent vitality." In other words, human beings can, without warning or thought, erupt into a ravaging mob. In the *National Post* Christine Blatchford was as much disturbed by those who stood by and watched the rioting with amusement, even taking pictures, as she was by the violence. And while the media properly pointed to Robert Mackay who tried to deter the vandals, the fact remains that the mob "fell on him like animals" and beat him mercilessly until another solitary soul intervened. As Cathal Kelly tells the story, "there is nothing in this that is good."[16] If mob violence can erupt in prosperous, Eden-like Vancouver, is the rest of the world inure? Or, to put it differently, it seems that human beings are prone to act without regard to the life or property of other human beings.

The standing of idyllic British Columbia is further undermined by the tragic story of Amanda Todd, stalked and harassed by live and internet bullies for almost four years until she felt compelled to take her own life in October 2012, one short of her sixteenth birthday. As terrible as her suicide was the aftermath. Amanda's indefatigable pursuers sent hateful messages to her Facebook Memorial page. She was as hounded in death as she was in her all-too-short life: a victim of human cruelty in a well-to-do Canadian community.

Human beings lie.[17] As any regular viewer of the American television series *House* would note, patients will lie even when their health and lives

---

16. Cathal Kelly's analysis appeared on the front page of the *Toronto Star* (June 17, 2011). He concludes with the realization that the Vancouver rioting leaves us with only shame and fear. Yet psychologist Bob Carrothers of North Ohio University told the CBC news (as reported in the *Toronto Star*, June 20, 2011) that "it's nothing they should be ashamed of as a city—it happens." The "it" that happens is what is both worrying and depressing.

17. Harvard Professor Sissela Bok's 1978 book, *Lying: Moral Choice in Private and Public Life*, still remains the classic work on the phenomenon, despite the attempts of some recent authors to supplant it. In *The Liar's Tale: A History of Falsehood*, Jeremy Campbell offers a guided tour through some of history's outstanding philosophers and their respective views on truth. Especially noteworthy are the later chapters on how postmodern thinkers have accepted "the death of truth." "Deception," says Robert Feldman in *The Liar In Your Life: The Way to Truthful Relationships*, "is deeply ingrained in our everyday interactions and in our broader culture." And making the case for the danger the palpable increase of incidents of lying presents to contemporary society is James B. Stewart, *Tangled Webs: How False Statements Are Undermining America from Martha Stewart to Bernie Madoff*. James B. Stewart is a Pulitzer Prize-winner for explanatory

are at stake. What ought to disturb viewers is not that Dr. Gregory House takes such a dim view of human nature but that he is always right: people do lie. And lying begins early. In his 2011 book *The Folly of Fools: The Logic of Deceit and Self-Deception in Human Life*, evolutionary biologist Robert Trivers reports that children as young as six months of age show a wide variety of deception, like fake crying, pausing to see if anyone is listening before resuming. By the age of eight months, infants are capable of concealing forbidden activities and distracting parental attention. Trivers also concludes that deceptiveness grows in direct proportion to intelligence.

In the United Kingdom, 70 percent of employers surveyed by Experian in 2007 claimed they discovered serious lying on job applications,[18] far exceeding the 17 percent of liars reported by Powerchex. *USA Today* (May 4, 2016) published the results of the HireRight survey of almost 3,500 human resources professionals. An astounding 88 percent reported finding lies and exaggerations in resumés.

According to an insurance company survey, 26 percent of British motorists lie on their insurance forms. This phenomenon of "application fraud" had increased by 12 percent in 2008 according to a report by the *London Independent*. The *London Times* recently reported a dramatic increase in the number of parents lying about where they live in order to secure a place for their children in a better school. Boston Realtors describe the overstated income on mortgage applications as "Liars' Loans," one of the factors responsible for the 2007 financial crisis.[19] Best estimates suggest that approximately 30 percent of those who use Internet dating sites for singles are actually married.

A 2008 study of 62 Northeastern University students is particularly revealing. Asked for their cumulative grade point average on a questionnaire, almost half the students lied by inflating their grades. At a subsequent interview while participants were connected to lie-detection equipment, researchers noted that none of the liars showed any heightened degree of stress normally associated with lying. In other words, the students were so comfortable lying that no physical signs were measurable. But this is only part of the story. Researchers Gramzow and Willard, now at Harvard,

---

journalism.

18. The UK statistics appear in www.I-resign.com, on the www.insurance.co.uk website, in the *London Times*, March 19, 2008, and on the *London Independent* website.

19. The Boston Realtors article was published on line on May 22, 2008 at www.boston.com/realestate.

rationalized the lies as mere "exaggerations" and explained it as "a statement of [student] aspirations" rather than deception. In other words, the researchers studying lying ended up justifying lying.[20]

That students lie about their grades might be expected. But that the university officials responsible for ensuring academic integrity would lie is not. Yet that is precisely what happened at the Massachusetts Institute of Technology where the dean of admissions who worked at the university for twenty-eight years resigned in April 2007 when it was discovered that she had lied about her credentials; it remains unclear whether she earned any academic degree at all.

When the organized response to Hurricane Katrina in 2005 seemed to be going terribly wrong, reporters for *Time* magazine learned that Michael Brown, director of FEMA, had been appointed to his position after lying on his resume. He did not, as he had claimed, oversee emergency services in Edmond, Oklahoma. He was, in fact, "more like an intern." He was forced to resign three weeks later.

Tom Williams was coaching football at Yale in 2011 when a player sought his advice on whether to play in a big game or interview for a Rhodes scholarship. Citing his personal experience, he advised the player to play in the game. It turns out that Williams neither applied for the scholarship nor had been a candidate to receive it. He resigned amid a university review.

David Edmonson, CEO of the now defunct Radio Shack, claimed he earned degrees in both psychology and theology when he joined the company in 1994. In 2005, when he rose to the top position in the company, reports surfaced that he was never awarded them. He eventually resigned.

Iowa State Senator Mark Chelgren claimed on his website that he held a business degree until NBC News and other media reported in March 2017 that all he earned was a certificate for completing a training program for the Sizzler restaurant chain. Chelgren explained that "apparently a degree and a certificate are different."

---

20. The Gramzow and Willard experiment was reported in the *New York Times*, May 6, 2008. The *New York Times* further reported (January 15, 2012) that Julia Hirschberg, professor of computer science at Columbia University, is programming computers to parse people's words for patterns that gauge whether or not they are honest. Perhaps changes in pitch and pauses will prove to be more useful in lie detection than the methods dismissed by Gramzow and Willard. The very fact that an entire industry of lie detection has blossomed, from the Brain Electrical Oscillation Signature test now legally validated in India to the California-based No Lie MRI, is an indication of the pervasiveness of lying.

Former Republican vice-presidential nominee Paul Ryan, later to become speaker of the House of Representatives, told radio interviewer Hugh Hewitt on August 23, 2012, that he had run a sub-three-hour marathon. Only elite athletes in whose company Ryan would like to be considered—presumably to impress voters—generally register such times. But the running world is a well-networked community that keeps track (excuse the pun) of superior performances. As it turns out, Ryan ran in one marathon in Duluth, Minnesota, when he was twenty-years old. His time was a very credible 4:01:25—a full hour more than he claimed. That so few Americans could enter a marathon, let alone finish, should be impressive enough. But Ryan felt compelled to embellish his athletic performance. It was not a strategy that worked for failed Democratic presidential candidate John Kerry in 2004 when he first claimed to have run the Boston Marathon and then withdrew his claim when journalists were not able to find his name on any list of entrants.

Rampant examples of lying impelled Dan Ariely, a professor of behavior economics, to author *The (Honest) Truth about Dishonesty: How We Lie to Everyone—Especially Ourselves*. Yet his conclusions were based on a variety of social experiments rather than anecdotal information. What he and his fellow researchers found is that everybody has the capacity to be dishonest and almost everyone cheats. That is precisely what disgraced Toronto Mayor Rob Ford claimed on his February 2014 YouTube show. After first denying using illegal drugs and the existence of an incriminating video, and then compelled to admit to it when the video surfaced, he mused: "Why did I lie? I think everybody in the world has lied." Sadly, this statement is probably true.

But more troubling than the lying itself is the tolerance of lying by others. For instance, when Robert Irvine, popular host of the Food Network's *Dinner Impossible* was shown to have lied about his claim to have served US presidents and cooked for the British royal family, he was still retained as host—with a corrected biography. Lying on resumés has become so acceptable that the British Columbia Court of Appeal, as reported in the *National Post*, October 20, 2016 (FP7), has now twice sided with complainants who were fired for lying on the grounds that a dismissal for lying is excessive when the dishonesty is not sufficiently severe.

Donald Trump's 2016 presidential candidacy birthed a growing industry of "fact checkers" who have uncovered an unprecedented pattern of half-truths, exaggerations, and outright falsehoods in his speeches and tweets. As reported in the *Toronto Star* on October 30, 2016, Daniel Dale, a Canadian journalist with no vested interest in the election outcome, has tracked 437 falsehoods within a mere 45 days during the campaign and 490 falsehoods by the campaign's end.[21] But the magnitude of mendacity has not really affected Trump's standing among the electorate or the allegiance of his supporters. Kellyanne Conway, President Trump's senior advisor, defended her boss's claim that "more than a million and half" people attended his inauguration when the photographic evidence and police estimates belied the claim, asserting that Trump's figures were "alternative facts." Telling the truth has all but been replaced with choosing the "facts" that best fit the story the speaker wants to tell.[22]

Under the title "The Brain Adapts to Dishonesty," the *Journal of Nature Neuroscience* (October 2016) published an article by N. Garrett et al. that reveals how negative emotional signals associated with lying decreases as the frequency of lying increases. In other words, the more people lie, the more lying becomes tolerable. Unless effectively governed, humans will lapse into dishonesty. And the consequences are serious. As ethicist Professor Harry Frankfort warns: "A society that is recklessly and persistently remiss in [supporting and encouraging truth] is bound to decline."[23]

Human beings steal. In 2001, *Reader's Digest* conducted a worldwide experiment testing honesty. Eleven hundred wallets were filled with personal items, including the name and local address of the "owner," and up to fifty dollars in cash and left them in various public locations. The goods news is that in Norway and Denmark every single "lost" wallet was returned. But in Germany and Mexico, 80 percent were never to be seen again. On average, 56 percent—just over half—were returned.[24] That

---

21. Dale has continued to monitor President Trump's flirtations with the truth and has tracked thirty-three lies in the first two weeks of his presidency (*Toronto Star*, February 5, 2017). He also counted 14 false statements in a *Time* magazine interview March 22, 2017, discussing President Trump's untruthfulness in the *Toronto Star*, March 24, 2017.

22. "Alternative facts" are an alternative articulation of Orwellian "double-speak." As reported by National Public Radio, January 25, 2017, since Kellyanne Conway invoked this explanation, a spokesman for Signet Classics announced an almost 10,000% increase in sales of George Orwell's 1984. According to Professor Peter McNight, *Globe and Mail*, January 28, 2017, Trump's tortuous relationship with the truth is a product of postmodernism that stresses the absurdity of universal truth. Since people have no way of accessing the world independently of their own perspectives, facts are meaningless. All that is available is interpretation. On this account, then, Conway is absolutely right.

23. Harry G. Frankfort, *On Truth*, 6.

24. The *Reader's Digest* experiment was reported in its April 2001 edition and online

means people are just as likely to keep lost property than return it to the rightful and identifiable owner: hardly an endorsement of human virtue. In February 2010 a massive earthquake struck Chile. Five hundred thousand houses were destroyed. The city of Concepcíon was particularly hard hit and the government did not react quickly to the catastrophe. But for the hundreds of people, according to the press reports, who looted the stores in the aftermath of the disaster, it was not food and water they were after but televisions sets and electronic goods. Some enterprising and ingenious looters used long tubes to siphon off gasoline from underground tanks at a closed gas station. The government had to send in the military to restore order after the looters had picked the stores clean.[25]

Looters in Mexico did not wait for a natural disaster. Andrea Navarro, reported for Bloomberg News, January 5, 2017, that at least 250 stores across seven Mexican states were sacked as a "protest" against a 20 percent rise in gasoline prices.

The July 2011 issue of *Popular Mechanics* reports that an unnamed Hawaiian resort reduced the rate of theft of towels from four thousand per month to 750 per month by installing radio-frequency identification tags on the linen with scanners at the pool entrance. The hotel also applied the same technology to their bed sheets.[26] It is hard to decide whether the worrying feature of this report is the need to use high technology devices to control stealing or the sheer numbers of items stolen.

More distressing still is the fact that contemporary thieves—unlike past criminals who tried to hide their identities—boast about their crimes. In 2011, Rodney Knight Jr. broke into a Washington, DC, home and before making off with the loot he posted a picture of himself with the soon-to-be stolen goods on the victim's son's Facebook page. And in 2012, nineteen-year-old Hannah Sabata posted a YouTube video boasting of her brazen bank robbery. The police quickly arrested her in her Nebraska home. What led to the arrest of members of the Bronx, New York, gang WTG was the social network pictures in which they showed off their guns, flashed wads of cash, and posted threats against their rivals.[27] It is not merely the

---

at www.readersdigest.com.

25. Associated Press reporters Michael Warren and Eva Vergara reported on the looting following the Chilean earthquake of 2010, *Toronto Star*, March 1, 2010.

26. The *Popular Mechanics* report appeared in the "Tech Watch" section of the July 2011 issue, 13.

27. *New York Times* journalist Ian Urbina reported on the brazenness of thieves who post their crimes on social media—and the police who find them—in his article

stupidity of these criminals that is exposed, but their apparent pride of accomplishment. According to a 2013 survey conducted by the International Association of Police Chiefs of 500 American police agencies, more than 80 percent use social media in criminal investigations. When criminals cease to hide their wrongdoing but instead publicize it, law enforcement has an advantage but respect for law is undermined.

Human beings cheat. Toronto-based Ashley-Madison has enjoyed rising success accommodating clients who are looking for assistance "when monogamy becomes monotonous." In less than two years after its launch in 2002, Ashley-Madison had 275,000 members. As of September 2008, Ashley-Madison boasted 2,540,000 registered users. As of July 2015 it claimed to have more than 36 million. And as of October 2016 the number of users has risen to 49 million. According to a 2004 *Newsweek* cover story, "The New Infidelity," 40 percent of married women are cheating on their husbands, almost as many as the 50 percent of married men who are cheating on their wives. One researcher, Kholos Wysocki, claims that the figures are much higher: 68 percent of men and 61 percent of women. Serving the need are American sites Married-match.com and Marriedsecrets.com. Even Yahoo and MSN offer chat rooms for married people who want to "flirt." By April 2009, OnlineBootyCall.com had exceeded by one million the registered clients of Ashley-Madison. But these pale in comparison with AdultFriendFinder.com that registered 32 million users who are seeking hassle-free hookups, meaning no-strings attached and no concern about a member's marital status.[28]

Logic would dictate that those in the public eye would be especially careful to avoid the slightest rumor of infidelity since scandal could irreparably damage their careers. But this is hardly the case. When it comes to affairs of the heart, adults turn into babies: ungovernable desires at one end and no control at the other. Former New York Governor Eliot Spitzer resigned from office in disgrace in 2008 after reports surfaced that he was regularly availing himself of the services of an aspiring singer/escort named Ashley Dupre. It was Spitzer who formerly prosecuted prostitution rings while serving as attorney general.

---

published February 15, 2014.

28. The Ashley-Madison phenomenon was reported by Valerie Gibson in the *Toronto Sun*, August 8, 2004. The SUNY Binghampton study was reported on the front page of the *Toronto Star*, June 17, 2011. Kholos Wysocki's research appeared in a *USA Today* article, "On the Web, a Growing Market for Philanderers," February 14, 2012.

While former Democratic presidential candidate and North Carolina Senator John Edwards was believed to have had a torrid affair with former campaign worker Rielle Hunter, it took months of hounding by the tabloids before Edwards stopped his furious denials and finally admitted to the affair. In early 2010 he further admitted to fathering a child with Hunter. He subsequently divorced his wife, suffering from a re-occurrence of cancer. His political career was all but ended.

When Republican Governor Mark Sanford of South Carolina went missing in 2009, his aides explained that he was hiking the Appalachian Trail. In fact, he was involved in a romantic tryst with Latin American television personality Maria Belen Chapur in Argentina. Sanford's wife served him with divorce papers and the state legislature is trying to impeach him. In 2011, then US Congressman Anthony Weiner first denied he had sent a lewd photograph of himself to a Twitter follower, claiming his account had been hacked. For ten days he reiterated his defense until he finally admitted that he not only had sent the photo but also had six inappropriate relationships over the past three years. He ultimately resigned in disgrace.

Roman Catholic priest Alberto Cutie, nicknamed "Father Oprah" for his relationship advice, was spotted by a reporter for a Mexican tabloid on a Florida beach engaged in sexual intercourse with Ruhama Buni Canellis, a licensed facial specialist and "body wrapper." Father Cutie was stripped of his parish in 2009. He resigned from the Catholic Church, became Episcopalian, and married his lover.

The clean-cut image of golfing billionaire Tiger Woods was soiled by the revelations following his mysterious late-night car crash in December 2009. It now seems that from Rachel Uchitel to Jamiee Grubbs and some porn stars between, Tiger Woods was a serial adulterer. Even before the notorious Tiger Woods scandal broke, comedian Chris Rock observed that "a man is basically as faithful as his options." The fact that human beings cheat is as old as time. But rather than finding ways of overcoming the cheating impulse, human beings have taken to justifying it! One of France's most prominent psychologists, Maryse Vaillant, claims that adultery can actually improve a marriage. In her latest book entitled *Men, Love, Fidelity*, she argues for rehabilitating infidelity as a liberating counterbalance for the suffocation of monogamy. And in a 2011 study published by the Public Library of Science, researchers at the University of New York–Binghampton led by evolutionary biologist Justin Garcia, the longer alleles of a gene identified as DRD4 are likely responsible for sexual misbehavior.

The Human Condition

Cheating extends beyond marital infidelity. No less than the bedroom, the playing field has been subverted by cheating. The scandal of performance enhancing drugs to gain a competitive advantage has resulted in the disqualification of Olympians, the undermining of the Tour de France, and the possible exclusion of star players from baseball's Hall of Fame. But cheating in the unlikeliest of places is what speaks most of its pervasiveness and pull. For instance, Pierre Bayard has written what one must hope is a satire entitled *How to Talk about Books You Haven't Read*. It is a step-by-step guide to bluff one's way through a reading club. Now reading clubs were established to encourage the reading of books and engage a group of like-minded people in discussion and analysis. The expected outcome was to enlarge a person's worldview, to open up new perspectives, to ultimately enhance one's life through the experience. Yet people seem to feel compelled to cheat in an activity that is entirely non-competitive where the only gain is achieved through doing the reading rather than avoiding it. And that a book is written to assist in the deception—assuming that the purchasers will not bluff their way out of reading it too—is mind-boggling.

There is no pastime inure to cheating: not even chess or dog shows. In 2011 the French Chess Federation accused three players of colluding at the 2010 Chess Olympiad in Russia by using coded text messages and a signaling system. The players, who have since appealed their suspension, were banned for five years. This followed after the notorious 2006 world championship match between Vladimir Kramnick of Russia and Veselin Topalov of Bulgaria. Topalov's handlers accused Kramnick of consulting a computer while using the lavatory. The organizers promptly locked the lavatory. Kramnick forfeited the game but refused to continue unless it was unlocked. Kramnick won that battle, and the match. And in August 2013, German International Master Jens Kotainy was caught receiving coded electronic messages on his cell phone even while it was in the "off" position. His remarkable play at the Sparkassen Chess Meeting in Dortmund—easily winning his first seven games including one against a grandmaster—could have been explained as the evolution of genius. But computer expert Kenneth Regan noted that every move conformed to the moves projected by a leading computer program; moves then sent to him electronically.

One of the oldest and most respected organizations for showing dogs is the British Kettle Club. Over the years, owners have tried to boost the chances of their dogs taking away top prizes by using a variety of "treatments" to give the dogs an edge. Hairspray was applied to keep the dogs' hair in place and chalk was applied to make white-haired dogs look whiter. The use of grooming products had become so routine that the club imposed mandatory laboratory testing, disqualifying those animals that had used "banned" substances. But complicating the attempt to eliminate widespread cheating was a group of owners who have—successfully—argued to legalize the banned substances. Their claim is that applying hairspray to a dog's hair is no different that applying hairspray to a beauty pageant contestant's hair. If the latter is allowed, so should the former. Ignore for the moment that the coat of a specific breed of dog is precisely one of the criteria by which the dog is judged, not so the hair of a beauty pageant contestant. What the rebel owners were arguing, in effect, is that cheating is long-established tradition in dog shows and should be accepted. It is not only the fact that cheating is pervasive that should be troubling. It is not even the fact that cheating is being justified. Cheaters have generally justified—or at least attempted to justify—cheating. It is that the public has accepted cheating as normative.

Indeed, researchers in the (growing) field of unethical behavior, see the acceptance of cheating as one of the reasons why academic cheating has become rampant.[29] Rutgers University Professor Donald McCabe explains that with easy Internet access cheating has become much easier. In addition, heightened competition and the pressure to succeed have impelled more students to cheat. Equally important is a relaxed societal reaction to cheating. Cheaters are abetted by a culture lacking clear and consistent boundaries that outlaw cheating as morally wrong. Consider the fact that a Montreal-based online service—unemployedprofessors.com—can even arrange for idle academics to do student-client research "so you can play while we make your papers go away!" As Harvard Professor Howard Gartner puts it, our "ethical muscles have atrophied."

Ironically, it is Harvard University that has experienced one of the latest academic scandals, perhaps the largest case of cheating in the university's

---

29. Curiously, *Time* magazine, July 6, 2015, included the Ethics and Behavior statistics on university cheaters in its "How We Learn" section. The world champion of academic cheating, however, is India. The latest cheating scandal was reported in March 2015 when more than 1000 students were caught cheating and expelled in three days of national examinations. A photograph published in the *Hindustan Times* shows dozens of men climbing up the exterior walls of the testing center to hand answers to students, often under the noses of proctors and sometimes with their collusion. Educators often vie for the posting of test supervisors since it often results in payouts from parents who will resort to bribery to advance their children's future prospects. *New York Times* journalist Richard Perez-Pena has reported extensively on academic cheating. See, for example, his article published September 8, 2012.

The Human Condition

storied history. More than 100 students were under suspicion of cheating on a take-home exam, as reported on August 30, 2012. The journal *Ethics and Behavior* reports that according to a 2015 survey, 82 percent of American college alumni admitted that they cheated during their undergraduate careers. According to the Josephson Institute of Ethics, university cheating should not be unexpected since high school students have already grown accustomed to cheating: 60 percent of high school students surveyed have admitted cheating in the past year. Remarkably, 80 percent of the same students claim their ethical standards are above average!

The problem is worsening. According to the results announced in August 2011, a survey conducted by the Pew Research Center revealed that the more than 1000 university presidents questioned indicated that plagiarism is a growing problem. No wonder that faculty members now must rely on services like turnitin.com to check the originality and honesty of papers submitted by their students.

Human beings deceive. Following the publication of the 2007 book *Love and Consequences*, a memoir of an embattled inner-city childhood in South-Central Los Angeles, a furor erupted when reputed-author Margaret B. Jones was revealed—by her sister—to be, in truth, Margaret Seltzer, raised in a middle-class suburb. The publishers subsequently recalled the book. Internationally honored Somaly Mam jeopardized the foundation established in her name to combat sexual slavery when in May 2014, after an investigation the foundation initiated, the rumors were confirmed that she had fabricated in large part her experiences in the Cambodian sex trade. That same month, a Massachusetts court ordered Misha Defonseca to repay her publisher $22 million when her book *Misha: A Memoir of the Holocaust Years* was determined to be fraudulent. Defonseca joins the ranks of Herman Rosenblat (*Angel at the Fence*) and Benjamin Wilkomirski (*Fragments: Memories of a Wartime Childhood*) whose memoirs were also exposed as fraudulent.

Such "false memoirs" no longer carry any shock value. Authors J. T. LeRoy and James Frey were already caught doing the same thing. And in 2011 Tom MacMaster, a US graduate student living in Scotland, confessed to the fact that he was the real author of the blog site ascribed to a Syrian lesbian Amina Arraf that featured the stolen photograph of Jelena Lecic, an administrator for the Royal College of Physicians. In 2012, thirty-one-year-old journalist and author of *Imagine: How Creativity Works*, Jonah Lehrer, confessed that he had manufactured a quotation attributed to Bob Dylan and recycled passages from his own published work.[30] Apparently, creativity works differently than anyone can honestly imagine.

Taking passages from one's own writing is simply lazy. But taking passages from someone else's work and passing it off as one's own is a writer's most serious sin. Yet it is a sin committed time and time again. High profile cases of journalistic plagiarism go back to 1981 when Janet Cooke was compelled to return the Pulitzer Prize she was awarded when it was discovered that her story published in the *Washington Post* was a fabrication. Star journalist (and lawyer) Stephen Glass was similarly shamed when he was forced to admit that he made up elements of twenty-seven stories he wrote for the *New Republic* and *George* magazine in 1998. Added to the list of "outed" plagiarists are Jayson Blair, Jacke Kelley, Jonah Lehrer, Michael Finkel, and Johan Hari. CNN host and *Time* magazine contributing editor-at-large Fareed Zakaria was one of the latest to be caught and suspended. His *Time* magazine piece on gun control published in August 2012 lifted paragraphs without attribution from Jill Lepore's essay in the April 23, 2012, issue of the *New Yorker*. Zakaria was reinstated after making a public apology.[31] Esteemed columnist Margaret Wente has been called to account for using another writer's words without attribution.

In 2006, publisher Little Brown recalled and destroyed the unsold copies of Kaavya Viswanathan's debut novel, *How Opal Mehta Got Kissed, Got Wild, and Got a Life,* when it discovered that the Harvard student plagiarized passages from others, including Salman Rushdie. Even respected primatologist Jane Goodall, lionized for her work with chimpanzees, was compelled to delay the publication of her book *Seeds of Hope* in March 2013 when the *Washington Post* revealed that entire passages were lifted from various websites including Wikipedia. The statement Goodall issued when the delay was announced included a pledge to ensure that "proper sources are credited." But there was no indication of how to account for these "unintentional errors."

---

30. Fellow journalist Michael C. Moynihan in *Tablet* magazine discovered Jonah Lehrer's confabulation, as reported in *Maclean's* magazine, August 13, 2012.

31. In an interesting twist, *National Post* columnist George Jonas, after examining the articles in question, argued, September 5, 2012, that Fareed Zakaria was not really guilty of plagiarism but admitted to the failing anyway. The "plague of plagiarism"—as he calls it—now demands that journalists abide by a higher standard. As to plagiarism itself, Jonas states that he is aware of only "one person of serious literary reputation" who defended it: Bertolt Brecht. It was Brecht who was reputed to have said that he did not recognize private property in art any more than in commerce.

And while some, like the *Washington Post's* Gene Weingarten, question whether the material published on the website *BuzzFeed* is of journalistic quality, the fact that it does include some serious matters makes the 2014 revelation that reporter/editor Benny Johnson was found to have copied material from others without attribution more than forty-one times troubling. Editor-in-chief Ben Smith promptly fired him. Meanwhile, Agnes Chauveau was accused in November of 2014 of plagiarizing significant passages from *Le Monde* and passing them off as her own in the *Huffington Post*. She denies ever having done so intentionally, admitting only to forgetfulness in citing her sources. She was still suspended as the executive director of the prestigious Sciences Po School of . . . Journalism!

New technology, incidentally, has opened the door to new means of deception. Writing positive comments under a false name to what appears on one's own website has become so pervasive it has acquired its own name: "sock-puppeting." Scott Adams, cartoonist of the popular *Dilbert* comic strip, was caught doing this very thing in 2011 when he posted some disturbing political statements and then reacted to them approvingly under a false name.[32] And in 2013 Rabbi Michael Broyde initially denied and later admitted to posting brief comments favorable to his work using Internet pseudonyms. He subsequently resigned from the Rabbinical Council of America's national Bet Din where he served as an expert on Jewish law.

Michael Jackson, the erstwhile "King of Pop," lost rights to his hit song "You Are Not Alone" when a Belgian court ruled in September 2007 that he plagiarized the work of twin song-writers Eddy and Danny Van Passel. (In 2005, a Belgian judge also found Madonna guilty of plagiarism.) Twenty-nine years earlier, almost to the day, a US court found former Beatle George Harrison guilty of plagiarism. British television psychiatrist and popular columnist Raj Persand was found guilty by the General Medical Council, to have passed off the work of other experts as his own.

Celebrity cases make the news. These cases, however, are not exceptions. Deceit is pervasive, universal, growing, and surfaces at early ages. According to a study of "Academic Dishonesty" recently published by Zoran Ercegovac and John V. Richardson Jr., 58 percent of high school students let others copy their work in 1969. Twenty years later, almost 98 percent did. By 1989, 68 percent of students surveyed admitted to cheating on exams. According to the *Plagiarism Handbook*, a free term paper website run by a

---

32. Damage to Scott Adams's reputation was the subject of a full-page article in *Maclean's*, May 23, 2011.

sixteen-year-old, receives no less than 13,000 hits per day. According to a 2004 *British Medical Journal* report, 25 percent of university students have plagiarized. As chilling as this statistic may be, it pales in comparison to the riots that rocked Bangladesh in May 1990 when 150 were arrested and 100 injured when students took to the streets over the "right to cheat." *Reuters* reported (May 14, 1990) that, dismayed by the expulsion of more than 4,000 students and the suspension of fifty teachers for complicity in cheating on nationwide college entry examinations, the students demanded that the government should allow rigging in examinations as they do in elections! Other protesting students chanted: "The right to cheating is as important as the right to freedom!"

While legal scholars may want to debate whether or not there is a "right" to cheat, students have certainly learned that it is *all right* to cheat. Consider the October 30, 2007, article entitled "When Plagiarism Is Academic" published in the *Guardian*. It reported that plagiarism was rampant among professors. In fact, a University of Minnesota study revealed that one in three scientists have plagiarized. And plagiarized work has been detected in prominent publications: *Nature, Science, Science News, Scientific American,* the *Journal of Information Ethics, Saturday Review of Literature, Business Week, Forbes, Harper's,* the *New Republic,* and the *Wall Street Journal,* among others. Albert Macfarlane calls this phenomenon "a plague of stolen words."[33]

In South Africa, Professor Abde Zegeye, the director of the Institute for Social and Economic Research at the University of Witwatersrand, was ultimately forced from his position when disclosures showed that he had extensively plagiarized over many years. He blamed his assistant. Professor Rene Lafreniere of the University of Calgary retracted a lengthy article that was the product of "cut and paste" plagiarism. The title of his manuscript was "Ethics in Surgical Treatment and Research." On June 11, 2011, Dr. Philip Baker, dean of the Faculty of Medicine at the University of Alberta, inspired the graduates with a stirring convocation address that was shortly discovered to have been largely plagiarized from a convocation address delivered by Dr. Atul Gawande at Stanford University one year earlier. The largely respected prime minister of Canada, Stephen Harper, delivered a foreign policy speech in 2003 that an underling had copied from a speech

---

33. Albert Macfarlane's observation was published in the *National Post*, June 16, 2011, along with his list of offenders. He promises that many of the words that comprise his article were actually written by him!

given by Australian Prime Minister John Howard. And Melania Trump "made plagiarism great again"—to quote the cheeky *Maclean's* magazine report (December 12, 2016)—when she included in her speech to the Republican National Convention of July 2016, several paragraphs lifted almost verbatim from a speech previously given by Michele Obama.

Harper and Trump seemed to have escaped these incidents unscathed. Harper was reelected in 2011 to a majority government. And Trump went on to become First Lady of the United States. Pal Schmitt, the president of Hungary, however, did not fair as well. When two separate investigations showed that his doctoral thesis was copied—almost word for word—from the work of a Bulgarian diplomat and a German professor, Semmelweis University revoked the degree awarded twenty years earlier on March 29, 2012. Schmitt did not deny his plagiarism. Instead, he claimed there was no link between the academic scandal and the ability to perform his largely ceremonial duties. Under public pressure, he nonetheless resigned a few days later. Similarly, in the cases of German Foreign Minister Karl-Theodor zu Guttenberg, who was detected as having plagiarized his doctoral dissertation in 2011, and Silvana Koch-Mehrin, a rising star in European politics, who plagiarized her own, both resigned their positions in disgrace. Guttenberg was stripped of his degree. And in 2014 the *New York Times* exposed US Senator John Walsh of Montana as a plagiarist, estimating that at least one-quarter of his masters thesis on American policy in the Middle East was taken word from word from other works without attribution. In his defense, Walsh admitted to only lifting a "few citations" left out "unintentionally" on account of post-Iraq war trauma.

Deception was taken to a higher (lower?) level when it was revealed in 2008 that the United Nation's Intergovernmental Panel on Climate Change had manipulated the data on global warming and climate change and worked behind the scenes to censor researchers who challenged the accepted view. The results, according to Danish environmentalist Bjorn Lomborg (who believes climate change is all too real) in his 2007 book *Cool It!*, would be the misapplication of funds amounting to forty trillion dollars which would have only a marginal impact on protecting the environment or saving lives.

Even scientists are not beyond deception. As early as 1974, immunologist William Summerlin created a sensation when he claimed to have transplanted tissue from black to white mice when he merely used a felt-tip pen to blacken the fur on white mice. Today, "blackening the mice" is the preferred term used to describe scientific fraud. When a team of researchers in New Zealand in 2009 were unable to reproduce the laboratory results of University of Manitoba researcher Fawzi Razem's data, he confessed to faking the numbers and that he had not, as he claimed, discovered the receptor of a hormone that could help plants better adapt to cold or drought. Razem promptly resigned.[34] And in 2011, Diederik Stapel was suspended from his post at Tilburg University in the Netherlands after three junior researchers blew the whistle on Stapel's scientific fraud, fabricating data in dozens of psychological studies, some of them quite prominent. A university investigation further revealed that two-thirds of the doctoral theses he had supervised were also based on fabricated data. Stapel subsequently admitted his wrongdoing. A Harvard evolutionary psychologist was also forced to resign in 2011 after he was found guilty of eight counts of scientific misconduct. (He is now rumored to be working on a book with the operating title *Evilicious: Our Evolved Taste for Being Bad*.)

Scientific fraud is a growing trend. Dr. Ferric C. Fang, editor-in-chief of the *Journal of Infection and Immunity*, reported in the fall of 2010 that he had discovered that one of his authors, Naoki Mori of Ryukyus University in Japan, had "doctored" six papers, all of which were retracted. Only nine articles had been retracted from this respected scientific journal in the previous forty years. According to Retraction Watch (that such a site exists is damning in itself), since this disclosure, twenty-four other papers published in scientific journals by the same author were retracted. The *Journal of Medical Ethics* cites the PubMed database figures indicating that between 2000 and 2009, 196 articles have been retracted from scientific journals because of fraud or fabrication. The *New York Times* (April 29, 2012) cites Dr. Arturo Casadevall of the Albert Einstein College of Medicine who sees the alarming rise in the number of retractions worldwide as a "symptom of a dysfunctional scientific climate." In fact, it is symptomatic of the human desire to get ahead at any cost. And that cost is to real people, not just to the reputations of scientists of dubious ethical standards.

Capitalizing on the need for academics to secure advancement through publication, some companies like OMICS International based in Hyderabad, India, and formally charged in 2016 by the US Federal Trade Commission with "deceiving academics and researchers about the nature of its publications and hiding publication fees," have charged thousands of

---

34. The disgrace of Fawzi Razem was reported by Jen Skerritt in the *National Post*, August 5, 2009.

dollars to have gibberish published in bogus journals. Revealing the extent of the subterfuge, a New Zealand professor submitted an article on atomic physics using the autocomplete feature on his iPhone. As reported in the *New York Times* (January 14, 2017) the abstract began: "Atomic Physics and I shall not have the same problem with a separate section for a very long way. Nuclear weapons will not have to come out the same day after a long time of the year he added the two sides will have the two leaders to take the same way to bring up to their long ways of the same as they will have been a good place for a good time at home the united front and she is a good place for a good time." The paper was accepted within three hours.

It took a team of lawyers working for a group of women suing Wyeth pharmaceuticals in 2009 for the alleged harm caused by hormones they were taking to discover the pervasive "ghostwriting" in the industry.[35] Drug companies hire firms to write glowing recommendations of their products and the firms, in turn, find doctors to sign off on them. Twenty-six ghostwritten papers were published in eighteen medical journals. Later, a US federal study revealed that the hormone drug carried an increased risk of breast cancer, heart disease, and stroke for menopausal women. That ghostwriting can result in harm has not deterred the expansion of the phenomenon. Houston-based Thewritersforhire.com posts a price between twenty-five to sixty-five thousand dollars for book manuscripts of 250 pages. Quick Delivery Ghostwriters claims they can provide the same service within a shorter time.

And now, there are even scholarly attempts to justify deceit. English Professor Marcus Boon of York University in Toronto has authored a (free and downloadable) book entitled *In Praise of Copying*. He contends that copying remains poorly understood. It is, in his opinion, "as essential part of being human." He points to camouflage in war and in nature and "faking" in sports as illustrative of the positive side to deception. Further, copying, he claims, is the ultimate compliment and a way of disseminating worthy ideas. "What if copying," he asks, "rather than being an aberration, or a mistake or a crime, is a fundamental condition or requirement for anything, human or not, to exist at all?"[36] (A better question to ask is what grade would he give his students if they copied from his book?) Leaving aside the

---

35. Robert Fulford exposed the phenomenon of ghostwriting in his column published by the *National Post*, August 6, 2009.

36. Professor Boon's thesis was also reported as part of an interview in York University's alumni publication, summer 2011.

legal issues of copyright infringements and intellectual property, Professor Boon grapples with what he believes to be an essential feature of human character. If he is correct, the implications are profound and disturbing. If he is wrong, then here is further evidence that deceit has become justifiable and even acceptable.

Reporting in the *New York Times*, Benedict Carey lists a number of scientists who are trying to understand cheating. Dr. Ajnan Chatterjee, a neurologist at the University of Pennsylvania, argues that it is an obsession with fairness that leads people to cheat in the first place. When a person feels victimized, resorting to cheating is not considered a failing but a restoration of fairness. Similarly, the urge to cheat may stem from a sense that in an unfair struggle against those with a decided advantage (e.g., family money, personal connections) cheating is an appropriate remedy. In other words, cheating can be justified. It turns morality on its head. According to this line of reasoning, the more a person asserts moral standards as determinative, the more likely that person will cheat.

Dominance and exploitation, selfishness, lying, and cheating presumably gain people happiness—albeit illicitly. But that is not the case. Human beings are increasingly miserable. Samuel Barondes reported in July 2003 that more than 100 million people around the world take some kind of psychiatric drug. In February 2003 *Time* magazine featured a cover story on "America the Anxious." That same year the United States' National Institute for Mental Health reported that 10 percent of the US population suffers from depressive disorder. The solution was Prozac, heralded by *Newsweek* in March 1990 as the "Promise of Prozac" and championed by *Time* in January 2003 that wondered "If Everyone Were on Prozac." That same month, Prozac was approved for children. But by January 2004 *Time* worried about "Generation Rx" and the long-term effects on children's health. Yet Prozac, Zoloft, Paxil, Effexor, Depakote, and Zyprexa are out-prescribed only by Viagra. Now, according to the Walter Reed Army Institute of Research, one of eight combat soldiers in Iraq (and one in seven in Afghanistan) are being provided with Prozac and other mood regulators, what Mother Jones called in 2003 "weapons of mass elation." Spending on prescription opioids in Canada more than doubled from 1998 to 2007 and prescription-opiate abuse increased by almost 25 percent from 2002 to 2005, according to a 2009 study in the Canadian Journal of Public Health.[37]

---

37. For additional reading on mood-altering drugs, see Elizabeth Wurtzel's *Prozac Nation*, David Healey's 2003 *Let Them Eat Prozac*, J. Phillips's summer 1994 article in

The Human Condition

And while people are more prosperous today than even before, happiness is more elusive. In *50 Facts That Should Change the World*, Jessica Williams notes that more people die each year from suicide than in all the world's armed conflicts. In the United States, more people die by their own hand than are killed by others. In the year 2000, there were almost twice as many suicides than homicides.[38] The Japanese enjoy one of the highest per capita incomes in the world. According to the World Bank, in 1950 the average worker in Japan earned US$1060; in 1980, US$8900; in 1991, US$26,930; and in 1997, US$42,000. In 1991 per capita income in Japan ranked number 3 in the entire world.[39] Although the Japanese economy has faltered in the last decades, the Japanese are still ranked highly. Yet thirty-four thousand Japanese killed themselves in 2007, the second highest total ever.[40] No doubt, there may be many factors accounting for the highest suicide rate in the world, but economic distress is not one of them.

Has the world become better? More than three hundred years ago Jonathan Swift wrote: "I never wonder to see men wicked, but I often wonder to see them not ashamed." The evidence shows little improvement since Swift. Human beings continue to be shamelessly wicked. As Mark Twain observed: "Man is the only animal who blushes . . . or needs to." But improvement is indeed possible: provided that the proper regimen is followed.

Vanity Fair, "Young, Depressed, and Self-Obsessed in America," and *Redbook's* December 1994 feature on "The Drugging of America's Children." Samuel Barondes's report appeared in *Science News*, July 5, 2003, under the title "Better than Prozac."

38. Williams's book, updated in 2007, lists the websites for the sources on child labor, torture, ongoing war, and slavery as well as suicide (257–60). Specific statistics on the US suicide rate are available from the Center for Disease Control.

39. The World Bank publishes statistics on per capita income.

40. *Time* magazine, August 4, 2008.

Chapter Two

The Four R's

> School days, school days, dear old Golden Rule days,
>
> Readin' and 'ritin' and 'rithmetic.
>
> Taught to the tune of a hick'ry stick.
>
> LYRICS BY WILL D. COBB, 1906

I HAVE NEVER QUITE grasped why the basics of elementary education were called the Three "R's": Reading, Writing, and Arithmetic. The last "R" is contracted into a slang-like term; hardly what we would want young minds to adopt as a model for proper composition or conversation. And the second "R" is not an "R" at all. It is a "W." In fact, by calling it an "R" we are really condoning a misspelling; again, hardly a virtue to promote. Nevertheless, the three "R's" they remain: a symbol for fundamentals since the beginning of the twentieth century.

I shall claim that Judaism has fundamentals as well. I will call them the Four "R's": Respect, Restraint, Responsibility, and Reverence for Life. (Note that, in fact, they are actual "R's.") By understanding these fundamentals, we can grasp what the goals and objectives of Judaism are. And by applying these fundamentals, that is, by making them operative in our lives, we can cure an ailing world.

RESPECT

Even for those familiar with the Bible, there is something unusual about a passage that appears in the book of Deuteronomy. According to the Torah, that is, what Jews call the first five books of the Bible—from Genesis to Deuteronomy—soldiers may not cut down fruit trees that may be of use to an enemy during war. This seems rather shortsighted, strategically speaking. An enemy could eat the fruit or use the timber for weapons or defenses or the branches for camouflage. Even so, the Torah (Deut 20:19) asks rhetorically: "Are the trees of the field human to withdraw before you into the besieged city?" Trees are not an enemy, though an enemy might use the trees. Trees cannot take shelter. They remain exposed and at our mercy. And trees are noncombatants. These trees, therefore, make a demand on us. Not only does this passage serve as an important underpinning for Judaism's concern for the environment,[1] it also teaches that respect in Judaism begins with inanimate objects, like trees. Trees, too, are part of God's creation. And trees must be treated with respect.

Respect in Judaism begins with inanimate objects but it surely doesn't end there. The same kind of respect for trees must be shown to animals. The Torah continues. When coming upon a bird's nest and the mother bird is sitting on the eggs of the nestlings, send the mother bird away before taking her eggs or her young (Deut 22:6).[2] Human beings are allowed to take and eat the eggs or the fledglings. That is part of the natural order of life since the time of Noah. But an allowance to use the eggs or the offspring does not absolve us from the responsibility to be mindful of the mother bird's feelings. Take her eggs away but not in a way that ignores what we imagine

---

1. Judaism's concern for the environment is based on the reason given for the first human being to be placed in the garden of Eden, namely, "to till it and to tend it" (Gen 2:16). The Hebrew for "tend" derives from the same root as the word meaning "protect." Hence, the first human being was given the dual task of cultivating the garden and protecting it. It is based on the idea that human beings are the stewards of God's creation that the seventh-century anthology of rabbinic interpretation, Ecclesiastes Rabbah (7:28), imagines God saying to the first man: "See My works, how fine they are! All that I have created has been for your sake; be careful not to destroy my world for if you destroy it, there is no one to restore it after you."

2. The reward for sending away the mother bird is long life, or as the New Jewish Publication Society of America translation puts it: "in order that you may fare well and have a long life" (Deut 22:7), the same as the reward for honoring parents (Deut 5:16): "that you may long endure and fare well."

to be her feelings. The fact that the Torah gives the same reward for respecting one's parents as for respecting a bird's feelings serves to emphasize the point.

It is not just the feelings that we attribute to trees and birds that must be respected; it is the entirety of creation. The Jewish tradition calls this "kavod ha-bri'yot"—respect for all creatures. And the reasoning behind it is solid. If we must treat inanimate objects with respect, and if we must treat lesser creatures (like birds) with respect, then we can and must treat every *person* with respect. First I shall present a rule and then tell a story to illustrate this point.

Those unfamiliar with Jewish practice need to note that three special meals are enjoyed by Jewish families every Sabbath, with the meal on Friday night the most widely observed. Before beginning the meal, a special prayer recognizing the centrality of the Sabbath is recited. The prayer incorporates a blessing over a cup of wine followed by a blessing over two whole loaves of bread. In what appears to be one of the more trivial rabbinic rulings, the Rabbis living about two thousand years ago determined that since bread, considered the staff of life and therefore more important than any other food or beverage, is relegated to the secondary position, it ought to be covered while the prayer and first blessing over wine is recited. We cover the bread so as not to "shame" it. After all, here is the staff of life set aside for the glory of the Sabbath: understandable, but deflating for the bread. Yet why should we worry about the "feelings" of some food we are about to eat?

A story is told about Rabbi Israel Salanter,[3] founder of a nineteenth-century system of ethical teaching. In a strange town one Sabbath, Rabbi Salanter was invited to dine with one of its most respected families. Returning from the synagogue after evening prayers, they all gathered together around the Friday night table. The host, to his horror, noticed that his wife had forgotten to cover the two loaves of bread, in violation of the rabbinical rule. Fearful that Rabbi Salanter would think his household was careless with tradition, the host berated his wife for her forgetfulness. Mortified, she ran to drape a cloth over the bread. When it came time to recite the appropriate prayers, Rabbi Salanter stopped his host and said: "I am not sure that the food in this house is fit to eat. It is a home that worries more about embarrassing bread than embarrassing people." The host, recognizing what

---

3. Alan Morinnis has become the contemporary champion of the Rabbi Israel Salanter and the Mussar Movement. See his *Everyday Holiness: The Jewish Spiritual Path of Mussar*.

he had done, apologized to his wife. And the lesson was well learned: if we worry about the feelings of bread, even the more so we must worry about the feelings of people.

This is not just the opinion of one historical figure. It is an opinion encoded in Judaism's most important commentary on the Torah, the Talmud. Jews hold that there are not just ten commandments, but actually 613.[4] The Ten Commandments that Moses received at Sinai were merely a sampling. With so many commandments it is not surprising that Jewish scholars have wondered if they could be ranked. Are some commandments more important than others? And is there one "most important" commandment? The Talmud records a famous debate between two colleagues in the second century of the Common Era.[5] Rabbi Akiva argued that the most important principle in the entire Torah is contained in the commandment to love your neighbor as yourself (Lev 19:18), a fine and noble sentiment. But his colleague, a teacher named Ben Azzai, argued that the single most important principle in all the Torah is not even a commandment. It is the narrative that human beings were created in the image of God (Gen 5:1). To Ben Azzai, this statement is the underpinning for everything else.

That all people are created in God's image means that all people have the same pedigree. No one is more important than another. Everyone is invested with the same sanctity. And since there is an aspect of the divine in each person, respecting another human being is tantamount to respecting God. As the prophet Malachi (2:10) asks rhetorically: "Have we not all one father? Has not one God created us?" And as the book of Job (13:13, 15) attests: both the slave and the master are born from the same womb. Status is an outcome of politics and economics. Biologically, however, all human beings are equal. Or to put it differently, the way to show our respect for God is by respecting all people since they are created in his image. An

---

4. That there are 613 commandments is first stipulated by Simon ben Azzai (Sifre, Deuteronomy 76, ed. Friedman, 90b) and according to Rabbi Simlai (*b. Makkot* 23b) are divided into 365 negative commandments and 248 positive commandments. The number 365 corresponds to the days of the year and the number 248 corresponds to the parts of the human body (bones and limbs) as the ancients counted them. The inherent idea is that God's will, represented by the 613 commandments, must be fulfilled every day and with the entirety of our physical capacity. It was ninth-century Simon Kayyara who first listed the 613 commandments in his *Halakhot Gedolot*. He was followed by Sa'adia Gaon, Solomon ibn Gabirol and Maimonides.

5. The debate between Rabbi Akiva and ben Azzai is recorded in the Jerusalem Talmud (*y. Nedarim* 9:4). It is the Yalkut Shimoni on Judges 4:4 that affirms that an aspect of the divine inheres in every human being.

early medieval text imagines God himself saying: "I bring heaven and earth to witness that the holy spirit dwells in a non-Jew as well as in a Jew; in a woman as much as a man; and in servants as much as masters." Contemporary teacher and scholar Alan Morinnis puts it this way:

> Honor, respect and dignity are due to each and every human being not because of the greatness of their achievements or how they have behaved, but because they are home to a soul that is inherently holy. Nobody created their own soul; everybody has been gifted with a rarefied essence.[6]

Citing the teachings of Rabbi Chaim of Volozhin, Morinnis concludes: "Honor all people simply because they are the handiwork of God."

Jewish law manifests the notion that all people are the handiwork of God and thus worthy of respect. The Talmud teaches that one may not call another by a derisive nickname, even if others commonly do so and that one should avoid meeting a person at the moment of his disgrace to spare any further embarrassment. Executed criminals, according to the Torah, had to be buried by the end of the day like everyone else since even criminals are people and every person needs to be treated with dignity. Moreover, according to the Torah, after execution criminals were hanged from a pole before burial at the end of the day. The hanging served as a public deterrent. Yet the Talmud adds that even the pole must be buried so no one should see it and recall who was hanged from it. That would be disrespectful. Even enemies had to be respected. Josephus Flavius, a first-century military commander as well as Jewish historian writes: "Let our enemies that fall in battle also be buried; nor let any body lie above ground, or suffer a punishment beyond what justice requires."[7]

---

6. See Alan Morinnis, *Everyday Holiness*, 109. The citation appears in the section captioned "The Map" consisting of eighteen chapters of traits the champions of Mussar considered important to the inner lives of human beings. In particular, the chapters on Honor, Loving-Kindness, and Responsibility are most related to my project. That the divine spirit resides in each and every person regardless of religion, gender, or social status is affirmed in *Tanna d'vei Eliyahu* and cited in the *Yalkut Shimoni* to Judges 4:4.

7. The Talmud (*m. Bava Metzia* 4:10; 58b) teaches that "if a person had repented, no one may say to him 'Remember what you once did' . . . ," since rehashing a person's past can be embarrassing. Rabbi Joseph Karo (Shulhan Arukh, Hoshen Mishpat 228:5) encodes the law as follows: "A person should take care that he not call his friend by a derisive nickname, even if he is used to being called by that name, if his intention is to embarrass him." See also pp. 29–36 on derogatory nicknames in Rabbi Daniel Z. Feldman's *The Right and the Good* that provides an excellent review of how the latest rabbinical authorities have understood this rule. *Pirke Avot* (4:23) includes the teaching

In fact, Judaism is replete with examples of how respect for others is an embedded value. Judaism, like all religions, includes prayer. In Judaism, some prayers are recited aloud, and some are recited silently. Few Jews, however, know why silent prayers were instituted. According to the third-century scholar Rabbi Yohanan, silent prayers were instituted so as not to shame sinners! Since the main prayer in each service used to include a personal confession of sins, the congregation would have heard the litany of transgressions committed by sinners were they reciting the prayer aloud. But even sinners, despite their failings, are people who merit respect. This is an extraordinary concept. Rather than deem sinners the architects of their own destruction, rather than dismiss any concern for the embarrassment of those who got what they deserved, Judaism was willing to alter the very nature of the prayer service in order to protect sinners from shame.[8]

Here is another example, one that Dennis Prager calls the "Storekeeper's Law."[9] The classic Abbott and Costello television show once featured a segment in which three children enter a candy store. The clerk asks the first child what he wants. He says he wants a penny's worth of peppermint candy. The peppermint candies were in a jar on the top shelf of the store. The clerk fetches a ladder, climbs all the way up, retrieves the bottle, weighs out a penny. The clerk then asks the second child what he wants. He says

---

of late second-century Rabbi Shimon ben Elazar: "Strive not to see [your fellow] in the hour of his disgrace." The book of Deuteronomy (21:23) commands that the executed criminal must be taken down and buried by the end of the day "so as not to bring undue indignity to his body" (Rabbi Abraham Bloch, *Book of Jewish Ethical Concepts*, 261). It is the Talmud (*b. Sanhedrin* 45b) that, upon close reading of the Hebrew text, concludes that the pole upon which the executed criminal was suspended had to be buried as well. Josephus mentions that enemies must be treated well on the battlefield, including the burial of their corpses, in his *Antiquities*, bk. 4, ch. 24). Decent treatment of enemies is an earlier biblical concern. A person must help relieve an animal of excess burden even if the animal belongs to an enemy (Exod 23:5).

8. Rabbi Yohanan's take on the origin of silent prayer is recorded in the Talmud (*b. Sotah* 32b). The passage reads: "Surely Rabbi Yohanan has said in the name of Rabbi Shimon bar Yohai: Why was it instituted that the Prayer be recited silently? So as not to put transgressors to shame; as is noted Scripture made no distinction as to the place of a sin-offering or a burnt offering" (based on the *Soncino Edition* translation of the Talmud).

9. The "Storekeeper's Law" is reported in the Talmud (*b. Bava Metzia* 58b): "Just as the law against defrauding applies to buying and selling, it applies to spoken words. A person may not say, 'How much is this thing?' if he does not want to buy it" (based on the translation of *Mishnah*, by Herbert Danby). Dennis Prager calls this "among the most ethically beautiful laws in Judaism" in his essay entitled "Legislating Goodness." It appeared in the October-December 1988 issue of the quarterly journal *Ultimate Issues*, that, sadly, Prager ceased to publish in 1996 after eleven years.

he also wants a penny's worth of peppermint candy. So the clerk, unhappily, fetches the ladder, climbs all the way up, retrieves the jar, weighs out a penny's worth of candy, but, before replacing the jar, turns to the third child and says, "I suppose you want a penny's worth of peppermint candy too." "No, sir," says the third child. So the clerk takes the jar in hand, climbs up the ladder, replaces the jar on the top shelf, climbs down and puts the ladder away. The third child then says: "I want two penny's worth!"

These children were not mean, and they certainly did not intend to put the clerk through so much for so little. They were just, well, children. So the fact that they had little regard for the time and effort of the clerk is understandable. But for those who are not children, such behavior is not acceptable. A storekeeper must be treated respectfully. A storekeeper's time is precious. And anything that we do that takes away from the storekeeper's ability to earn a living is improper, in fact, disrespectful. It suggests that our time is more important than the storekeeper's. Thus the Talmud teaches that one is not permitted to ask the storekeeper the price of an item if he knows he will not purchase it. This does not mean that Talmud precludes comparison-shopping. A person may certainly ask the price of an item from as many stores as necessary to find the best deal. It is only if a person knows that he or she will definitely not buy from that particular store that the rule applies. To deliberately mislead a storekeeper into thinking that you are a potential customer when you are not is disrespectful.

Here is another example. Gratitude for a favor rendered is properly acknowledged with a "Thank you." And the courteous response to "Thank you" is "You are welcome." But the once courteous response has been replaced by the typical "No problem." Ostensibly, "no problem" means that there was no extra effort expended. That sentiment, Judaism argues, would be disrespectful. No favor or service should be minimized by saying "It's only a small matter" (or, "No problem" in today's jargon) because it suggests that the beneficiary was not worth any extra effort. Instead, the service provider ought to respond in such a way to suggest that the service was valuable and that it took some effort to render it, implying that the beneficiary deserved the special treatment. Hence, "You are welcome." It is a matter of respect.[10]

10. "Doing favors for people," says Rabbi Abraham Bloch in *A Book of Jewish Ethical Concepts*, "accomplishes two goals. It renders a useful service by filling an avowed need. It also lifts the morale and builds up the ego of the recipient of the favor. A benefactor should not minimize the value of his service by saying 'It is only a small matter.' On the contrary, by agreeing that the service was valuable and that it took some effort to render

Here is another example. The Torah includes a detailed description of the kinds of sacrifices that were offered when the portable tabernacle and then the Jerusalem temple were extant. Modern readers often gloss over these details since today—absent a temple—they are inoperative. Others may find the entire system of animal sacrifice too gory to contemplate if not outright offensive. But some of the most valuable gems are mined from these overlooked or underappreciated details. Thus, when fowl is offered as a sacrifice, the Torah (Lev 1:17) commands that the officiating priest "shall tear it open by its wings, without severing it." In his commentary on Leviticus, Rabbi Hezekiah ben Manoah explains that the reason for leaving the wings intact is because "[the bird] is small and if it is severed there would be only small pieces which would be unseemly to bring before God."[11] Rabbi Jacob Milgrom, in his extensive modern analysis of the book of Leviticus, concurs.[12] He writes that "its purpose may be to increase the size and give the appearance of a more substantial gift." What needs to be added is that the bird offering was brought by the poor; those who could not afford to bring a cow or sheep or goat. So in deference to the poor who might otherwise be embarrassed, the Torah insists that the bird's wings remain intact. Moreover, since the feathers remained attached to the wings and the entire bird was placed on the altar, this sacrifice would give off a less-than-pleasing smell. Anyone who has smelled singed pinfeathers will attest to this fact. Yet despite the smell of the burning feathers, the slight to the poor would be far more offensive. In order to respect the dignity of even the Israelite with the lowest social status, everyone in the temple had to bear the smell of burning feathers. But that is a small price to pay for giving due respect to all.

Here is another example that comes from the celebration of one of the three main festivals of the Jewish year, what Jews call Sukkot and what others refer to as Tabernacles. One obligation requires Jews to live outdoors

---

it, one raises the esteem of the beneficiary by the implication that he was worthy of it (*Sifre*, Deuteronomy 3:25)." In her book *The Gift of Thanks*, Professor Margaret Visser notes that the German word *danken* (to thank) is related to the word *denken* (to think). Thanks and thinking, are closely related through the fact that when one is given a gift, one is compelled to think about the one who took the trouble to give it. The result is that the recipient feels beholding to the provider. While gratitude is a virtue, Judaism aims at making the recipient feel important, rather than needy. That is the power of respect.

11. *Hazzekuni* (Lemberg, 1859). Rabbi Hezekiah ben Manoah is known as Hizquni. He lived in France during the middle of the thirteenth century.

12. Jacob Milgrom, *Leviticus,* is probably the most illuminating and comprehensive study of the third book of the Torah.

in temporary shelters or booths for the duration of the seven-day festival. Another obligation is to gather together four species of plants and use them during prayers. Many reasons are given for taking these four disparate plant species and bundling them together. My favorite, and perhaps the best known, is offered by an ancient textual commentary.[13] Each one of the four species has a different quality, representative of each kind of Jew. The *etrog*, or citron, has both a pleasing aroma (it smells like a lemon) and an appealing taste, albeit a tart one. Hence, the *etrog* is taken to represent the Jew who is both learned in Torah (suggested by the pleasing aroma) and performs good deeds (suggested by the appealing taste). The *lulav*, or palm frond, has no smell but, when mature, bears dates which have a good taste. Hence, the *lulav* represents the Jew who is learned in Torah but does not act on it. The *hadas*, or myrtle, has a wonderful aroma but no taste. Hence, the *hadas* represents the Jew who, although not learned, still performs good deeds. And the *aravot*, or willows, have neither any smell nor any taste. They represent the Jew who is neither learned nor performs good deeds. Three of the four species represent Jews who are deficient in some way. Yet the Torah commands that those Jews who are partly or even wholly deficient must be "taken together," that is, incorporated into the community. All Jews, no matter their background or qualities or accomplishments must be respected[14] and, therefore, included. Diversity of opinion and behavior must be honored.

Accepting diversity of opinion and behavior is one reason why Judaism has never made proselytizing others an article of faith.[15] To advocate

13. The symbolism of the four species appears in Leviticus Rabbah 30:12. The end of the passage reads as follow: "Says the Holy One, praised be He, let them all be tied together in one bundle and they will atone for one another. If you have done so [says God], then at that instant I am exalted." The Rabbis assert that respect for others exalts God.

14. The Mishnah (*m. Mo'ed Katan* 1:6) teaches that during the intermediate days of the festival of Sukkot or Passover, no preparations may be undertaken for an anticipated burial. The exception is for "an important person." Fourteenth-century Rabbi Obadiah MiBartenuro comments that these days everyone is an important person. In other words, while there may be cultural distinctions based on wealth and power and even achievement, fundamentally all people are of equal merit and must be treated with equal respect.

15. The second-century BCE forced conversion to Judaism of the Idumeans by John Hyrcanus, the Hasmonean ruler of Israel, was an exception. Professor Shaye J. D. Cohen writes in his reliable *From the Maccabees to the Mishnah*, that "there is no evidence for an *organized* Jewish mission to the gentiles, but individuals seem to have engaged in this activity on their own." This does not mean to say that outsiders did not find Judaism attractive on their own. Josephus narrates that the royal house of Adiabene adopted Judaism in the middle of the first century. Among the Roman nobility that converted

changing the religious commitments of others or encourage the acceptance of new religious commitments implies no respect for their choices. The proselytizer assumes that he or she possesses the right answers and the ultimate truth and that the targets of proselytizing are ignorant, stubborn, or worse. Judaism does not proselytize because Judaism affirms that respect for others means acceptance of their choices and opinions even though we may fundamentally disagree. That is what the very word respect implies. It derives from the Latin root meaning "to look at again." Respect entails taking another look at others before shaping an opinion; being open to the fact that we are not always right and others are not always wrong. "Respect" means giving credit and due regard to the opinions of others. That is precisely what any casual reader of the Talmud would note. The Talmud records disputes among rabbis on almost every page. Yet even when the law is settled, contrary opinions are retained and even enshrined. That is the hallmark of every valued judicial system: minority views are not just retained but treasured.

Eighteenth-century Rabbi Jacob Emden was a living example of religious respect. Undoubtedly aware of the all-too-many instances of Christian persecution of Jews and Judaism, he nonetheless offers a paean to Christianity. He writes that he sees Christianity as a theological ally of Judaism bringing an appreciation of monotheism and respect for the Bible to places in the world that Judaism could not reach. He extols Christian clergy for taking up the defense of Judaism against the scurrilous charges of certain extremists. And he praises Christian publishers for printing Jewish books that would otherwise go uncirculated.[16] Rabbi Emden chose to see the good in another tradition and set the standard for later inter-religious dialogue.

Accepting diversity of opinion and behavior is also one reason why Judaism has never condoned the censorship of ideas. Rabbi Samuel ben Meir

---

to Judaism were Fulvia, the wife of a senator serving under the emperor Tiberius and Flavius Clemens, a nephew of the emperor Domitian. And sometime during the eighth century, King Bulan of the Khazars of the Caucasus formally adopted Judaism for his entire realm. Cohen's analysis stands in stark contrast to that of Rabbi David Max Eichhorn who states unequivocally that "Judaism, by its very nature, is, and for a long time actively was, a proselytizing religion" (*Conversion to Judaism*, 3). Cohen's point, however, is irrefutable. That is, any attempts at conversion to Judaism were not due to a concerted effort supported by communal funds and institutions and formally set as a religious objective.

16. Rabbi Jacob Emden's appreciation for Christianity was published as part of his commentary on *Pirke Avot* under the title *Etz Avot*. It appears as part of his explanation of Avot 4:10, p. 41a.

and Rabbi Abraham ibn Ezra were two of the most celebrated Jewish commentators of the Middle Ages. They were also two of the most independent thinkers. Contrary to Jewish practice that holds that all "days" begin the previous evening, Rabbi Samuel ben Meir wrote that a proper reading of the scriptural text would show otherwise. Since the sun was not yet created, in Genesis 1:5 "evening" and "morning" could only signify the end of the period of light called "day." Divine creativity resumed with the renewal of light. Accordingly, "day" begins with sunrise. And contrary to the standard view that the entire Torah as we read it today was given by God to Moses at Sinai, Ibn Ezra suggests that some editing was done subsequent to Sinai.[17] These positions are both radical and controversial yet both these commentaries continue to be printed on the pages of every standard explicated Torah text published today. Their opinions have been challenged and rationalized, but never silenced. In fact, their opinions have been preserved and continue to be studied.

17. The book of Deuteronomy begins with the verse "These are the words which Moses spoke unto all Israel beyond the Jordan." The phrase "beyond the Jordan" refers to the land to the east of the Jordan River. Thus the verse speaks from the perspective of someone already standing in Israel. But in Moses' day the Israelites had not yet crossed over and entered into Israel. Ibn Ezra's comments to Deut 1:2 are cryptic: "If you know the secret of the twelve, and of 'And Moses wrote,' and of 'And the Canaanite was then in the land,' and of 'in the mountain where the Lord is seen,' and of 'Behold, his bedstead was a bedstead of iron,' you will know the truth." Joseph ben Eliezer Bonfils, in his commentary called *Tzofnat Paneah*—Revealer of Secrets—effectively demonstrates that Ibn Ezra makes the claim that this verse and the others included in his "riddle" show that the Torah includes editorial comment that could only have made sense to readers well after the time of Moses. The "secret of the twelve" refers to the last twelve verses of the Torah that could not have been recorded by Moses since he had already died. And, for example, when the Torah says, "The Canaanites were then in the land," could only be relevant to readers who lived at a time when there was no longer a trace of the Canaanites in Israel, well after the time of Moses. Consequently, Ibn Ezra was arguing that the Torah as we have it today could not have been written at the time of Moses. There is evidence that there are passages that were written some time later. This controversial notion runs counter to the traditional account that Moses received the entire Torah at Sinai and that Torah is exactly the one we have today. There is an alternative account in the Talmud, ascribed to Rabbi Yohanan (*b. Gittin* 60a), namely, that the Torah was given piecemeal over time and as the events occurred. But it was the opinion of Rabbi Shimon ben Laqish, a colleague of Rabbi Yohanan, which was adopted by Maimonides, namely, that the Torah was given all at once and has remained immutable. See Rabbi Louis Jacobs, *Principles of the Jewish Faith*, 232–37, who runs through all of Bonfils's explication of Ibn Ezra and shows why Friedlander's attempt to offer an alternative, orthodox reading of Ibn Ezra fails. Yet despite holding an unorthodox opinion of a central tenet of Judaism, Ibn Ezra's commentary was never banned or censored.

Even in the formative stages of Rabbinic Judaism when certain texts had to be excluded from the canon, like the book of Ben Sira, there was never a ban on the possession or reading from these "external books." In fact, the Talmud occasionally quotes from Ben Sira in approval of some of its wisdom. And when Elisha ben Abuya lost his faith and was excluded from the rabbinic community, his teachings were retained and transmitted, albeit without his name attached.[18] Maimonides, that is Rabbi Moses, son of Maimon, was arguably the greatest mind that Judaism ever produced, not just in the twelfth century. He was a physician, philosopher, and teacher. Thomas Aquinas credits Maimonides with many of his ideas. Maimonides understood the "external books" to refer to works on idolatrous worship rather than any writings that would be harmful to faith or morals. Even so, he argues that these "external books" need to be studied if we are to understand precisely what is forbidden and how to combat their influence. In other words, censorship would be counterproductive.

And while there have been—and continue to be—instances where some rabbis somewhere have called into question the writings of other rabbis, the fact is that Judaism has never institutionalized censorship and never worked to silence the opinions or ban the ideas of non-Jews no matter how caustic they may be. That is the by-product of true respect.

To be sure, these days much is made about respect but little is understood or practiced. One of the ugliest moments in organized sports took place near the end of a basketball game between the Indiana Pacers and the Detroit Pistons on November 21, 2004. During the last minute of the game, with one team clearly ahead and the outcome no longer in doubt, one Indiana player intentionally fouled a Detroit player igniting a fight that moved from the basketball court into the crowd. Nine people were treated for injuries and nine players from the teams were banned for a combined 143 games, one for almost an entire season. Mitch Albom, covering the game for the *Detroit Free Press*, wrote the following analysis of the incident:

> Respect is what started this in this the first place.
> Oh, not real respect. Real respect has traces of kindness. Real respect is deferential, like a young apprentice and his patient mentor. Real respect knows, at its core, humility.
> I'm talking about the bastardized "respect" in today's sports world—where the word means nobody does anything to you that you don't like, want, accept or appreciate.

---

18. The story of Elisha ben Abuya is dramatized in Rabbi Milton Steinberg's 1939 novel *As a Driven Leaf*.

Or you let them have it.

Ben Wallace felt "disrespected" by Artest's hard foul late in an already decided game. So he had to shove Artest in the neck. Artest, "disrespected" by Wallace's retaliation, couldn't shrug and say "sorry," he had to jaw back, then argue, then ultimately lie on the scorer's table mocking Wallace in order to even the "disrespect" ratio.

Some idiot fan, who felt "disrespected" by Artest's mocking of Wallace, was compelled to throw a beer on Artest, to teach him a "respect" lesson. And Artest had to show that such "disrespect" would not be tolerated, so he thundered into the stands—over a table and a railing and seats—until he found someone whom he could punch, even though he had no idea if this were the culprit.

Artest's teammates couldn't let the "disrespect" go on, so they joined him and found others to punch. More fans, emboldened, couldn't let the Pacers "disrespect" them, so they confronted several on the floor, where fans should never be. And those confronted players couldn't allow such "disrespect"—after all they had egos to protect—so they swung away.[19]

Sad to say, what occurred in the basketball arena that November evening is repeated in the inner-city schoolyards almost every day. The notion that respect is something that must be demanded from others rather than given to others is what motivates renegade countries and terrorist organizations to pursue dangerous policies. Albom concludes with the following observation: "Only fools are deluded about 'respect.' That word is not something you lose when someone does something you don't like, and it is not something you gain with a fist. Respect comes by behaving respectfully." And behaving respectfully, that is, treating all people with deference and the generosity of spirit intended to shield people from embarrassment and uphold their essential dignity is fundamental to Judaism.

A basic question regarding the Creation saga did not escape the attention of Judaism. Why did God create a solitary human being from whom all others would descend? (Woman is created out of man and the couple subsequently becomes the progenitors of all humanity.) Since God is omnipotent, He could have just as well populated the world instantly with a hundred people or with billions. Starting with one seems to be inefficient. The answer is included in one of the central, and oldest, rabbinic texts:

---

19. *National Post*, Monday, November 22, 2004.

> A single man was created for the sake of peace among humanity, that none should say to his fellow: "My father was greater than your father."[20]

Were there many people created at the same time, people would naturally and childishly contend with each other. But with all human beings descending from one individual, our pedigrees are identical, no one has any claim of superiority over another, and—importantly—we are all members of the same family. And while it is true that family members may quarrel, in the end, the recognition that family ties are deep and powerful makes conflict less likely. Without mutual respect, however, conflict is inevitable. Realizing that all human beings share the same ancestry ought to foster mutual respect. And that is point of the story of the creation of the first human being. It is Judaism, through the Torah text that has given the world a recipe for conflict avoidance.

RESTRAINT

With well over five million copies in print, *The Road Less Traveled* is probably the most popular contemporary book on spiritual growth. Author and psychiatrist M. Scott Peck provides practical and experiential advice on how to address and solve the difficult problems of life. The first quarter of the book is devoted to discipline because, as Dr. Peck explains, "Discipline is the basic set of tools we require to solve life's problems. Without discipline we can solve nothing. With only some discipline we can solve only some problems. With total discipline we can solve all problems."[21]

What was "discovered" by Dr. Peck when he first wrote the book in 1978 was long ago realized by Judaism. The finest example of discipline in Judaism is the dietary laws, called Kashrut. Many people today would assign Kashrut to a vestige of the past when survival depended upon assuring good health by eating proper food. Others suggest that the dietary rules are no different form any other Divine command and required only our obedience. But the real purpose of Kashrut is to train us to practice restraint, self-control, and discipline. Here is how.

Social scientists and evolutionary psychologists have concluded that every human being is a bundle of impulses they call "drives." Almost

---

20. The reason for the creation of a solitary, first human being appears in the Talmud (*b. Sanhedrin* 40a).
21. Peck, *Road Less Traveled*, sect. 1, "Discipline," 15.

instinctively, human beings are compelled—some say "hardwired"—to behave in a certain way because of ingrained patterns for genetic survival. There is a sleep drive, a power drive, a pleasure drive, a survival drive, and a very powerful sex drive. But the most powerful drive of all is the food drive. Their appetites drive human beings. It is not only true that an army marches on its stomach. Every human being is directed by the drive to eat. So if we can control our eating, we can effectively control our lives.

But left on their own, people, like the pets they keep, would eat whatever they want, whenever they want, however they want. This kind of behavior is described so well and so briefly by the Torah that characterizes the reaction of Esav, the epitome of the brutish, coarse personality, who buys a bowl of lentil soup from his brother, Jacob. The narrative puts it this way: "He ate, he drank, he got up and left" (Gen 25:34).[22] The four words in Hebrew convey a kind of mechanical, peremptory approach to eating, devoid of any etiquette, mindfulness, or control. In other words, much like any dog or cat, Esav gobbled his food to satisfy his hunger. He simply was, to use Irving Berlin's descriptive expression, "doin' what comes nat'rally."

Judaism, however, through its system of Kashrut, insists that we cannot and should not behave like animals, as natural as that may be. We are more than just a bundle of impulses. Through our will we have control over our impulses; they do not have control over us. There are days we can chose not to eat at all. In religious terms, we call them Fast Days (although sometimes they do no pass so fast at all.) We can suppress the food drive because we decide that there are some things more important than food. The rules of Kashrut teach that when we eat, we must eat only certain foods, in certain ways, and at certain times. These are not restrictions for their own sake, impositions on our freedom. They are a form of discipline, training us how to control our lives. For if we can control what, and when, and how we eat—the most basic and powerful of all drives—then we can control anything and everything in our lives. As Dr. Leon Kass remarks in his book *The Hungry Soul*: "Good habits and thoughtful attitudes regarding food and eating will have far-reaching benefits. Self-restraint and self-command, consideration for others, politeness, fairness, generosity, tact, discernment, good taste, and the art of friendly conversation—all learnable and practiced at the table—enrich and ennoble all of human life."[23]

---

22. My translation.
23. Kass, *Hungry Soul*, 229–30.

THE FOUR R's

Kashrut is a fundamental part of Judaism because the discipline of Kashrut develops will power, inculcates restraint, and builds self-control. In a world that often seems to have gone out of control, where there are no restraints except those self-imposed, Judaism offers a vehicle to regain control of our lives. I'll never forget a congregant who once bemoaned the fact that he could not maintain a healthy diet. I told him, "What you need is will power." "Rabbi," he replied, "I've got lots of will power. What I need more of is won't power." Judaism gives us "won't power." We won't surrender to our impulses. We won't yield to what's harmful just because it's popular. We won't let our urges control us.

Included in the dietary laws is the requirement of waiting between eating meat and eating dairy. Customs among Jews vary, with some waiting only an hour, others waiting three hours, and yet others waiting six.[24] Ostensibly, the reason behind the waiting period is to conform to the rule against mixing milk with meat, even when the mixture is in our digestive tract. But while that may be the reason, it is not the purpose. The purpose of the waiting period, I contend, is to condition delayed gratification. I may really want to have the Baked Alaska following the roast beef, but I can't, meaning, I won't. By overriding my strongest dietary desires, by restraining my impulse to eat what I want now, I learn that good things can be enjoyed in due course.

The discipline of Judaism[25] allows us the ability to delay gratification, precisely what Dr. Peck identifies as essential to success. He reports about

---

24. According to Rabbi David Halevi (known as TaZ) the reason for the waiting period between meat and milk is that meat leaves a lingering taste in the mouth that must completely dissipate before eating dairy. As well, particles of meat may be lodged in the teeth and they are not dissolved by saliva until six hours have elapsed (*Shulhan Arukh*, Yoreh De'ah 89, subparagraph 1). German Jews, however, have typically waited only three hours, and Dutch Jews only one. Of the many books written on the Jewish dietary laws, some of the more notable are Rabbi Jacob Cohn's 1970 outline entitled *The Royal Table*, Dr. I. Grundfeld's 1972 comprehensive two-volume treatise, *The Jewish Dietary Laws*; and, more recently, Lisë Stern, *How to Keep Kosher*. Also useful is Rabbi Isaac Klein, *A Guide to Jewish Religious Practice*, units 21 through 26. Professor Louis A. Berman, *Vegetarianism & the Jewish Tradition*, builds on the fact that meat eating was a divine concession, a point emphasized by Samuel Dresner and Seymour Siegel in *The Dietary Laws*. See also the introduction to Aviva Allen's 2007 *Organic Kosher Cookbook*.

25. The discipline of Judaism if further reflected in ritual. Ritual may seem to be unnecessarily repetitive. Yet it is through constant repetition that the values inherent in the actions become automatic. In *Values of the Game*, Rhodes scholar, basketball champion, and former US senator from New Jersey Bill Bradley talks about how he came to realize that discipline was the secret to success. He tells how he practiced from June to

his treatment of a thirty-year-old financial analyst who complained about her incessant procrastination. After several months of analysis it appeared that little progress was being made. Dr. Peck writes: "Finally, one day, we dared to look at the obvious. 'Do you like cake?' I asked her. She replied that she did. 'Which part of the cake do you like better,' I went on, 'the cake or the frosting?' 'Oh, the frosting!' she responded enthusiastically. 'And how do you eat a piece of cake?' I inquired, feeling that I must be the most inane psychiatrist that [sic] ever lived. 'I eat the frosting first, of course' she replied. From her cake-eating habits we went on to examine her world habits, and, as was to be expected, discovered that on any given day she would devote the first hour to the more gratifying half of her work and the remaining six hours getting around the objectionable remainder. I suggested that if she were to force herself to accomplish the more unpleasant part of the job during the first hour, she would then be free to enjoy the other six. It seemed to me, I said, that one hour of pain followed by six of pleasure was preferable to one hour of pleasure followed by six of pain. She agreed, and, being basically a person of strong will, she no longer procrastinates."[26]

Note that Peck links her improvement to her strong will, her ability to control her behavior, what I argue is the objective of the dietary laws. Peck concludes: "Delaying gratification is a process of scheduling the pain and pleasure of life in such a way as to enhance the pleasure by meeting and experiencing the pain first and getting it over with. It is the only decent way to live."[27] Of course the pain to which Dr. Peck refers need not be actual physical discomfort. It could be no more than hard work or effort. And it can be emotional as well as physical.

The Talmud anticipated Peck's conclusion two thousand years ago. It is one of the most well known of all Talmudic legends[28] and involves a mysterious wonder-worker named Honi. Honi once came upon an old

---

September, four days a week, three hours per day and from September to March, three to four hours a day during the week adding two more hours each day on the weekend. He trained and conditioned himself extensively. He kept shooting at the basket until he sank twenty-five consecutive shots from five different spots on the court. And then, after practice, he would play games. He learned that the harder he worked, more "automatic" things became for him. That is precisely what Judaism offers. The repetitive routine and regular demands in Judaism that strike many as monotonous is actually the way to ingrain values, to make doing the right thing "automatic."

26. Peck, *Road Less Traveled*, 18–19.
27. Ibid.
28. The story of Honi, the circle-maker, is told in the Talmud (*b. Ta'anit* 23a).

man planting a carob tree and asked him: "How long will it be before the tree bears fruit?" "Seventy years," replied the old man. "Surely you will not live seventy years to enjoy the fruits of the tree you have planted," Honi challenged. But the old man was very wise. He retorted: "Just as my ancestors planted for me, so I plant for my descendants." This man took the concept of delayed gratification to the extreme. He is not just working now to enjoy the benefits later. He knows that he will not enjoy the benefits at all but nonetheless sees value in his labor. He is prepared to forego personal gratification in favor of providing for the future. This old man could have planted vegetables or fruits trees that would have provided him with more proximal benefits. But he intuited that if everyone simply acted on his or her own selfish impulses, the future would be untenable. Those who operate on the principle of play now, pay later, those who live without restraint and aim to satisfy their impulses as quickly and as frequently as possible, will set a pattern that may result in dropping out of school, landing them in disastrous relationships or no relationships at all, in accidents, psychiatric hospitals, or in jail. The practice of Judaism is the practice of restraint and self-control, a discipline that is drilled into every Jew by the very way we eat. Properly observed, Judaism conditions us to delay gratification and gain us control over every aspect of our lives.

Intimately connected with the value of restraint is the concept of limits. When we control ourselves we set limits to our behavior. Limits are all pervasive. Borders are the limits of a given country's control. When we drive we notice that there are posted speed limits. In playing games or for some examinations there are time limits. At some amusement parks admission to certain rides is based on a height limit, although here the limit is actually a minimum height. We may not always like these limits and sometimes we may not follow them but we understand why they are important.

Most people who read the Bible, particularly the opening chapters of the book of Genesis are hardly aware of the fact that it is a story about setting limits. When God creates the world, He set limits. God limits the light to the daytime and the darkness to night. He limits the sun to rule over the day and the moon and stars to rule over the night. He limits the fish to the sea, the birds to the sky, and the other animals to the earth. He limits the animals to breed only with animals of the same species. Even the episode of the first two human beings[29] in the garden of Eden is a narrative

---

29. I refer to the first two human beings rather than to "Adam" and "Eve" because "Adam" and "Eve" are not their names. The Hebrew uses the definitive article "the"

about limits. They are given limits about what they could eat and what they must not do. When they disobeyed and were evicted from the garden it was because they failed to respect the limits.[30]

Interestingly, the action in the garden of Eden revolves around two trees rather than around rocks or rivers because trees are consistent with the theme of limits. As tall as some trees grow, they do not grow without bounds. There is an internal, biochemical mechanism that controls how high trees may grow: only so high, and no higher. The unspoken but underlying message is that if trees operate according to self-imposed limits, so should human beings.

And almost always overlooked in this early biblical episode is the description of the location of the garden.

> A river issues from Eden to water the garden, and it then divides and becomes four branches. The name of the first is Pishon, the one that winds through the whole land of Havilah, where the gold is . . . The name of the second river is Gihon, the one that winds through the whole land of Cush. The name of the third river is Tigris, the one that flows east of Asshur. And the fourth river is the Euphrates.[31]

To most casual readers of the scriptural text this geographical addition seems rather unnecessary. After all, it adds nothing to the development of the plot. But it is entirely consistent with the theme of limits. The garden of Eden itself generates limits by which lands are bounded. Mesopotamia, that is, the geographical area centered at the confluence of the Tigris and Euphrates Rivers, is, literally, "the land between the rivers." The Bible is preoccupied with limits, as we should be. So from the very outset we are impressed by the existence of limits in life. And failure to observe the limits brings disaster.

---

preceding the word "Adam" from the Hebrew root meaning the red earth from which he was created, rendering the term "the earthling." Logically, he needed no name since he was the only person alive. "Eve" is not a name either. It is a description: "mother of all life."

30. In ch. 1 of the book of Genesis God sets limits to the darkness (v. 4), differentiates the species of plants thereby setting limits to which plants could breed with other (vv. 11–12), sets up the boundaries of day and night by creating the sun and moon (v. 16), and differentiates the animals species (v. 25).

31. The four rivers circumscribing the garden of Eden as well as other lands are described in 2:10 and following.

The Four R's

Jewish tradition identifies four kinds of people.[32] The first kind of people says: "What's mine is mine and what's yours is mine." These people are selfish. The second kind of people says: "What's mine is yours and what's yours is yours." These people are generous. The third kind of people says: "What's yours is yours and what's mine is mine" are neither selfish not generous. They just maintain the status quo. The fourth kind of people says: "What's mine is yours and what's yours is mine." These people are stupid as well as confused. That is because they fail to understand limits. If what is mine is mine and what is yours is mine, then I want everything. If what is mine is yours and what is yours is yours, then you can have everything. But if mine is yours and yours is mine, everything is mixed up. It means that I have as little regard for you or your possessions as I have for my own. In effect, it means that I'm not me and you are not you. It sounds ridiculous. But that is precisely what results when people fail to observe limits.

One of my favorite cartoons shows a woman at a supermarket checkout counter. She stands at the "Express Lane" for "Ten Items or Less." Both the customer and the clerk who was scanning her purchases are looking up at the loudspeaker mounted above the nearest aisle as it blares: "You have eleven items! Drop the Orange Juice and come out with your hands up!" In reality, that doesn't happen. Most customers don't care whether the number of items in their cart complies with the maximum allowed. They are interested only in avoiding having to wait on the other, usually longer and slower moving, lines. Most clerks don't care whether the number of items complies with the maximum either. And most supermarkets don't bother to enforce the limits they set, presumably for the benefit of all their customers. I am simply waiting for the time when the customer ahead of me on the "Express Line" about to unload her pile of groceries far in excess of the posted limit is pulled aside by the cashier who would ask her: "So which ten items would like to buy?" Perhaps that day will come, but not in the current culture where limits are generally ignored. The supermarket is a microcosm of the world in which limits are unknown or, when known, violated.

In biblical account of creation, it is God who sets the limits.[33] On the highways, it's the government that sets limits. But more often than not,

---

32. The four kinds of people are listed in *Pirke Avot* 4:13.

33. Limits are also reflected in the Sabbath laws. According to the book of Numbers (35:5) the agricultural domain of a given city extends 2000 cubits in all directions. The Talmud (*b. Nedarim* 56b) fixes this area as the full extent of human habitation. Hence, since the Torah (Exod 16:29) states that no man shall go beyond "his place" on the Sabbath, the 2000 cubit limit is intended (Maimonides, Laws of the Sabbath 27:1).

it is people who impose limits on themselves. Sticking to a diet is a self-imposed limit. But diets are very hard to maintain without "won't power." Judaism, through the training of restraint, builds the discipline necessary for "won't power." More importantly, if we can say "No!" to things that we could eat—and we out things in our mouths all the time—then we can say "No!" to stealing (even though no one is watching) and we can say "No!" to cheating (even though others may be doing it).

Joseph is a biblical hero. When we are first introduced to him, he does not seem to be a very nice young man. He is not very heroic at all. He is boastful and he tattles on his brothers. But Joseph shows another side to his character. He was brought to Egypt against his will but he manages to become very successful. He was also very handsome. His master left him in charge of his entire house and trusted Joseph with everything. One day, when no one was at home, the wife of Joseph's master grabbed him and attempted to seduce him.[34] Her argument was simple and it would have been easy for Joseph to go along: his master trusted Joseph implicitly and would not suspect anything, and, besides, no one was around to notice. It was probably very tempting. But Joseph knew that it was wrong for him to be with a married woman so he said "No!" Joseph had "won't power," that is self-control, restraint. That is what makes Joseph a hero, a "righteous man."

Sabbath-observant Jews thus have their appreciation of limits reinforced every week. In an essay on "The Publication of the Mishnah" in *Hellenism and Jewish Palestine*, 83n3, Professor Saul Lieberman, arguably the greatest Talmudist of the twentieth century (see Meir Lubetski, *Saul Lieberman [1898–1983] Talmudic Scholar and Classicist*, and Elijah J. Schochet and Solomon Spiro, *Saul Lieberman: The Man and His Work*, and for a contrarian view, Marc Shapiro's *Saul Lieberman and the Orthodox*), explains that the Hebrew word *halakhah*, meaning Jewish law, may not come from the root meaning "to walk [along the right path]" but from the word for "boundary." In the biblical book of Ezra (4:13), Professor Lieberman points out, a tax called the "halakh" is mentioned. From ancient Aramaic documents we learn that a land tax was called "halakha." Hence it is possible that term for Jewish law, "halakhah," had as its origins the name of the fixed land tax having the same valence as the Greek *oros*, meaning "boundary." That means that what Jewish law does is determine which practices are within bounds and which are out of bounds. In other words, Jewish law sets limits.

34. The story of Joseph and Potiphar's wife is told in Gen 39:7f.:

> After a time, his master's wife cast her eyes upon Joseph and said, "Lie with me." But he refused. He said to his master's wife, "Look, with me here, my master gives no thought to anything in this house, and all that he owns he has placed in my hands. He wields no more authority in this house than I, and he has withheld nothing from me except yourself, since you are his wife. How then could I do this most wicked things, and sin before God?" And as much as she coaxed Joseph day after day, he did not yield to her request to lie beside her, to be with her.

And the point is that Joseph is not perfect. He had flaws, just as we do. But we, like him, have the power—the "won't power"—to control ourselves. "Won't power," however, needs to be cultivated and Judaism provides the regimen to do so.

Scientists have long known of a rare condition called adermatoglyphia, the absence of any clear patterns of swirls and ridges at the tip of human fingers. Dr. Eli Sprecher, a geneticist and dermatologist at the Tel Aviv Sourasky Medical Center have now identified the gene mutation that causes the disease. Simply put, adermatoglyphs have no fingerprints. Since crime detection has been largely based on fingerprint evidence, this would put adermatoglyphs at an advantage. They could commit all kinds of crime with impunity. The only things that would deter them (assuming there were no witnesses or video surveillance-and even sometimes when there is!) would be their own conscience; their own "won't power." It is only when people develop a value system that judges actions by standards of right and wrong rather than on the basis of with what they can get away will civilization have advanced to the stage of nobility we could celebrate.

Judaism teaches that three things can judge a person's character. The Hebrew words are useful here because they sound alike: Kisso, Kosso, and Ka'asso.[35] A person can be judged by how he controls his money (*kisso* = his pocket). A person can be judged by how he controls his drinking (*kosso* = his cup). And a person can be judged by how he controls his anger. All three things are related. They all are ways we demonstrate self-control. A person who is careful not to spend more than she has and be generous and prudent with she does spend is a person with self-control. A person who is careful not to drink too much alcohol is a person with self-control. And a person who gets upset but doesn't let her anger explode is a person with self-control. The more self-control a person demonstrates, the more that person is to be admired and respected.

This last idea is particularly important because it shows the connection between restraint and respect. Here is another. Self-control means having the power to say "No!" Self-control also means having the power to respect someone else who says "No!" Nonconsensual sexual relations remain a persistent concern in North America and throughout the world where the sexes mingle freely. According to a 1987 study by Andrea Parrot at Cornell University, an estimated 20 percent of college women were forced into

---

35. The three things upon which a person's character is judged appears as a statement in the Talmud (*b. Eruvin* 65b).

sex by a date or acquaintance. Kent State psychologist Marry Koss spent three years studying 32 campuses. She put the rate of nonconsensual sex at 15 percent. By 1994, the University of California at Santa Clara Rape Prevention Education Center put the figure at 25 percent. That means that one out of every four women attending a university has been forced into sexual relations she did not want. According to US Bureau of Justice statistics, in the year 2000, 13 percent of college women are forced into nonconsensual sex by their dates. And according to the latest figures collected and published by the Pennsylvania Coalition Against Rape, 90 percent of rape victims on college campuses knew their attackers. It seems that familiarity does indeed breed contempt. When others are respected, 'No!" is accepted. The problem is as much related to a lack of respect for others as it is to power and dominance. But the problem could be overcome, if not eliminated altogether, had the men involved a greater respect for their dates and restraint over themselves. What is needed-as much as severe criminal penalties-is a regimen that would cultivate respect for others and build self-restraint. That regimen is Judaism.

A comparison of two champion professional basketball players will help illustrate the value of restraint related to limits and self-control. Wilt Chamberlain was one of the most dominant players ever. Nicknamed "Wilt the Stilt" and "The Big Dipper," he would frequently overcome double-teaming and triple-teaming. He once scored 100 points in a single game. He remains the only player in the history of the National Basketball Association to average more than fifty points per game for an entire season. He won several championships, was elected to the Basketball Hall Fame in 1978, and was voted one of the fifty greatest players the game has ever known. But he was a prolific "scorer" off the court as well. His lawyer and agent Sy Goldberg once said about his client: "Some people collect stamps. Wilt collected women." In his second autobiography, *A View From Above*, published in 1991, he claimed that he had bedded 20,000 women, an extraordinary number. It would be the equivalent of having sexual relations with the entire population of Augusta, Georgia. Or, as one calculation determined, it would require Chamberlain having sexual relations with eight women per week from the age of fifteen until his death in 1999! A lifelong bachelor, Chamberlain once explained to a television interviewer: "I was doing what was natural." No doubt that's true. But Judaism maintains that human beings are part of the animal world but with the will and power to rise above it. Judaism insists that we do not behave like animals but like those the psalmist says are "a little lower than the angels." What Chamberlain admits to be lacking is self-control. His sexual impulses knew no limits. Without restraint Chamberlain merely did what came naturally. Swedish Olympic high-jumper Annette Tannander, who met Chamberlain when she was 19 and he was 40, said Chamberlain was "always respectful . . . never bad or rude."[36] But she misses the point. It is not a question of what he said to women but that he considered them conquests. They were in service to his natural urges. And that is not respectful.

Another champion basketball player, A. C. Green, is a study in contrast. Green played sixteen seasons for the Los Angeles Lakers and three other teams from 1986 to 2001, winning multiple championships. During that span of time he played in 1192 consecutive games, a "perfect attendance" record. It is a record that will be difficult to ever break, and a tribute to his durability, skill, and intensity. He scored a career-high 41 points in one game while suffering from pneumonia. (Tristan Thompson had the longest recent streak of consecutive games played ended at 477 on April 5, 2017 when he was sidelined by injury.) But Green also holds a more impressive record: he remained sexually abstinent until his marriage at the age of thirty-eight to Veronique Shipley in 2002. Said Green after the event: "It was worth the wait."[37] During his playing days, teammates would tempt him by sending women to his room in attempts to seduce him. But he resisted. His dedication to sexual abstinence before marriage motivated him to start the A. C. Green Youth Foundation to promote the values he personified. Green is a paradigm for restraint and self-control.

I suspect that if a survey were conducted today most of those questioned—especially college age males—would hold Chamberlain in higher regard than Green. Green's self-control would be considered prudish and old-fashioned, if not repressive, and certainly laughable. Chamberlain would be hailed as supremely virile, and his accomplishments enviable. But were the survey to ask parents to choose who they would prefer to date their daughter, I suspect the results would be quite different. Further, were

---

36. For all the quotations on Chamberlain, see Robert Cherry's 2004 book, *Wilt: Larger Than Life*, 343–56. Less extensive but just as telling as Chamberlain's exploits are those of singer Gerardo Mejia whose hit song *Rico Suave* topped the charts in the 1990s. As widely reported in December 2014, Mejia claims to have slept with between 500 and 600 women and justifies his conduct on the basis that his Ecuadorian heritage normalized infidelity for him.

37. *Los Angeles Times*, June 30, 2002.

the survey to ask who would be preferred as a teacher or a political leader, I suspect the results would favor Green.

When I was a child, every school report card included grades for character as well as for academics, a procedure, I sadly note, did not persist through my children's elementary school years let alone survive to this day. Children were once graded on "Punctuality," "Citizenship," and most importantly, "Self-Control." Children were expected to know the limits of proper behavior and exercise restraint. Failure to respect the limits resulted in punishment, sometimes as severe as suspension or expulsion. Children learned that an absence of restraint resulted in consequences, a hard but necessary lesson to learn. And if the school failed to reprimand them for misbehaving (hardly likely), their parents (painfully) would not. But a far better, wiser, and, I believe, more effective way to inculcate self-control is being raised in a system that teaches restraint through diet rather than through fear. That system is Judaism.

RESPONSIBILITY

The story is well known. God places the first couple in the Garden of Eden. The male has no name. In fact, he needs no name. There was no one else around. Since he is created from the red earth, *adamah*, in Hebrew, the narrative refers to him as *ha-adam*, meaning, "the earthling." He calls his mate, the first female, *Havah*, from the Hebrew word for life, because she is the progenitor of all future human life. They are given dominion over the garden, entitled to eat of its bounty and required to tend it. But there is one tree from which they are instructed not to eat: the Tree of Knowledge of Good and Evil. The female is convinced by the cunning serpent to eat from the forbidden fruit. (Nowhere, by the way, is the kind of fruit actually specified.)[38] She shares it with her mate. And both are expelled from the Garden for their disobedience. But the details are particularly important so I will quote directly from the *New Jewish Publication Society of America* translation:

---

38. The fruit eaten by the first two human beings has been suggested to be a citron (related to a lemon), a fig (since they did use fig leaves as clothing after eating), a grape (which seems to be the oldest tradition), wheat, nuts, and even carob. See Louis Ginzberg, *Legends of the Jews*, vol. 5, 97n70, for all the speculations. It is based on Genesis Rabbah 15:7.

The Four R's

They heard the sound of the Lord God moving about in the garden at the breezy time of day; and the man and his wife hid from the Lord God among the trees of the garden. The Lord God called out to the man and said to him, "Where are you? He replied, "I heard the sound of You in the garden, and I was afraid because I was naked, so I hid." Then he asked, "Who told you that you were naked? Did you eat of tree from which I had forbidden you to eat?" The man said, "The woman You put at my side—she gave me of the tree, and I ate." And the Lord God said to the woman, "What is this you have done!" The woman replied, "The serpent duped me, and I ate" (Gen 3:8–13).

The scene is so striking in depicting the reaction of the first two human beings to being held accountable. The earthling's first impulse was to evade detection. When that fails, he tries shifting the blame. "She made me eat it!" he claims. And she, in turn, blames the serpent: "He tricked me!" To parents intent on disciplining their mischievous children it is an all too familiar sequence. It is a classic display of how to escape responsibility, or at least how to try to escape responsibility. The fact that all are punished is a clear indication that evading responsibility is as wrong as much as it is futile.

Now compare this scene with one from a later book of the Bible. King David set his eyes on a beautiful woman and was intent on making her his wife. But she was married. In fact, her husband was one of the king's most loyal soldiers. But King David connives with his military chief of staff to arrange to send this soldier to the fiercest point of combat to ensure his death. Then the king could marry the widow. And so events unfolded. But the prophet Nathan was sent by God to come before the king to hold him accountable for the terrible sin he had committed. To scold or reprimand a king would be impertinent. So Nathan contrives a case for the king to adjudicate. The passage is worth quoting directly, again from the *New Jewish Publication Society* translation:

And the Lord sent Nathan to David. He came to him and said, "There were two men in the same city, one rich and one poor. The rich man had very large flocks and herds, but the poor man had only one little ewe lamb that he had bought. He tended it and it grew up together with him and his children: it used to share his morsel of bread, drink from his cup, and nestle in his bosom; it was like a daughter to him. One day, a traveler came to the rich man, but he was loath to take anything from his own flocks or herds to prepare a meal for the guest who had come to him; so he took the poor man's lamb and prepared it for the man who had come to him." David flew into a rage against the man, and said to Nathan, "As the Lord lives, the man who did this deserves to die! He shall pay for the lamb four times over because he did such a thing and showed no pity." And Nathan said to David, "That man is you!" (2 Samuel 12:1–4).

And the prophet Nathan proceeds to tell David how he shall be punished. And then comes David's reaction: "David said to Nathan, 'I stand guilty before the Lord'" (v. 13).

The most important lesson from this passage is King David's reaction. He does not evade. He does not deny. He offers no excuses. He admits his wrongdoing and takes full responsibility. King David is lionized by Jews and counted as the forebear of the Messiah not solely for his military conquests and the establishment of Jerusalem as Israel's capital. King David is a paradigm for accepting responsibility.

Evading responsibility has become legend in our days. When Homer Simpson, of television cartoon fame, believed he was going to die, he wanted to leave his son Bart with some fatherly wisdom. Among the three most important things he wanted his son to learn was the phrase "It was like that when I found it." Celebrities and politicians will often blame the media for reporting their foibles, failings, imbroglios and peccadilloes rather than take responsibility for them. The Bush administration blamed the media for bad war news rather than accepting responsibility for the mismanagement of the war in Iraq and its aftermath. Hillary Clinton blamed the media for rarely reporting on the intensity of her support thereby costing her the 2008 nomination for president. Ralph Nader, in his 2001 book *Crashing the Party*, blamed the media for most of his poor showing in the 2000 presidential campaign. He claimed that "inept reporters," rather than his own unpopular policies, undermined his election chances. Political pundits blame terrorism on poverty and powerlessness even though most terrorists come from well-to-do families. President Robert Mugabe blamed Zimbabwe's runaway inflation on British meddling rather than on his own corrupt government and failed economic policies. And we mustn't forget how Dan White blamed the sugar rush from eating "Twinkies" for his mood disorder that led him to commit a double murder in 1979.

After the 2008 Summer Olympic Games, Cuban Angel Matos was upset at being disqualified for taking too much injury time during his Bronze Medal tae kwon do match. His reaction was to kick referee Chakir Chelbat in the face. Worse still was Fidel Castro's defense of Matos in the August

26 edition of the Cuban political journal *Gramma* in which Castro blames "European chauvinism, corrupt referees . . . and a strong dose of racism" for the loss and for Matos's understandable reaction. The extent to which people go to find excuses rather than take responsibility is discussed and criticized by Vincent Barry in his 1997 book *The Dog Ate My Homework*. It's always someone or something that's at fault. But laying the blame on others is not the Jewish way. That is not the way King David behaved.

In the ancient world, people tended to blame the stars for everything. Astrology is a vestige of the ancient notion that somehow the alignment of the planets and constellations have an influence on our lives.[39] That even the most highly educated among us still glance at the horoscopes that even the most respected newspapers continue to publish is a testament to the attractiveness of the concept that we are not wholly responsible for our actions. Shakespeare acknowledges the allure of astrology as a convenient evasion of personal responsibility in *King Lear*, where he writes: "When we are sick in fortune, often the surfeits of our own behavior, we make guilty of our disasters the sun, the moon, and the stars." But in the end, Shakespeare, with his profound understanding of human psychology, would have us admit as Marc Anthony puts it: "The fault, Dear Brutus, lies not in our stars but in ourselves."[40]

Judaism, too, preserves a leftover piece of assigning influence to the stars. When good wishes are extended to another, they are accompanied with the expression "Mazal Tov," literally, "a good star." The underlying assumption is that the stars are responsible for one's good fortune. But noteworthy here is that even in this case, Jews do not assign blame to the stars. A "bad star" is not responsible for *mis*fortune. We are. (There is no parallel expression of comfort, "Mazal Ra," "a bad star," to those who suffer a reversal of fortune.) While the expression "Mazal Tov" remains, it is effectively dismissed by the Talmud that proclaims: "There is no [guiding] star for Israel."[41]

---

39. For Judaism's view on astrology, see Jacobs, *What Does Judaism Say*, s.v. "Astrology," 48–49.

40. The lines from Shakespeare are cited from *King Lear*, act 1, scene 1, line 134 and *Julius Caesar*, act 1, scene 2, line 134. See Allan Bloom for a superb analysis of Shakespeare's insight into human nature.

41. The Talmud declares that there is no guiding star (or constellation) for Israel in *b. Shabbat* 146a. Maimonides, a champion of science and reason, in his *Letter on Astrology*, writes: "I know that you may search and find sayings of some individual sages in the Talmud and commentaries whose words appear to maintain that at the moment of

In later times, people tended to blame other supernal or supernatural powers. Comedian Flip Wilson made a career out of dressing as a woman character named Geraldine, who, when caught in some unseemly act would proclaim her innocence with the expression: "The devil made me do it." But normative Judaism puts no stock in the devil as a nemesis of God, with distinct powers, and who can lure people into sin. In the Hebrew Bible the word "satan" is used to describe a military adversary, an accuser, and an antagonist. The closest that the Hebrew Bible comes to the popular notion of a devil is in the prologue to the book of Job (1:7) where "satan" appears as a member of God's heavenly council with the purpose of exposing human sins. Critical to note, however, is that he has no independent powers. And while he can bring accusations to God for investigation and punishment, he cannot "make" anyone do anything. The Apocrypha, that is, those books that were not included in the official canon of the Hebrew Bible, does include mention of "satan" as a seducer in the *Wisdom of Solomon* and the *Slavonic Book of Enoch*. But these books were excluded from the Hebrew Bible. Scholars believe that they were written under the influence of other religions. The rabbinic tradition, however, assigns wrongdoing to an inner impulse, not to an external power.[42] As God tells Cain (Gen 4:7): "Sin crouches at the door, its urge is towards you, yet you can be its master." It is within each person to control, subdue, and overcome the evil we might think of doing. When we fail to exercise that power and control, we have no one and no thing to blame but ourselves.

In fact, even when blame can be placed on others legitimately, Judaism does not. The destruction of the Jerusalem temples by the Babylonians in the year 586 BCE and by the Romans in 70 CE could rightfully be attributed to their military might. But in the prayers that Jews recite in which the destruction and subsequent expulsions are mentioned, the blame is placed squarely on our own shoulders. "Because of our sins have we been exiled from our land," we say. The proximal cause of the destruction was indeed foreign armies. But the underlying cause was our own faithlessness. By emphasizing the underlying cause every Jewish worshipper learns that

---

a man's birth, the stars will cause such and such to happen to him. Do not regard this as a difficulty . . . it is not proper to abandon matters of reason that have already been verified by proofs, shake loose of them, and depend on the words of a single one of the sages from whom possibly the matter was hidden. Or there may be an allusion in those words; or they may have been said with a view to the times and business before him . . . A man should never cast his reason behind him, for the eyes are set in front, not in back."

42. Cf. *b. Kid.* 30b, 40a; *b. B. Bat.* 16a.

ultimate responsibility is personal responsibility. The Talmud (*b. Avodah Zarah* 17a) teaches that when Rabbi Eliezer ben Doradia came to realize the error of his ways, he also understood that no one and nothing else could intervene on his behalf. Rather, he acknowledged, "It all depends on me."

The most solemn day of the Jewish year is the Day of Atonement. I prefer to think of it as the Day of At-One-Ment.[43] It is the time specifically set aside to make amends for the wrongs committed during the previous year and thus become at one with God and at one with those we have wronged. Central to the process is making confession and restitution to the parties we have wronged. Taking personal responsibility means having the courage to face the victims of our misdeeds rather than revealing them to a third party. Those we injured by word or deed need to hear from us directly. They need to hear an accounting of the wrongdoing and we must be contrite enough and sincere enough to offer one.

So far, I placed the value of personal responsibility in the context of wronging another. Jewish tradition, however, also maintains that taking responsibility for us translates into not harming ourselves. In a moving prayer recited during the most solemn period of the Jewish year, we affirm that our bodies as well as our souls are God's. And, to borrow a term from the Marriage Encounter movement of the 1980s, "God does not make junk." Figuratively, the prayer means that we owe our entire existence to God. But there is also a literal meaning that does not escape notice. Our bodies do not "belong" to us in the sense that they are our personal property with which we can do whatever we want. That is why the criminal code in Jewish law forbids intentionally wounding oneself or doing anything that puts our lives in jeopardy. Our bodies are conceived as a temporary loan that can be reclaimed by God in due course. And just as any borrower must return the object lent in good order and condition, so must we. Accordingly, Maimonides's code of Jewish law begins with a lengthy section on proper diet and exercise; with advice on the kinds of things that ought to be included or avoided so that we remain healthy. And anyone, Maimonides rules, who does put him- or herself at risk, saying, "I am only endangering myself, and no one else has the right to interfere," is subject to disciplinary flogging.[44]

---

43. I am grateful to Rabbi Robert Gordis, of blessed memory, for the reading of the Day of Atonement as the Day of At-One-ment.

44. The law against putting oneself in jeopardy is based on Deut 4:9 that reads, in part, "Take utmost care and watch yourselves scrupulously." The law against wounding oneself is the subject of the Mishnah, *Bava Kamma* 8:7: "If a man said 'Blind my eye' or 'Cut off my hand' . . . he [that does so] is liable." The Talmud (*b. B. Kam.* 91b) bases

Prescription for an Ailing World

Judaism demands that we take responsibility for ourselves. It further demands that we take responsibility for others. A first-century teacher of Judaism framed it this way: "If I don't look after myself, who will? But if I only look after myself, what am I?"[45] In these two rhetorical questions Hillel expresses how Judaism moves from personal responsibility to responsibility for others. Following the teaching of the Talmud, every person must say: "For my sake was the world created." But while this may assure self-esteem, it can easily degenerate into a kind of antisocial solipsism. To be truly human, Hillel contends, one must be socially concerned and communally involved. Our very humanity is contingent upon our sense of responsibility for others.

By tradition, every synagogue must have windows.[46] At first glance, this seems to be a rather trivial requirement. But upon closer inspection, this requirement teaches volumes about how Judaism teaches responsibility to others. Insisting that synagogues are equipped with windows is not simply a practical matter that ensures sufficient light. Putting windows in synagogues is intended to teach that even when we pray, that is, when we turn inwards, we must look outward. We have a responsibility to care for our souls. But we have an equally profound responsibility to care for other lives. Windows in synagogues make us realize that we can never become so insular and aloof from what goes on outside in the world-at-large. We certainly have responsibilities to ourselves. But we also have responsibility for others.

We have a profound and enduring responsibility for other Jews. That sense of responsibility begins with Abraham, who, at great personal risk and against tremendous odds, went to war in order to free his captive nephew,

---

the rule against self-inflicted wounds Gen 9:6: "For your own life blood I will require a reckoning." Self-inflicted wounds are forbidden since one's body is not to do with as one pleases. See also, Rabbi Solomon Ganzfried, *Kitzur Shulhan Arukh*, sect. 32, translated into English by Hyman Goldin as *The Code of Jewish Law*. Maimonides's advice on keeping in good physical condition is incorporated into his *Mishneh Torah*, Laws of Opinions, 1:4 and 4:1f. in which he writes: "It is a man's duty to shun whatever is harmful to the body and cultivate health-preserving habits."

45. Hillel's rhetorical questions are cited by *Pirke Avot* 1:14. Contrary to some attributions, Hillel was not a rabbi. He lived at a time when rabbinic ordination was not yet institutionalized.

46. The rule that every synagogue must have windows is encoded by both Maimonides (*Mishneh Torah*, Laws of Prayer 5:6) and by Rabbi Joseph Karo (*Shulhan Arukh*, Orah Hayyim 90:4).

Lot.[47] That sense of responsibility continues with Moses who, after leaving the insular life of luxury in Pharaoh's palace, first defended an Israelite slave from the beating of a taskmaster and then intervened in a quarrel between two Israelites.[48] That same sense of responsibility for other Jews is enshrined in the Torah that demands that even the most financially disadvantaged are given a fresh start every seventh year, and that no Israelite should ever perish under the weight of financial hardship.[49] The Talmud succinctly states the operative principle: "All Israelites are responsible one for the other."[50] It is that sense of responsibility that has, in recent times, motivated Jews in the free world to actively work for the freedom of Jews imprisoned in the Gulags of the former Soviet Union for those refused exit visas, and for those suffering under anti-Semitism. And it is that same sense of responsibility that has driven the State of Israel to rescue the Jews of Ethiopia and the Jews who lived in fear in Syria.

That dual sense of responsibility, to ourselves as individuals and to other Jews as a consequence of joint membership in the people of Israel, is reflected in one of the most central prayers of Judaism called the *Sh'ma*.[51] The first of its three paragraphs taken from the Torah and formulated in the singular addresses the individual: "You shall love the Lord your God with all your heart, and with all your soul, and with all your might." But the second paragraph addresses the entire community of Israel and is formulated in the plural. It describes the collective responsibility for the future of the Jewish people. Reciting this prayer twice daily is a constant reminder that

---

47. Abraham's rescue of his nephew Lot is narrated in the book of Genesis, ch. 14. With only 318 retainers he attacked the combined forces of four kingdoms.

48. Moses' intervention on behalf of the beaten Israelite is described in Exod 2:11–14. That Moses looked "this way and that" is not an indication that he was checking to see of he could get away with it. Rather, he was waiting to see if anyone else would come to the aid his fellow.

49. The book of Deuteronomy (ch. 15:1ff.) declares:
> Every seventh year you shall practice a remission of debts. This shall be the nature of the remission: every creditor shall cancel the debt that he claims from his fellow . . . There shall be no needy among you.

50. The Talmud proclaims that "all Israelites are responsible for one another" in *b. Sanhedrin* 27b and *b. Shevu'ot* 39a.

51. The three paragraphs of the *Sh'ma* consist of Deut 6:4–9, Deut 11:13–21, and Num 15:37–41 in that order. It is Rabbi Louis Jacobs, in *What Does Judaism Say*, 185, who brought its connection of responsibility to oneself with responsibility to the community to my attention.

although we must value ourselves as individuals with singular worth, we are concomitantly part of a larger group for which we bear responsibility.

We also have a profound sense of responsibility for all people. This, too, is rooted in the Torah that demands that we care for the resident alien as much as for the native born: a revolutionary idea in its time.[52] And all people are to be treated the same way. The same civil laws apply equally to Jews and non-Jews alike. It is an ineluctable outcome of both the principles of respect and responsibility for others. And it is perhaps this sense of responsibility for others that is characteristic of all Jews today, regardless of religious affiliation or interest. According to the latest statistics available, 62 percent of American Jews give to general causes, compared to 41 percent to specifically Jewish causes. Just looking at the wealthiest Jews, of the more than 29 billion dollars of philanthropic giving, only 318 million went to exclusively Jewish causes. According to the research published by sociologist Gary Tobin, 80 percent of the dollars from the 50 most prominent Jewish foundations went to general—not Jewish—causes.

That Jews have historically been leaders of almost every reform movement or social cause in the history of humanity is a testament to the sense of responsibility for others with which Jews are raised. It is rooted in the idea that the world is essentially good, but not perfect. That is at the very heart of the Genesis narrative. God sees the world he created and declares it to be "Very good." Of course an omnipotent God could have created a perfect world. But, instead, God created an imperfect world into which he inserted human beings and gave them the responsibility to not only maintain it but to improve it.

Rabbi Moses Chaim Luzzatto emphasizes this idea of human responsibility when he writes that God was certainly capable of making all

---

52. Twice in the book of Numbers (9:14 and 15:15) the Torah requires that the same law be applied to foreigner and Israelite alike. The revolutionary nature of Judaism is reflected in the principle of merit rather than that of status. While the book of Deuteronomy (21:15) reflects the standard right of primogeniture, that is, the preferred treatment of the firstborn, universally acknowledged in the ancient world, the book of Genesis consistently defies it. Thus the sacrifice of the younger Abel is preferred over that of the elder brother Can, the younger Isaac is preferred over the elder Yishmael, the younger Jacob is preferred over his older twin Esav, Joseph is favoured over his ten older brothers, and Menashe is preferred over his older brother Efraim. In all these instances, the principle followed is worth over birth. Moreover, it is quite possible that the law in Deuteronomy is not really about supporting the rights of the firstborn son but about supporting the status of the first wife. If this is so, then the radical departure from the ancient system is complete. Since worth emerges as the ideal, it stands to reason that worthy causes must similarly be supported.

creation perfect. Furthermore, it would have made much more sense for God to do so since that would befit a perfect God. But, he adds, in his great wisdom he ruled it better to leave to people the completion of creation. God intentionally created the world as less than perfect and empowered human beings to perfect it and themselves.[53]

The origins of humanity, according to Judaism's reading of Scripture, are paired with the responsibility to make the world better; to move the world into which we are placed from "Very Good" to "Excellent." Judaism takes this responsibility seriously. We see ourselves as (junior) partners with God in perfecting the world. That is our mission.

We affirm this mission through the rite of circumcision, according the fourteenth-century author of *Sefer Ha-hinukh*. If the absence of foreskins were so important to God, he could have simply created all males without them rather than require a procedure to surgically remove them. This could have saved the parents some distress and the infants some discomfort. In fact, babies are born without foreskins infrequently, but it does happen. However, argues the author, this would deprive human beings of being active partners in fixing God's creation. Circumcision is thus a regular reminder of our mission of repairing the world. And we affirm this mission in a prayer that concludes every worship service: "to perfect the world under the kingship of God."[54]

To complete this mission, several things are needed. First, we must be willing to be engaged with the world, not isolated from it. The Jerusalem Talmud advised that to settle a legal dispute the disputants ought to "go out and see how the public is accustomed to act."[55] It was not just good advice for the case under discussion. It was a warning against being too insular. But for one notable exception, Jews have never been ascetics, living the cloistered life of hermits in splendid isolation. The possible exception was the Dead Sea sect, or Essenes, who lived out their lives in poverty, celibacy, and silence some two thousand years ago. But recent scholarship has now called into question the conclusion reached by Pere de Vaux about the Qumran community.[56] Apparently, the residents were not poor, or celibate,

---

53. Luzzatto, *Way of God*, vol. 1, ch. 1, 30–36.

54. It is in the discussion of circumcision that the *Sefer HaHinukh* (Law no. 2) comments that the surgical procedure necessitates human beings acting as partners with God: "God wanted Jews to be made complete by human means." Thus circumcision is an act of partnership with God in the perfection of humanity.

55. b. *Berakhot* 45a.

56. The study of the Dead Sea sect has occupied scholars for many years. Louis

or silent—at least in the first and longest period of occupation. To be sure, there have been attempts by others to relegate Jews to remote or undesirable areas. But that was not what Judaism advocates or what Jews wanted. And the communities or neighborhoods into which Jews voluntarily move today are intended to allow for mutual support and provide essential services, not as a retreat from what was perceived to be the vices of civilization. Jews may reside in Jewish enclaves but remain fully engaged with the world: in business, in education, in politics.

The second thing needed to fulfill the mission of perfecting the world is empathy. Human beings take on responsibility when they feel the suffering of others. A Jewish folktale illustrates this point. A terrible Russian cold wave was causing great distress to the poor. One bitingly cold day, the local rabbi went to solicit the only wealthy man in town for the funds to help shield the poor form the cold. The wealthy man had a reputation of being miserly. The rabbi knocked and the wealthy man opened the door. "Come in," he said to the rabbi. Unlike everyone else in town, he was only in shirtsleeves because his house was well-heated. But the rabbi declined. Instead, he asked the wealthy man to step outside for a moment while the rabbi engaged him in casual conversation. In just a few minutes, the wealthy man was shivering in the bitter cold. He asked, "Rabbi, what did you come here for?" The rabbi responded, "I need money from you to buy coal to heat the homes of the poor." "So why don't you come in and we'll discuss it by the fire?" "No," said the rabbi, "if we sit by the fire you will be warm and comfortable and you really won't understand how the poor are suffering so. You can only appreciate their pain when you also stand out here in the cold."[57]

This is one reason Jews fast on the Day of Atonement, the most solemn day of the Jewish year. By not eating or drinking Jews are directed to focus on the spiritual rather the physical aspects of life. But there is an auxiliary benefit. Fasting engenders within us empathy for those who have no food to eat; those who do not choose to fast, but those who are compelled to fast. We better understand and appreciate our responsibilities when we can empathize with those in need.

A story is told of two Jewish girls who arrive late to school. The teacher demands an explanation. One little girl says: "Sarah's doll broke

---

Ginzberg published *An Unknown Jewish Sect* in 1970. Amir Drori and Yitzhak Magen's finding, that the Qumran complex was founded by Hasmoneans as part of a line of fortresses, is mentioned by Michael Wise, Martin Albegg Jr., and Edward Cook, *The Dead Sea Scrolls: A New Translation*, 22, 23.

57. Telushkin, *Jewish Humor*, 171–72.

and I helped her fix it." "But," said the stern teacher incredulously, "you don't know anything about repairing dolls." "I know," said the little girl, "I helped her cry." Edmund Fleg, in his *Dynamics of Emancipation*, expressed the same thought. "I am a Jew," he affirmed, "because in all places where there are tears and suffering, the Jew weeps."[58]

Remarkably, we find the same sense of empathy integrated into ritual law. Those appointed as prayer leaders for the days of Awe must be married with children for only those who have others dependent upon them and only those who must take into account the sentiments of others can serve as appropriate prayers leaders for the community.

The third thing required in order to fulfill the mission to improve the world is the realization that our actions can and do make a difference. The story is told of Rabbi Israel of the town of Vishnitz who, along with his aide, used to take nightly strolls looking for an opportunity to do some good deed. One evening, the rabbi turned to his aide and motioned him to join him inside the home of the local bank director. The rabbis sat down and said absolutely nothing for twenty minutes. Then he arose, bid the banker farewell and began to leave. Before he reached the door, the bank director asked, "Rabbi, why did you come here?" The rabbi replied, "To do a good deed." "What good deed?" asked the bank director. The rabbi explained: "It says in the Talmud that just as you are required to admonish someone if you know the reproof would be heeded, so too are you required to keep silent if you know your reproof would be ignored." Now what kind of service would I be performing if I just sat in my own house and was silent? No, I knew that I had to go the house of the person who would not listen to reproof and sit there quietly and not offer it. So I came here to perform that requirement." "But perhaps I will listen?" the banker objected. "I'm afraid you won't," said the rabbi. But the banker was insistent so the rabbi relented. "There is a certain widow who has not been able to make her mortgage payments and you have sent her a notice that you will repossess her house." "That has nothing to do with me," protested the banker. "I am not the owner of the bank. I am just the director. I don't have the power to forgive a loan; it's not my money. There is nothing I can do." "Exactly as I said," said the rabbi, "you will not listen." And he walked away without saying another word.

---

58. Edmund Fleg is an interesting personality. Writing in French, he authored biographies of Moses and Solomon. Yet perhaps his greatest contribution was his 1927 defense of Judaism entitled *Why I Am a Jew*.

The bank director could not sleep that night. The next morning, he paid the widow's mortgage out of his own pocket.[59]

Judaism teaches that to be truly human means taking responsibility for others. It means being dedicated to making the world a better place. It means being *part of* the world, not *apart from* the world. Judaism condones no monasteries because Judaism insists that there is a mission to constructively engage the world and improve it. Judaism is far less interested in teaching people how to get to heaven than in teaching people how they must make this world heavenly. Life after death—as significant a theological issue it is for Jews—is less important than life before death. The task of human beings, as Judaism sees it, is to make life before death better for all. In fact, it would be no overstatement to suggest that Jews get to heaven by getting others there first.

This thought was well expressed by Wilhelm Jerusalem in 1921 reflecting on the biblical phrase imploring Abraham to "become a blessing." It requires, he says, "that everyone shall so order his life that the lives of others also shall be thereby vigorously speeded on and made happy . . . the commandment also tells me clearly that I am not alone in the world, that my life is destined to make the lives of other human beings easier, and that my actions and aspirations fulfill their purpose only if through them the lives of others and the life of all the world are vigorously aided."[60]

Vigorously aiding others, physically and spiritually, is a crucial theme of the biblical book of Jonah. Jonah is a reluctant prophet. God wants to send him on a mission to Nineveh, a thriving—and Gentile—metropolis. The mission is to induce the residents to repent of their sins and thereby avoid Divine punishment. But Jonah does not want to go. He books passage on a ship going in the opposite direction, but to no avail. A sudden violent storm forces the ship's crew to take drastic and reluctant action. Thrown overboard, he is swallowed by a big fish (no mention of a whale in the Hebrew text) and spewed out on shore some three days later. He is ultimately convinced that he must accept the mission and fulfill his responsibility to the men, women, and children of the city of Nineveh. His mission is successful: the inhabitants heed his message and are saved.

---

59. Zevin, on Exod 6:12. Hasidism began as a movement with the disciples of Rabbi Israel Ba'al Shem Tov, who lived in Poland during the eighteenth century. Hasidism emphasized the joyous practice of Judaism and espoused many mystical elements. Hasidic masters were revered as exemplars and mentors.

60. Wilhelm Jerusalem's comment is published in *Du Sollst Zum Segen Werden*, translated into English in *Foundations of Jewish Ethics*, 62.

Two ideas are noteworthy. First, the entire book is predicated on God's desire for the salvation of all people. It is Jonah who had to learn the lesson that salvation is not reserved only for a select group, namely, Jews. And Jonah had to take responsibility as an agent of God to ensure that salvation was secured. From this we learn that Jews have a sacred responsibility for others. Second, the book of Jonah reinforces my earlier point regarding respect. Jonah was not sent to convert the inhabitants of Nineveh but to convince them to repent. In other words, God, as Jews read the book of Jonah, did not want Gentiles to be Jewish but simply to be good. Respect for others means accepting others for who they are rather than trying to make them into what you want. That Jews read the book of Jonah publicly throughout the world on the holiest day of the year speaks volumes for how central the theme of taking responsibility for others is in Judaism. What is given prominence of place and time indicates more than anything else what is most important in a given religion. For Judaism, it is responsibility.

Noteworthy is the fact the Hebrew word for responsibility comes from the same root as the word for "another person." It is as if the Hebrew language itself emphasizes the point that to be a responsible person means looking after others. As Elie Wiesel notes: "The emphasis on the *other* is paramount in Judaism: *Achrayut*, responsibility, contains the word *Akher*, the Other. We are resposible for the other."[61]

The Torah describes in detail the sacrificial ritual to be performed by the high priest on the Day of Atonement. First he makes expiation for himself, then for his household, and then for the entire community.[62] It is a noteworthy progression. Responsibility begins with oneself, then extends to those closest to us, and then widens to everyone. As Rabbi Israel Salanter once taught: "First a person should put his house together, then his town, then the world." Similarly, the entire people were liable to bring a sin offering even though a fraction of the people had, unintentionally and under the assumption that the action was warranted, violated a prescription of the Torah. The underlying idea is that everyone bears at least some responsibility for the ills of society.

When Philo of Alexandria tried to explicate the Torah for a Greek audience, he needed to explain how it is that Moses, and all the patriarchs

---

61. Wiesel, *Sages and Dreamers*, 184.
62. The ritual of the Day of Atonement appears in ch. 16 of the book of Leviticus. In v. 6, Aaron first makes expiation for himself and for his household. Later, in v. 17, he then makes expiation for the whole congregation. The law of sacrifice for a communal sin follows the opinion of Rabbi Yehudah in the Mishnah (*Horayot* 1:5).

before him, were shepherds. In Hellenistic society shepherds were held in low esteem. In his essay on Moses, Philo explained that shepherds make exceptionally fine leaders. That is because shepherds act to protect each and every lamb in their care. They must remain always vigilant to ward off wolves and always ready to recover all stragglers. What Philo describes is, in essence, responsibility for others. It is not just an attribute of the historic leaders of the Jewish people. It is an attribute, Philo argues, that well serves every nation.[63]

Judaism also demands that we take responsibility for our planet and the creatures that inhabit it. When the first human being is placed in the garden of Eden, he is given the task "to cultivate it and to protect it" (Gen 2:15). The rabbis later derive from this narrative a requirement to be diligent custodians of the earth, anticipating the science of ecology by almost two thousand years. Moreover, the animals on the earth must be properly tended not because they have "rights," but because human beings have responsibilities. Consider this otherwise unremarkable verse in the book of Deuteronomy (11:15) that describes how God gives "grass in your fields for your cattle and you shall eat and be satisfied." The untrained reader glosses over both the content and the order, but not the rabbis. The untrained reader reads this verse as a statement that the bounty of forage available to animals in the field will result in their growth and, when slaughtered for food, provide ample sustenance for the inhabitants of the land. But the rabbis see something more. The fact that forage for animals precedes the description of human satisfaction results in the Jewish tradition concluding that animals must be fed before humans may eat.[64] Domesticated animals rely on humans for their survival. Humans derive benefit from raising animals but in exchange for that benefit comes serious responsibility.

The final word on responsibility belongs to Homer Simpson. He noted: "Weaseling out of things is important to learn. It's what separates us

---

63. Philo, *On the Life of Moses*, in *The Essential Philo*, bk. 1, sect. 11, 205: "For the business of a shepherd is a preparation for the office of king" since the good shepherd must manage the flock and protect it form harm.

64. It is the Talmud (*b. Berakhot* 40a) that rules how animals must be fed before their masters. An excellent book on the Jewish responsibility to protect the environment is Dr. Richard H. Schwatrz's *Judaism and Global Survival*. Schwartz cites the commentary (Midrash Ecclesiastes Rabbah 7:28) that describes how God took the first human being and let him pass before all the trees of the Garden of Eden and said: "See My works, how fine and excellent they are! All that I have created, for you I have created them. Think upon this and do not corrupt and desolate My world, for if you corrupt it, there is no one to set it right after you" (*Judaism and Global Survival*, 37).

from the animals . . . except the weasel." As usual, Homer has gotten things right, but in the wrong way. Lacking what philosophers call a rational will, animals have no sense of responsibility at all. Human beings are endowed with a rational will and should have a sense of responsibility. Thus evading responsibilities is only something that human beings can do. But that is not the objective. In Homer's world—a world much like our own—evading responsibility and avoiding blame is a worthy pursuit. That accounts, in part, for the sorry state in which we find ourselves today. If that is to change, then it is not important to learn how to evade responsibility. It is important to learn to accept responsibility. And Judaism emphasizes that point through texts, exemplars, and even in ritual.

REVERENCE FOR LIFE

Two very different kinds of weapons were deployed in the 1970s and the contrast between them serves as a fitting point of entry into any analysis of reverence for life. As early as 1958 the United States developed the technology for an enhanced radiation weapon. It was a thermonuclear device designed to release far less explosive energy than was the norm but emit enormous pulses of deadly radiation. For military strategists, this technology was particularly useful as a tactical weapon during the Cold War. The radiation could penetrate the armor of Soviet tanks and kill the crews, countering the Soviet advantage in the sheer number of tanks they could assign to an attack in Europe. But the weapon, dubbed the "neutron bomb," proved to be controversial. The Soviets called it the "capitalist bomb" because it was engineered to kill people yet preserve property. Even Americans were troubled. But the weapons were deployed and remained in service until the final series was retired in 2003. However, it was not moral compunction that compelled taking these weapons out of service. Rather, it was the fact that new tank designs and more sophisticated materials protected tank crews from radiation rendering the neutron bomb ineffective.

In 1978 the first battalion of Israeli-made Merkavah tanks was introduced. The Merkavah tank was the second generation of domestic tanks made in Israel, adopting the best aspects of other tanks shaped by battle experience in Israel's previous wars. The critical feature of the Merkavah tank was that it was designed—above all else—to protect the crew. Unlike all previous tanks, the crew compartment was placed in the rear and the engine in front. The gun turret was also mounted further to the rear of its platform and the crew accessed the tank through a rear door allowing especially for undetected exit. And the armor was attached in such a way as to allow for rapid repair of battle damage. In other words, the tank crew was nestled within a protective cocoon. This was a tank that could only be designed in Israel where every soldier's life was considered precious and where the value of reverence for life infuses military strategy.

To be sure, the "neutron bomb" was also designed to save lives by serving as a deterrent against any potential attack. But if actually used, the "neutron bomb" would kill the soldiers inside it while leaving the tank intact (not to mention any surrounding structures). The Merkavah was designed so that even if the tank did not remain intact, the soldiers inside would be safe: sacrifice the property to save the people. A society that reveres life sets its priorities in this way. And Israeli society is built upon essential and historical Jewish values.

In the Middle Ages, areas where Jews lived (often by compulsion) were traversed by narrow alleyways in tightly confined neighborhoods. As difficult as things were in the European Ghetto or Arab *mellah*,[65] life went on. And in the course of daily life the residents were often faced with a variety of problems, including what to do when certain events came into conflict. For instance, if two processions—one for a funeral and the other for a wedding—came to an intersection such that one would have to yield to another, which takes precedence? According to Jewish law, the wedding procession has the right of way.[66] This is not because the dead do not deserve respect. But it is because of the greater emphasis Judaism places on life. A wedding is an event that celebrates life. And the celebration of life takes precedence over the rituals of death. That life trumps death is a hallmark of Judaism.

---

65. The ghetto, as an institution, existed well before the term came into use. For example, a restrictive Jewish quarter existed in Speyer in the eleventh century and introduced in Frankfort in 1462 and in Venice in 1516 while the actual word "ghetto" only appears in a papal bull in 1562. The consensus of scholarly opinion is that the word "ghetto" derives from the Italian meaning, "foundry," the site in Venice to which Jews were relegated in the sixteenth century. But there are far earlier accounts of gated sections of a city where Jews were forced to live. The "mellah" was the Arabic term for the restricted part of the city to which Jews in Morocco were confined. For more on the treatment of Jews under Islam, see Bernard Lewis, *The Jews of Islam*, Norman Stillman's classic *The Jews of Arab Lands*, and Martin Gilbert's more recent *In Ishmael's House: A History of Jews in Muslim Lands*.

66. The law giving the right of way to a wedding procession over a funeral procession is encoded in sixteenth-century Rabbi Joseph Karo's *Shulhan Arukh*, Yoreh De'ah 360:1.

The Four R's

Under Roman rule thousands of Jews were sent to their deaths in the gladiatorial arenas. So aside from considering Roman "sporting events" as a prolific waste of time, there was a natural aversion to attending the very events where one's fellow Jew might meet his end. Further, distancing Jews from all things Roman was a rabbinic predilection. Nevertheless, the Talmud allows for attendance on the grounds that a life might be saved. To be sure, there was no guarantee. But even the prospect that one more vote—a thumbs up—might save a human life was sufficient grounds to allow a Jew to attend.[67]

About two hundred and fifty years ago, a noted scholar from Prague was consulted on the question of hunting for sport. It seems that with the advent of the modern period Jews had the possibility to engage in the popular leisure activity of the day. Rabbi Ezekiel Landau[68] considered all the arguments and ruled that hunting is prohibited on the grounds that it may cause unnecessary cruelty to animals and that it may endanger the hunters engaged in the chase. But beyond these matters of Jewish law, he asks a philosophical question: why would anyone *want* to go hunting? Rabbi Landau simply could not understand what possible satisfaction a person could derive in taking the life of animal for no good reason. What led Rabbi Landau to ask this question are millennia of Jewish conditioning that all life is sacred and the preservation of life is supreme.

In Judaism there is no principle more important. The Sabbath, for Jews, is more than just a commemoration of God completing creation. It is a day of renewal and regeneration. The Sabbath involves a host of regulations designed to reconnect us with spiritual needs and set aside our preoccupation with the physical needs that pervade the other days of the week. As such, Asher Ginsberg, writing under the pen name *Ahad Ha'am* (One of the People) in the nineteenth century, remarked: "More than the Jews have kept the Sabbath, the Sabbath has kept the Jews." Yet as important as the Sabbath is for Jews, it is set aside to preserve life.[69] All Sabbath laws

---

67. The Talmudic discussion on the relative merits of attending Roman theatres, circuses, and gladiatorial combat is discussed in *b. Avodah Zarah* 18b. As an interesting aside, one third-century scholar, Rabbi Shimon ben Lakish (known as Resh Lakish), was a champion gladiator, winning 92 matches, before "retiring" and beginning his rabbinic career.

68. Rabbi Ezekiel Landau's responsum on hunting is published in Hebrew in a collection called *Noda B'Yehuda*. A fine English summary is available to non-Hebrew readers in David Novak, *Law and Theology in Judaism*, 55.

69. See Rabbi Isaac Klein's *A Guide to Jewish Religious Practice*, on Sabbath Laws, ch. 5, 76–94.

are suspended for women in childbirth or for the dangerously ill. And the Talmud gives the very practical reason: "Violate one Sabbath for them so that they may observe many others." In fact, when the laws of the Sabbath must be suspended for the ill, no less than the most prominent and pious Jews must tend to their needs to clearly signal that the suspension of Sabbath laws is something we do willingly and intentionally. That life is more important than the Sabbath would only be properly conveyed when the "violations" are performed by the most honored, rather than relegated to others. Jewish laws, says the Talmud emphatically, based on the Torah (Lev 18:4), are designed that we may "live by them, not die by them."[70]

In keeping with this general principle, two examples of its application are focused on Yom Kippur, the Day of Atonement. According to the Torah it is a mandated fast day. As essential fasting is to the commemoration of the day, it is set aside when life is at risk. In that case, it becomes a requirement to eat what is necessary rather than fast. (During a cholera outbreak, a Rabbi Israel Salanter insisted that his entire congregation eat on the Day of Atonement to keep up their strength and, leading the way, he ate in their presence during public prayer.)[71] Preserving life takes precedence over fasting.

And so great is the principle, Jewish tradition holds it to be subjective. Thus while the Talmud (*b. Yoma* 83a) rules that one who feels ill on the Day of Atonement is fed on the advice of a physician, it also concludes that even if the physician deems him to be healthy enough to fast, we reject the physician's opinion in favor of the patient. Citing the proverb "The heart knows its own bitterness" (Prov 14:10), the Talmud concludes even a perceived

---

70. The Talmud posits that matters of health are more important than matters of ritual (*b. Hullin* 10a) so it is not surprising at all to see the extent to which the rabbis will go to preserve and protect life. "You shall live by them" and not die by them becomes the overarching theme of Judaism as the Talmud (*b. Yoma* 85a) puts it. In his excellent review of the pertinent sources in *Health and Medicine in the Jewish Tradition*, 23, Rabbi David M. Feldman cites this passage: "How do we know that avoidance of a threat to life sets aside the Sabbath?" asks the Talmud (*b. Yoma* 85b). Rabbi Simon ben Menassia: "We are told: 'You shall keep the Sabbath, for it is holy unto you' (Exodus 31:13). That means, unto *you* is the Sabbath given over, but you are not given over to the Sabbath." Rabbi Nathan: "We are told: 'The people of Israel shall keep the Sabbath, to observe the Sabbath through the generations' (Exodus 31:16). That means, violate one Sabbath if necessary in order to keep many Sabbaths afterward." Rabbi Yehudah in the name of Rabbi Samuel: "We are told: 'Keep My commandments and ordinances, which if a man do them he will live by them' (Leviticus 18:5). That means live by them and don't die because of them."

71. The noted Yiddish writer I. L. Peretz offers a fictionalized account in his short story "Three Who Ate" (see *Three Gifts and Other Stories*).

danger is compelling enough to supersede the fast. As Rabbi Joseph Karo sums up in his code of Jewish law *(Shulhan Arukh,* Orah Hayyim 329:3): All laws of the Torah are suspended on the possibility that life is in danger, however remote the likelihood.

The second example that illustrates the principle involves an emergency of the Day of Atonement, called by the Torah (Lev 16:31) "the Sabbath of Sabbaths," that is, the ultimate Sabbath. Excavations on the Sabbath or on the Day of Atonement would be a fundamental violation of the law. Digging is an activity that is connected to agriculture (or mining), workday pursuits that are prohibited on the Sabbath. But should a building collapse and people are suspected of being buried under the rubble, we are required to dig out all the survivors. Importantly, the text makes no distinction between Jews and non-Jews. All human life is sacred. All human life must be saved.[72]

And all life must be safeguarded. Indeed, the Torah is filled with laws that speak to the preservation of life. The roofs of ancient houses were part of the living area. Accordingly, when a house was constructed, parapets, that is, railings or fences were required for every roof lest someone fall off (Deut 22:8). On this basis, the Talmud (*b. Bava Kamma* 15a) rules that no well or construction trench was allowed to remain uncovered lest human beings or animals fall in. Even animal life needs to be preserved. As the biblical book of Proverbs (12:10) puts it: "The righteous regard the life of his animal." And since attaining righteousness is the objective of every person, it is more than just selective advice. It is a general rule.

That animals may be eaten for food does not contradict the rule. Eating meat is a divine compromise. Recall that the first two human beings were permitted to eat only of the fruits of the garden of Eden, except for the fruit of the Tree of Knowledge. Human beings were given domain over the animals, but no permission to eat them. In other words, the first human beings were vegetarians. The prophet Isaiah foretells of a future time when predatory animals of all kinds will become herbivorous. In other words, the Messianic period will also be characterized by vegetarianism. From this we may deduce that according to the Bible vegetarianism is, in fact, the

---

72. The Mishnah (*Yoma* 8:7) teaches: "If a person is buried under rubble [from a collapsed building]—even when there is doubt if a person is beneath it, even when there is doubt that the person below is still alive, even when there is suspicion that the victim is an idolater—we dig until we reach his nose. If he is still breathing, we dig him out [even on the Day of Atonement]. If not, we leave the body there [until after the Holy Day is over.]"

ideal. It was required of the earliest people and will be the standard later in history.[73]

But since the expulsion of the first two people from Eden and until the coming of the Messiah, human beings live in an imperfect, rather than ideal, world. In this less than ideal world, human beings are driven by their animal impulses, including a desire for eating meat. God recognizes that to forbid meat entirely would be impossible for human beings to endure. So the Torah permits meat eating, but in a very limited way. Not every kind of animal may be eaten. Permitted animals must be properly and painlessly slaughtered. No blood may ever be eaten since the blood was considered the source of life. And no flesh may ever be eaten from a living animal. But this allowance—the Divine compromise—is temporary. The principle of the preservation of all animal life is affirmed, although not yet fully operational in terms of diet. But in terms of ritual it surely is. Thus while thanks to God is recited in the form of a prayer when acquiring any new clothes, that prayer is omitted when acquiring new shoes. Shoes are made of leather and leather comes from animal hide. That an animal had to die in order for us to wear shoes is no cause to be thankful.

Reverence for human life in particular is the subject of one of the most important passages in all of rabbinic literature. In an earlier section I mentioned how the principle of respect for others is generated from the biblical account of creation. By creating a single, solitary human being, potential conflict is reduced since no person can argue that he or she has a finer pedigree. But the creation of a single, solitary human being also leads the rabbis to draw another conclusion, one that explains the Jewish preoccupation with the preservation of life. A single man was created in the world, says the Talmud, to teach that if any man causes a single soul to perish, Scripture imputes it to him as if he has caused an entire world to perish; and if any man saves a single soul, Scripture imputes it to him as if he has saved an entire world.[74] This single sentence unambiguously encapsulates Judaism's regard for all human life. Every person represents all humanity-an entire world, just as the first human being was all humanity. And the whole world, borrowing from an old spiritual, is in our hands. That is why God, through

---

73. It is only after the flood that meat is permitted (Gen 9:3), provided that the animal is dead. In the book of Isaiah (11:6–10), vegetarianism is implied when Isaiah describes how carnivores will eat straw. For a fuller account of the implications, see Berman, *Vegetarianism and the Jewish Tradition*.

74. A single soul equals an entire world is included in the admonition to witnesses in Mishnah Sanhedrin 4:5.

Moses, reminds us that life and death, blessing and curse are placed before us all the time, and then exhorts us to "Choose life!" (Deut 30:9).

To choose life means to put the preservation of life ahead of any other concern. As much as Judaism demands prompt burial of the dead as matter of respect for the body even after life has ended, and as much as Judaism considers autopsies as a desecration of the dead, autopsies are not only allowed but even required when the medical information that can be gleaned from the procedure is helpful in saving a life. Again, while there are some specific concerns related to organ transplantation, Judaism endorses cadaver transplantation since it is a life-saving technique.[75] And there has never been any concern whatsoever about live-donor transplantation, including blood transfusions. To choose life has historically meant to become expert in those techniques that save lives and to shun those activities that take lives. That is why a disproportionate number of Jews have become doctors. That is why so few Jews go hunting. And that is why no Jewish boy grows up with the ambition of becoming a ritual slaughterer.

To choose life means to reject voluntary martyrdom. The first-century historian Josephus (*War of the Jews*, bk. 7, chs. 8 and 9) tells the story of the defenders of Massada who, rather than be captured alive by the besieging Roman, took their own lives. Interestingly, it is a story that finds no confirmation in any of the rabbinic texts of the same period. The story is not likely true. Josephus even records what he claims is the last speech given by the leader of the defenders. How he could have known what was said when there were no survivors and no Romans present to overhear he never explains. It was probably a story concocted by Josephus to play for his Roman audience who would have found the story heroic. If the story were true, the rabbis would have condemned the act of mass suicide rather than condone it since it is contrary to the principle of reverence for life. There are firsthand accounts of Jews in the Rhineland who, rather than be raped or tortured by crusaders on the way to the holy land, threw themselves into the river and drowned.[76] But these sad events were never glorified. Judaism has never sanctioned taking one's own life for any cause. And Judaism has

---

75. The conditions under which autopsies are permitted—even necessary—in Judaism appear in Klein, *Guide to Jewish Religious Practice*, 274–75. The permissibility of transplants and transfusions are explained by Rabbi David Feldman, *Health and Medicine in the Jewish Tradition*, ch. 12, 103ff.

76. The sad story of Jewish communities that chose death over torture and rape emerges from the firsthand accounts of witnesses. See Marcus, *Jew in the Medieval World*, 115ff.

never sanctioned taking the lives of others. Suicide bombers could never be accepted or defended or justified or rationalized, let alone celebrated.

Needless to say, if life is sacred and Judaism is averse to taking lives, then capital punishment seems anomalous. Yet the execution of those convicted of committing heinous crimes is indeed required by the Torah. But rather than an anomaly, it is an irony. The irony is that to uphold the principle of the sanctity of life, violators must forfeit their own lives. Any lesser punishment would fail to establish the primacy of the principle. The ultimate punishment is applied to the ultimate violation of the ultimate principle. Even so, the rabbis during the second century of the Common Era insisted that while capital punishment still applied in theory, it hardly ever would be acted on. Two rabbis, for example, boasted that were they members of the Supreme Court, no criminal would ever be executed.[77] Executions, in any case, would nearly be impossible since the rabbis attached so many qualifications to the law that would make conviction a challenge. For example, two eyewitnesses to the crime were needed. And the witnesses had to warn the perpetrator of the consequences before the act was committed. And the perpetrator had to acknowledge the warning. And the witnesses' testimony had to agree in every minor detail. And the judges' decision could not be unanimous. In effect, the threshold for conviction was set so high that it was never likely to be crossed. Of course, the question is why would the rabbis undermine a penalty prescribed by the Torah? And the answer is that it is the Torah itself that conditioned the rabbis to preserve life.

Imagine what the world would be like if all people were conditioned to choose life, to take responsibility for themselves and for others, to exercise restraint, and to treat everyone with respect. My contention is that the world would be a much better place than the one in which we live today. That better world is indeed possible if the fundamentals of Judaism were learned and embraced.

77. The Mishnah (*Makkot* 1:10) reports: "A Sanhedrin which executes [a criminal] once in seven years is known as destructive. Rabbi Elazar ben Azariah says: once in seventy years. Rabbi Tarfon and Rabbi Akiva say: if we had been members of the Sanhedrin, no person would ever have been executed. Rabbi Simon ben Gamaliel says: They would have been responsible for the proliferation of murderers in Israel." While Rabbi Simon ben Gamaliel takes the position that executions serve as a deterrent as well as eliminating a threat to civil society, his colleagues believed that capital punishment was not warranted, presumably because human justice is flawed and once a life is taken, if a mistake is recognized there is no remedy. The rigorous demands of examination listed in *m. Sanhedrin*, ch. 5, thus made conviction highly unlikely.

Chapter Three

The Three H's

JUST BEYOND THE FUNDAMENTAL values are three additional values that inhere in Judaism and are essential to making life better: helpfulness, holiness, and hopefulness. Helpfulness is obviously a concept that, when applied, impacts on conduct toward others. Holiness, as I shall explain, does the same thing. But hopefulness is not quite the same. While there is an aspect of hopefulness that will have a practical external benefit, it is primarily an inward directed concept. Judaism is more than just a regimen of social service. Judaism includes guidance on how we can *feel* good, not only *do* good, as undeniably important that is.

HELPFULNESS

What happened to Mohn Asyraf Haziq is one of the most appalling sights ever captured on camera. Haziq, a foreign student from Malaysia, was studying in London when the riots broke out in the summer of 2011. On his bicycle, he was riding to a local store to buy food one evening in order to break his fast during the Muslim observance of Ramadan. He was attacked by rioters and left on the street bleeding profusely. Video surveillance captured what happened next. A small number of men approached him, appearing to be offering help. One person helps him to his feet and leads him away. But while he is being helped along, another man rummages through the pack on Haziq's back, taking some electronics. Soon a bicyclist arrives and has a look through as well. And even the first man to render assistance has a look through as well. People are robbed all the time. But what is particularly galling to most observers is the fact that an innocent man was robbed under the pretext of being helped. This violates our very understanding of the meaning of rendering assistance. There is an essential cognitive dissonance between helpfulness and deceptiveness. When helpfulness becomes a ruse, a strategy employed for exploiting the needy, there is something profoundly wrong. It demands that we look deeply and carefully at human conduct and what might be done to change it for the better.

The very first woman, as you might recall, named "Mother of All Life," Havah, in short, had no courtship problems whatsoever. There was only one man in the world for her, literally. But ever since, and especially in liberal Western democracies, finding the right mate has become a challenge. Judaism has always maintained that *finding* that right person follows from *being* the right person. But even being the right person does not assure success. And as we find ourselves busier and busier pursuing our studies and then our careers, we find less and less time to devote to dating. So today more and more people, young and old, rely on some assistance. Computer dating services have become especially popular—and successful. As a former congregational rabbi, I can personally attest to the dramatic increase in the number of couples who meet with me after their engagement and tell me how they met through a computer dating service. Some computer services provide only the particulars and leave the subscribers to figure out whom they wish to meet. But other more sophisticated services determine what they think make two people compatible and provide only those names to each. The ancients thought marriage was far too important to be left to the young or to strangers or, nowadays, to computers. The ancients arranged marriages. And it is a practice that endures in many parts of the world.

The Torah (Genesis 24) narrates the events surrounding the first arranged marriage. Abraham, unhappy with the standards of the local population, did not want his son Isaac marrying anyone outside his circle of kin. So he entrusted his faithful servant Eliezer to return to the "Old Country," that is, Mesopotamia—a very old country—to bring back a wife. Eliezer took on the mission but he was given no particulars from Abraham as to what qualities would make a woman suitable for Isaac. It was Eliezer who would have to sort this out on his own. Before he reaches town, Eliezer decides on a plan. With his camels in tow, he would go the local well. Whichever woman comes forward to fetch him water and water for his camels as well will be Isaac's bride. As it happens, Rebecca sees the stranger and his caravan, and runs to fetch him water and water for his camels too. Eliezer presents her with gifts, negotiates with her family, and brings her back to Isaac, his mission successfully accomplished.

This biblical story tells us about more than ancient marital practices or about the continuity of Israel's patriarchy. The story tells us about what quality makes for a good person, a person worthy of Abraham's son. That quality is helpfulness. Eliezer did not settle on a plan that would determine the status, or net worth, or attractiveness of a potential bride. Eliezer believed that the ideal quality, the one quality that was more important than anything else, was helpfulness. Jewish tradition has always looked at the stories of the patriarchs and matriarchs as more than just history. These stories are lessons for good conduct. Hence, the selection of Rebecca is not just a story about our distant ancestors. It is an example of the kind of character we all should have.

To add to the impact of this story, I offer a short lesson in rabbinic hermeneutics. Hermeneutics refers to the method by which a text is interpreted. Some rabbis long ago deduced that Rebecca was a mere three years old when she came to the well and was subsequently "engaged." It sounds quite incredible and I will attempt to make it sound less so in due course. But first, I will explain how these rabbis came to this startling deduction. It is based on a simple rule of operation. The rule holds that events that appear in adjoining passages of Scripture occurred at the same time, unless specifically stated otherwise. With this rule in hand, some simple arithmetic is all else that is needed. The text tells us that Sarah gave birth to Isaac at the age of ninety and died at the age of 127. That means that Isaac was thirty-seven years old at the time of his mother's death. Since the passage describing Sarah's death is followed by the passage relating Rebecca's birth, and applying the rule just cited, Rebecca was born when Isaac was thirty-seven. Since the Torah tells us that Isaac was married at the age of forty, the ineluctable conclusion is that Rebecca was three years old when she was engaged and married.[1]

While it sounds incredible, there is supportive evidence from the narrative itself. First, Rebecca's family reluctantly gives her away in marriage. They appeal to Eliezer to let her reside with them for ten years. That makes sense if she was merely three at the time of "engagement." In effect, they wanted to raise her until she reached puberty. Second, accompanying her on her trip to Isaac's location was a nursemaid. A nursemaid would only be

---

1. For the calculation of Rebecca's young age at marriage, see RaShI on Gen 25:20 whose source is *Seder Olam*, an early rabbinic text that locates each biblical event in time.

useful to a small child. And third, when Rebecca sees Isaac from afar she falls off her camel. For hopeless romantics, Rebecca, it seems, was in love at first sight. More likely, however, absent infant car seats back then, toddlers were not secure on camelback.[2]

But my point here is not to defend this reading of the text. Instead, I ask the questions, of what benefit would it be, as the rabbis read it, if Rebecca were determined to have been three years old? How does it affect the lesson of the story? If Rebecca were three years old the story shows that she was helpful from a very early age. Helpfulness was part of her character early on. And so must it be with us.

The Ammonites and Moabites are forever excluded from the ranks of the people Israel (Deut 23:4), even though their origins make them kin.[3] The Amalekites are excluded because of what they did. They brutally attacked the weakest segment of Israelites following the exodus from Egypt. The Ammonites and Moabites, however, are excluded because of what they did not do. They did not come forward and provide food and water for the weary Israelite wayfarers. It is not an act of barbarity that warrants their exclusion; it is an absence of helpfulness. They failed to live up to the expectations of Judaism that help must be provided to those in need. Since they violated the basic code of conduct, they could not be counted among Jews. They simply did not belong.

In an earlier chapter I mentioned how the Talmud allowed for attending a gladiatorial combat in the hope that a life might be saved. In the same Talmudic discussion Rabbi Nathan offers another reason. According to Jewish law a woman may only remarry after she is properly divorced or after her husband dies. In ordinary circumstances, the husband's death is easily ascertained. Death was at home and in the presence of family or later in history, in a hospital under the care of medical professionals. There were

---

2. Rebecca's family requests that she remain with them an additional ten years in Gen 24:55. If she were three, the ten years would put her at thirteen, roughly the age of puberty. In other words, her family requested that she reside with them until she comes of age; a perfectly sensible request. Genesis 24:59 reports that her nursemaid accompanied her. That she fell off her camel is reported in Gen 24:64.

3. Both the Moabites and Ammonites are descendants of Abraham's nephew Lot (Gen 19:36–38). The Amalekites brutally attacked the vulnerable Israelites following the exodus (Exod 17:8) preying on the weak and weary (Deut 25:18). The scriptural exclusion of the Ammonites and Moabites (Deut 23:4–5) is based on the fact that neither offered the Israelites bread and water before they asked. The implication is that helpfulness was expected. In fact, the Moabites attempted to destroy the Israelites through magical means.

ample people there to attest to the death of the husband. That is precisely what Jewish law demands: witnesses. Without such witnesses, a woman had no permission to remarry. Given this legal requirement, Rabbi Nathan argues that going to the gladiatorial arena serves another important purpose: it allows Jews to witness a death and provide that information to the widow. So aside from the role of potentially saving a life, attending the arena games could prove helpful to the survivors. First, it gave the survivors information that allowed them to grieve. And second, it allowed for the widow to remarry. There could be little more helpful than this. So important was the value of helpfulness that Rabbi Nathan construed it as a reason for doing what might otherwise be considered off-limits.

In 1964, Kitty Genovese, a decent, pretty young woman of twenty-eight, was stalked through the streets close to her Kew Gardens, New York, apartment and stabbed again and again by a man who followed her home and took almost half an hour to kill her. During that bloody eternity, according to an extraordinary account published in the *New York Times*. "Oh my God!" she screamed at one point, "He stabbed me! Please help me! Someone help me!" Minutes later, before the murderer, Winston Mosely, came back and attacked her for the final time, she screamed, "I'm dying! I'm dying!"

The reason why the murderer's actions and the victim's calls for help are so well documented is that the police were able to find thirty-eight of Kitty's neighbors who admitted they witnessed the awful event. They heard the screams and understood her cry for assistance. Peeking out their windows they saw enough of the killer to provide a good description of his clothing and appearance. On especially sharp-eyed person was able to report that the murderer was sucking his finger as he left the scene; he had cut himself during the attack. Another witness had the distinction of being the only person Kitty Genovese recognized in the audience taking in her last moments. She looked at him and called him by name. He did not reply. No one really came to help Kitty at all. Only one person shouted four words at the killer—"Let the girl alone!"—and the only phone call to the police came after the murderer had walked to his car and driven away.

I dredge up this ghastly episode because one generation later, it seems to have repeated. Albeit the site and circumstances are somewhat different, the same indifference has reoccurred. Forty people stood by in 1996 as a terror-stricken, thirty-three-year-old Deletha Word was beaten and brutalized and compelled to escape her attacker by jumping off the MacArthur

Bridge that spans the Detroit River even though she could not swim. Apparently, a scuffle erupted following a fender-bender accident and it quickly escalated. The perpetrator repeatedly thrashed her with a crowbar and chased her to her death. Incredibly, some people cheered the attacker or laughed at the spectacle. One brave latecomer tried unsuccessfully to reach Deletha Word in the river, but the others did nothing but gather on the bridge and watch as if the spectacle was staged for their entertainment.

Dortha Word, Deletha's tormented mother, said: "The ones who were standing there and looking, they were just as guilty." Her message is true; but it remains unheeded. On March 18, 2017, a fifteen-year-old girl in Chicago went missing after going to church. Three days later, she was discovered to have been abducted and sexually assaulted by at least four men. Her story came to light when a relative was informed of the assault and reported it to the police. Investigators determined that the entire assault was posted online by the perpetrators and witnessed live by forty viewers, none of whom bothered to alert the authorities! Commenting on the story, Northwestern University Law Professor Jeffrey Urdangen points out that is not illegal to watch a live broadcast of a crime or to fail to report it.

In contrast, the Torah (Lev 19:16) commands us never to stand by idly when a person's life is in danger. I have already argued that preserving life is fundamental. But what the Torah adds here is that one must *act* on that principle. As the Talmud expands: Do not watch with indifference when a fellow human being is in mortal danger by without hastening to the rescue.[4]

The stories of Kitty Genovese, Deletha Word, and an unnamed Chicago teenager disturb us. But the detachment of those who could help but did not offends us. The difference resides in the difference between good citizens and good people. Good citizens obey the law. Good people respond to a higher law. Most people will drive past a roadside accident rather than stopping to assist. To be sure, there are many excuses that might be offered. Stopping to assist may expose the helper to a potential lawsuit if the aid offered results in further injury of death. The paramedics are probably on the way, we sometimes reason. Someone better qualified to assist will be

---

4. The requirement to intervene and save those drowning or under attack is included in the Talmud, *b. Sanhedrin* 73a. The requirement to intervene stands in contrast with many other examples of indifference. In 2010, for instance, a homeless man named Hugo Alfredo Tale-Yax attempted to save a New York City woman from being assaulted and robbed. He was stabbed for his trouble by the attacker. Even the woman he saved failed to call the police. By the time someone finally called the police and help arrived, Tale-Yax was dead.

around shortly. Or using the cell phone to alert the authorities is sufficient. We might have passengers in the car who need to reach their destination without delay. But whatever the rationalization, of one thing we can certain: the police will not track us down for failing to stop, arrest us or charge us with a crime. (That is unless you are in the Province of Quebec, Canada, or other similar jurisdictions where so-called "Good Samaritan Laws" require you to stop and assist.) The operative principle is that so long as you were not involved in the accident you are not required to stop. A person who failed to stop and assist and broke no law is, by any objective account, still a good citizen. Good citizens are simply obliged not to hurt others. But Judaism teaches that is insufficient. Judaism teaches that we are obliged to help others.

The principle of helpfulness is articulated near the very beginning of the Bible. God declares that it is not good for the first human being to be alone. He needs "a fitting helper" (Gen 2:18). That is to say, the purpose of the second human being is to help the first human being. Companionship was a bonus to her presence. Helpfulness was the purpose of her existence.

The principle of helpfulness is also deeply encoded in Jewish law. One prayer, called the *Sh'ma* by Jews, is often called the central affirmation of the Jewish faith. (Incidentally, Judaism is not a faith but a way of life.) It reads: "Hear, O Israel, the Lord Our God is One." This prayer forms the central core of both the morning and evening prayer services. The *Sh'ma* is also the proclamation with which Jews conclude the Day of Atonement and the last prayer recited by Jews about to die. There is an entire section in the books of Jewish law that deal with the regulations of how and when the *Sh'ma* is recited. One law stipulates that all kinds of labor must cease when the time comes to recite the *Sh'ma*. In other words, this prayer is so important that it merits our undivided attention. So all kinds of labor must be suspended for the recital of the *Sh'ma* . . . except one. As sixteenth-century Rabbi Joseph Karo formulates the exception in his authoritative and influential code: "If a person is preoccupied with looking after the public welfare when the time for reciting the *Sh'ma* arrives, that person may NOT stop."[5] That is to say, as central as the recital of the *Sh'ma* is for Jews, looking after the needs of others is more critical. I would put it this way: we don't stop being helpful to others even for the recital of crucial prayers. Helpfulness outweighs piety.

---

5. As important as the *Sh'ma* is, time is not taken for its recital when engaged in looking after the public welfare according to Rabbi Karo's *Shulhan Arukh*, Orah Hayyim 70:4.

Prescription for an Ailing World

According to Maimonides, helpfulness is also the highest degree of charitableness. Hebrew has no word for charity. The word commonly assumed to mean charity (*tzedakah*) is actually the Hebrew word for righteousness. Charity is merely one aspect of doing what is right. While the word for charity may be in question, the principle certainly is not. Maimonides asserts that there are eight degrees of charity, which later interpreters suggested could be arranged in the form of a ladder.[6] The lowest degree of charitableness, and hence positioned on the lowest rung of the ladder, is giving begrudgingly when asked directly. Higher than that is giving begrudgingly but not waiting until asked. Giving anonymously is higher still. But the highest degree of all has nothing to do with giving. Maimonides ranks teaching a person a trade so that he can become gainfully employed and self-sufficient as the highest form of charitableness. Note that this ultimate degree of charitableness has nothing to do with money. It has to do with dedicating the time and effort to train a person to be employable. I would call this being helpful more than being charitable. Helping someone learn to earn outranks making a donation for the duration.

Sharing our knowledge and skill is an expression of helpfulness. It is the highest form of righteousness. Refusing to share our knowledge and skill must therefore be its antithesis. And that is precisely what the Talmud teaches. There were several families, or more precisely, guilds, that had special expertise in preparing the necessary elements for the temple service. One such family had the exclusive knowledge for preparing the incense. In what today might be called a "salary dispute," they refused to produce and refused to share their expertise with others. Their unhelpfulness resulted in being cursed by the community.[7]

The principle of helpfulness finds expression in a number of scriptural laws. For example, the Torah teaches that a bystander is commanded to assist in unloading an overburdened animal. And lost property must be returned to the rightful owner (Deut 22:1). The extent to which the finder must go is mentioned in the continuation: "If your fellow does not live near you or you do not know who he is, you shall bring it home and shall remain with you until your fellow claims it; then you shall give it back to him" (Deut 22:2). Regardless of what the lost object may be and independent

---

6. Maimonides's "Eight Degrees of Charity" appears in consecutive paragraphs of his code of Jewish law called *Mishneh Torah*, Laws of Gifts to the Poor 10:7–12.

7. The Talmud (*b. Sheqalim* 14a) condemns the House of Avtinas for refusing to disclose their technique.

of its value, "so shall you do with anything that your fellow loses and you find." The passage concludes with the admonition: "You must not remain indifferent." Apathy is the antithesis of helpfulness.

In July 2004 Eliyahu Ben-Porat was walking along Menachem Begin Street near his home in the Israeli city of Ashkelon when he detected an envelope lying on the ground. He picked it up and, when he opened it, was surprised to discover $6,500 is US currency. There were no immediately visible identifying marks. "It was obvious that I would return the money," he said later, adding: "After all, all of us here in this neighborhood live, thank God, from hand to mouth, and everyone needs money. But this wasn't mine, someone else worked for it, and it's his." Ben-Porat took the money to the local police station where an investigation was begun. With no overt clues to go on, the police looked at every single bill and noticed a name scribbled on one. It was the name of an eighty-year-old woman who lived on the same block as Ben-Porat. They called by phone and asked if she had an envelope of foreign currency. She replied in the affirmative. So they asked her to check if the envelope was where it was supposed to be. It was missing. She was asked how much was missing and she answered: "US$6,500." It turns out that her older sister had placed the envelope near the window when she was cleaning their apartment. It fell outside in the process. Ben-Porat arrived with the police to return to her what was the sisters' entire savings. Ben-Porat assured reporters: "Even if it were a million dollars, I would run to the police to return it." Eliyahu Ben-Porat wanted no reward. He did, however, accept a Model Citizen Certificate from the police, and, no doubt, the gratitude of two neighbors.

I have no idea whether Ben-Porat was religiously observant or whether he was familiar with the precise passage in the Torah. But he was infused with the spirit of helpfulness that inheres in Judaism.

And from a remarkable passage in the book of Deuteronomy (21:7), we learn how much helpfulness was to be incorporated into the human personality. If an unidentified corpse was found in a field, the elders of the nearest city had to declare: "Our hands have not shed this blood nor have our eyes seen it." In other words, to be exonerated from responsibility, the city officials had to publicly attest that they had nothing to do with the death. But this declaration raises an interesting question: why on earth would anyone ever suspect the elders of committing a crime? The rabbis explain that the declaration has nothing to do with suspicion of guilt. Rather, the elders were required to assure all the people that they had not failed to do anything that might have averted the tragedy, like giving the victim food or protection from harm. The assumption is that people are expected to help other people.[8] That also explains why so many volunteers came forward to assist when the tabernacle was under construction that Moses had to turn them away.[9]

A later book of the Bible tells the sad story of Uzzah.[10] When King David was determined to replace the tabernacle with a permanent temple in Jerusalem, he moved the contents of the tabernacle to Jerusalem. The single most important furniture item in the tabernacle was the holy ark that contained the broken shards of the first set of tablets and the replacement set that Moses had engineered. This golden chest was placed on an ox cart and slowly made its way to David's capital city. Along the route, the oxen stumble and the ark tilts to the side, threatening to fall off the cart. Uzzah, being the helpful person everyone ought to be, rushed to hold the holy ark in place, failing to remember that only the authorized few were entitled to handle this sacred treasure. He died on the spot. This story reinforces the point I made in the last chapter, namely, violating the stated limits results in disaster, in this case, death. Uzzah crossed the boundaries. And no matter his good intentions, he failed to honor the proper limits. But understanding Uzzah's motivation is equally important. Uzzah, in that brief moment of time when holy ark was wobbling, did not think about the consequences of illicitly touching a scared object, he thought only of being helpful. Helpfulness was so ingrained in his character that he could not think of doing anything else.

And helpfulness is a lesson learned early. The foundational ceremony of Judaism is the Passover *seder*. It is a ritual performed around the table, including but not limited to, a sumptuous meal. Near the beginning of the proceedings, the leader announces: "Let all who are hungry come in and eat, let all who are needy come and be satisfied." Today, it is unlikely that such an invitation is going to be heard by those in need, let alone accepted. The needy don't seem to linger in the suburbs or condominiums. But in the ancient world, the invitation was serious and would likely be taken up. In any case, it is not necessarily the practical results that count, but the

---

8. The declaration made by the elders of the city that the corpse found in their jurisdiction was not dead as a result of a lack of assistance is mentioned by RaShI in his commentary to Deut 21:7. Its source is the Talmud (*b. Sotah* 45b).

9. Exod 36:6.

10. 2 Samuel 6.

impression it makes and the lesson it teaches. Anyone in need is welcome in our homes. Anyone in need must be assisted. And since the Passover *seder* is designed to be a learning experience particularly for children, it launches them into adult life with the abiding message that help must be extended to all. What is important is not who is in need but to do what is needed.

A six-year-old girl once visited New York City with her father. As many tourists do, they took the ferry to Liberty Island and visit the Statue of Liberty. As they approached, the two were mesmerized by its beauty and meaningfulness. After staring intently at the statue, the little girl looked up to her father and asked: "Tell me, Daddy, doesn't she need someone to help her hold up the light?" That is the ultimate Jewish question; a question addressed at each Passover *seder*. The world needs people to hold up the light of caring and hope, never to be extinguished by indifference of despair.

The principle of helpfulness also finds expression in the Talmud. If a person asks for directions because they are lost or unsure of the way, we are duty bound to give them, even though it may interrupt what we are doing. And were we to give false information just to be rid of the bother, we would have committed a serious sin. To be of helpful service to another person is what defines a society and what describes our purpose from creation.[11] The Talmud further teaches that all the poor and all who are ill must be supported and visited, not just those who are Jewish.[12]

The principle of helpfulness finds expression in the "Physician's Prayer." Writing for Canada's *National Post* (August 13, 2008), Dr. Yoel Abells explains why his graduating class of physicians opted to commit to the physician's prayer attributed to Maimonides, rather than the traditional Hippocratic Oath: "We did so because we saw in the former principles of practice that we hope would guide us in our chosen profession. Maimonides's words formed a humbling prayer in which the physician asks God for the insight, tools and direction needed in order to provide effective and humane care." In truth, the physician's prayer first appeared in print in

---

11. The rule against giving false directions and other deceptive practices is encoded by Rabbi Joseph Karo in the *Shulhan Arukh*, Hoshen Mishpat 228:4f.

12. That the non-Jewish poor must be supported and non-Jewish ill visited is demanded by the Talmud (*b. Gitin* 61a) as a manifestation of the "interests of peace." A 2003 study of philanthropy by Gary Tobin et al. revealed that of the $5.3 billion donated by Jewish mega-donors, only 6% went to Jewish causes. While this is cause for consternation among some Jews, it is evidence of the magnanimity and open-minded compassion advocated by the Talmud.

1793 and was likely written by Marcus Herz, a Jewish physician and pupil of the noted German philosopher Immanuel Kant. The prayer was translated into English in 1917. Since Maimonides served as the paradigm of Jewish scholarship as well as superb medical care, attributing the prayer to him is fitting. In fact, if Maimonides himself did not write this prayer he very well could have.

The Hippocratic Oath has physicians pledge to teach healing at no fee and to abstain from whatever is deleterious and mischievous, particularly giving no deadly medicine or any drug that would induce abortion. The physician's prayer, however, appeals for God's support "in these great labors that they may benefit mankind," mirroring Judaism's emphasis on helpfulness and responsibility to all people. And the prayer implores: "Do not allow thirst for profit, ambition for renown, and admiration to interfere with my profession, for these are the enemies of truth and love for mankind and they can lead astray in the great task of attending to the welfare of Your creatures." The physician's prayer reminds every doctor that there is a spiritual component to healing and that there is a person to be treated, not just a bundle of symptoms. As Abells notes: "We were inspired by the words' religious and spiritual focus. They gave context (why we should practice medicine) and texture (how medicine should be practiced). They defined the art of medicine for us, guiding us in our approach to patients. We realized that if the science of medicine is not transcended by spirituality, it is like a body without a soul, fixed and lacking in substance. It is compassionless rather than compassionate, robotic rather than human."

Consider the case of Dr. Ciamak Morsadegh as reported in the *New York Times* on February 9, 2014. Dr. Morsadegh is the director of the Dr. Sapir Hospital and Charity Center in Tehran, Iran. The hospital is named after an earlier Jewish doctor who died in 1921 trying to cure patients during a typhus epidemic. The hospital was founded by Persian Jews and staffed by Persian Jews but offering low-cost medical services to all Iranians. (Only five Jewish doctors still remain on staff.) Today, 96 percent of those treated are Muslims. Dr. Morsadegh explains: "Here all people can come no matter what religion, color or race"—a generous attitude coming from a Jewish doctor whose status in Iran is at risk. He went on to say: "I speak English, I pray in Hebrew, but I think in Persian." I would contend that because he prays in Hebrew he is compelled to think in Persian. That is to say, it is in the words and laws of Judaism to place helpfulness above parochial concerns.

The Three H's

The principle of helpfulness also finds expression in the Jewish literary tradition. Writing in the early twentieth century, I. L. Peretz's stories reflect centuries of Jewish communal life in Eastern Europe, its values and culture. He tells of a community where the local rabbi is considered a sort of miracle worker. The locals assumed that since the rabbi did not appear in the synagogue for late evening prayers services during the intensely spiritual period of the year around the New Year, he must have gone up to heaven. A visitor to the town heard of this commonly held assumption and was skeptical. To prove to the residents that they must be sorely mistaken, he surreptitiously enters into the rabbi's house and hides under his bed . . . and waits. In the middle of the night, when Jews would head to the synagogue, the rabbi awakes and, while reciting under his breath the same prayers his followers would be reciting in the synagogue, he goes to his closet and dresses as a local peasant woodcutter, replete with an axe. He goes out into the woods, with the skeptic behind, all the while reciting his prayers. He chops up some wood, bundles the twigs, and hauls it to a distant shack, all the while reciting his prayers and with the skeptic behind. In the shack lived an old, bed-ridden Gentile woman. The rabbi, dressed as a woodcutter, enters the shack, puts some wood in the fireplace and checks on her well-being. When he is sure that she needs nothing further, he makes the trip back home. The next day, when the locals ask the visitor: "Well, were we not right? Didn't the rabbi go up to heaven?" The visitor, no longer a skeptic, answered: "If not still higher." Those words become the title of Peretz's instructive story. Those words also celebrate the Jewish concept of helpfulness. It is helpfulness that raises us up. It is helpfulness that can lift up the world.[13]

Many people are familiar with what is called the "Jewish Star" or the "Shield of David," a six-pointed star considered to be an ancient and revered Jewish symbol. The popular etymology is that the young King David had inscribed upon his round shield a six-pointed star. But there is no mention of this in all of rabbinic literature. Ancient Jewish sarcophagi, ossuaries, and burial sites were frequently decorated with the candelabrum or menorah and never a six-pointed star. The oldest archaeological record of a six-pointed star was a third-century Jewish tombstone found in Italy, although its dating remains in dispute. A seventh-century inscription found in what is now Lebanon is thus the oldest reference to the six-pointed star

---

13. The story I cite, entitled "If Not Still Higher," appears in many different anthologies like, *A Treasury of Yiddish Stories*, edited by Irving Howe and Eliezer Greenberg, 231ff., and *Three Gifts and Other Stories*, 13ff.

as a Jewish symbol. A Jewish sectarian writing in the middle of the twelfth century was the first to discuss the symbolism of the six-pointed star. It turns out that the six-pointed star was more likely a Christian symbol than a Jewish one. When I was serving a congregation in Brooklyn, New York, it was not uncommon for guests coming to attend a religious service to end up coming late. The synagogue had no overt Jewish symbols on the exterior. But the Catholic Church across the street had emblazoned on its façade a six-pointed star. The six points were historically held to represents the six sacraments of the church and, in the medieval period, to distinguish Christianity from sorcerers that used the five-pointed star, or pentacle, as a symbol. Thus any visitor to Florence or to Salt Lake City will notice churches with six-pointed stars. But by the late middle ages, the six-pointed star had become a recognizable Jewish symbol.

The question of what the six-pointed star represented still remained. My favorite explanation is that the symbol is constructed of two intersecting arrows: one pointing upwards, and another pointing downwards. The one pointing upwards symbolizes the human yearning to reach to the heavens. The upward reach of humanity is characterized by our devotion to doing those things that help others. And when we reach upwards, God reaches down to raise us up further and brings us close. Thus the use of the six-pointed star is a reminder of the constant striving to be helpful and the perception that helpfulness is what God desires.

The popular bumper sticker and refrigerator magnet that urges "Practice random acts of kindness and senseless beauty" is on the right track but wrong, as Judaism sees it. Acts of kindness, particularly helpfulness, should not be random. Helpfulness is not a matter of choice or feeling. Helpfulness is not something subject to mood or whim. Helpfulness is obligatory. In Judaism, we refer to obligations as "mitzvot," literally, commandments. The eighteenth-century Scottish philosopher David Hume once wrote that "the end," meaning the purpose, "of all moral speculations is to teach us our duty."[14] Human beings, Hume insisted, have obligations to each other. Bringing relief to the miserable is principal among them. Hume was intent in creating a philosophical system that would encourage, not just explain, the performance of our duties. Beginning with the Torah, more than three thousand years ago, Judaism came to the same conclusion. Helpfulness must not be left to chance. It must be ingrained in our personalities and

---

14. Hume, *Enquiry concerning the Principles of Morals*, sect. 1, 4.

insinuated in our conduct. Judaism provides the context that succeeds in doing both.

HOLINESS

Being holy is the most important mandate in the Torah. I say this even though being holy is not counted as a commandment in any of the traditional lists. That is because being holy underlies *all* the commandments. The book of Leviticus, in what biblical scholars call the Holiness Code, says: "You shall be holy" (Lev 19:2). Commenting on this verse, thirteenth-century Rabbi Moses ben Nahman, known as Nahmanides, takes issue with eleventh-century RaShI. RaShI is the acronym for Rabbi Shlomo Yitzhaqi of Troyes, France, perhaps the greatest Jewish commentator of all time. RaShI explains that when the Torah commands us to be holy it means separating from all vice or avoiding all the wrongs things. Nahmanides disagrees, not that avoidance of the wrong things is bad advice. Nahmanides links holiness more with doing permitted things in the right way than with avoiding doing wrong things. Nahmanides gives an example. The Torah really prohibits only a small range of foods. All grains and fruits and vegetables and much fish and meat are available for Jews to eat. But eating too much of permitted foods is nevertheless wrong. Gluttony, that is, eating to excess, is a sin, even when eating the right kinds of food. The person who eats too much of permitted foods is not technically violating the dietary laws but is violating the mandate to be holy. He calls such a violator a "Torah-sanctioned scoundrel." In Judaism, not all activities that are permitted by law are right. Judaism is concerned not just about doing what is permitted, but doing what is right and good. According to Nahmanides, holiness demands doing what is right and good.

A person who publishes pornography may not be breaking any law. But Judaism would contend making a living through the sale of pornography is not holy. Prostitution, in some jurisdictions, is legal. But sex for money is not an activity that we would consider holy, even though some participants may invoke God's name while vigorously engaged in it.

The word in Hebrew for holy is "Kadosh." A prominent name for God in rabbinic literature is "HaKadosh Barukh Hu," the Holy One, praised be his name. The sanctification of the Sabbath and holidays is affirmed through a prayer called Kiddush, derived from the world for holy. The doxological affirmation of a merciful God even in the face of death is called "Kaddish," from the same root as holy. There is another form of the word that is not as well known but is, nonetheless, equally important. An entire institution in Judaism is called *Kiddushin*—Holiness. It is the institution of marriage. In Judaism, marital relationships are sacred, holy. Faithfulness requires maintaining a sacred trust. The larger world in which we live has never and does not now accept this idea.

I am reminded of a conversation between two friends. "Boy am I scared," one fellow says to the other. "I just got a note from a guy who said he'll break my legs if I didn't stop sleeping with his wife." "Well," said the other, "I guess you'll just have to steer clear of her." " Easy for you to say!" "Why," he asked, "do you like her that much?" "It's not that," said the philanderer, "the guy who left me the note didn't sign his name." Rampant disregard for the holiness of marriage is characteristic of our society in which serial, anonymous sexual liaisons are more the norm than the exception. What used to be scandalous is now normative and even acceptable. And the acceptability—even the justification—of all kinds of sexual activity is symptomatic of today's world.

Mozart's comedic-tragic opera *Don Giovanni* ("Don Juan") culminates with the scene in which the notorious womanizer is literally dragged down to hell. The principal character was considered a villain in 1787 when the opera was completed and da Ponte's libretto included. But in today's world, boasting of ravishing 2065 women from all over the world would more likely earn kudos than condemnation. In fact, in promoting its 2008 production, the Canadian Opera Company chose to use as its advertising catch-phrase: "To be faithful to one woman dishonors all others." It plays to the contemporary listener who might find the logic convincing. Convincing it might be to some; but contrary to the holiness of matrimony it certainly is. Faithfulness is the handmaiden to holiness.

Dalma Heyn, while executive director of *McCall's* magazine, published a 1992 book entitled *The Erotic Silence of the American Wife* in which she contends that troubled marriages can be saved by adultery. Her research and interviews with hundreds of women led her to conclude that in some cases infidelity may even enhance and preserve marriages. And anthropologist Helen Fisher, in her 1993 book *Anatomy of Love: The Natural History of Monogamy, Adultery, and Divorce*, justifies infidelity on the grounds that there is, in her opinion, a biological force that supports a human tendency to extramarital liaisons. One of the most popular and entertaining sex-advice columnists, Dan Savage, agrees. In an article that appeared in the

New York Times Magazine (July 3, 2011) described monogamous relationships as boring and lacking variety that leads to despair. Occasional flings, he argues, can actually strengthen a relationship. Savage describes his own marriage to another man as "monogamish." The Heyn-Fisher-Savage opinion is subsequently shared by other social scientists. A 2011 study from the University of Guelph, for instance, concludes that performance anxiety experienced by many married men and women may be overcome through sexual encounters with an extramarital partner. In other words, infidelity can be good for you. Little do people need scientific endorsements for their sexual proclivity. The culture in which we live is a culture of acceptance: whatever goes on behind closed doors between consenting adults is nobody's business. Judaism, however, insists on *Kiddushin*, the sanctity of marital relations. Fidelity, exclusivity, loyalty, trust—these are at the core of the Jewish concept of marriage. These are the elements that raise up a relationship from the category of casual to the category of holy.

Robert Wright focuses on the last generation in particular. In his 1995 book *The Moral Animal: Why We Are the Way We Are*, he cites some frightening statistics. The American divorce rate, relatively level in the 1950s and early 1960s, doubled between 1966 and 1978, until reaching the present level. Between 1970 and 1988, although the average age of a woman marrying for the first time was rising, the number of eighteen-year-old girls who reported having sexual intercourse grew from 39 percent to 70 percent. For fifteen-year-old girls, the numbers went from 5 percent to 25 percent.[15] And the number of unmarried couples living together in the United States grew from half a million in 1970 to nearly three million in 1990. At the same time, the number of American women between thirty-five and thirty-nine years of age who had never been married rose from 5 percent to 10 percent and of the women in that same cohort who did marry, about a third were also divorced.[16] In examining these figures Wright sees what he calls the "double whammy": as easy divorce creates a growing population of formerly married women, easy sex creates a growing population of never-married women. And reflecting on all this, Wright concludes: "A quarter-century of indulging these impulses has helped bring a world featuring, among other things: lots of fatherless children; lots of embittered women; lots of complaints about date rape and sexual harassment; and the frequent sight of lonely men renting X-rated videotapes while lonely

---

15. Wright, *Moral Animal*, 133.
16. Ibid.

women abound."[17] Only by reinjecting holiness into matrimony will we have any chance of turning things around. And the holiness of marriage is what Judaism prescribes.

Holiness relates to how we speak to one another as well. The Talmud emphasizes that coarse expressions are beneath all human beings. When two students of one Talmudic scholar wanted to express their utter exhaustion, one said he felt like a pig, another said he felt as tired as a kid. The teacher refused to speak to first student who had used an expression that was improper, not because pigs are unfit for Jewish consumption but because the comparison was unrefined. The Bible is filled with euphemisms, some quite quaint to the modern ear. For instance, couples do not copulate, they "know" one another. This is not because the ancients were ashamed of sexual relations. There are many passages in the Talmud that discuss sexual relations quite frankly. Euphemisms were preferred because the ancients held that certain things should not be discussed overtly. To paraphrase the Talmud, everyone knows why the bride enters the bridal chamber, but that doesn't mean everyone should talk about it. Maimonides argued that this sense of propriety is why the Hebrew language is called the "Holy Tongue." Maimonides also alludes to a reason why we ought to be circumspect about what we say. Human speech is a gift that distinguishes us from all other animals. As such, it should not be used in ways that make us think or behave like animals. Conforming our speech to the requirements of holiness will also enhance the respect we ought to show to others.[18]

In his book *Less than Human*, philosopher David Livingstone Smith argues that because of "our cognitive architecture" human beings are predisposed to divide living things—including people—into categories. And those who are judged not to fit the pattern of what is essentially human are ranked as "counterfeit human beings." This is the process of

---

17. Ibid., 145. In her book *For Better*, Tara Parker-Pope takes issue with the oft-cited statistic that half of today's marriages end in divorce. But *Time* magazine, May 24, 2010, concludes that "what seems clear is that less educated, lower income couples split up more often than college grads and may be doing so in higher numbers than before."

18. Proper language as an expression of holiness is emphasized in many texts. The Talmud (*b. Ketubot* 8b) teaches that no reference ought to be made of what the bridal couple does in the bridal chamber. It is based on the verse in Isaiah (9:16) that includes the phrase "and every mouth speaking wantonness." A series of statements advocating avoiding coarse language appears in the Talmud (*b. Pesahim* 3a–b) from which I have selected two. Maimonides's description of Hebrew as "the holy tongue" averse to coarse language is found in his *Guide of the Perplexed*, bk. 3, ch. 8. In the Shlomo Pines English translation, the passage appears on 435–36.

"dehumanization." According to Smith, this explains why enemies resort to labeling each other as animals, vermin, and so on. It is not simply propaganda but a manifestation of human nature. Some may want to challenge Smith's contention that "sub-humanity is typically thought to be a permanent condition."[19] But assuming for the moment that all of what Smith claims is true, to act on the call to holiness requires that we rise above the tendency to dehumanize and, instead, aim to re-humanize those who are different. That is precisely what Judaism necessitates.

One of the most overused words in current use is "community." It seems that every profession, disability, lifestyle, religion, and ethnic group are now communities. There is the legal community, the medical community, the handicapped community, the gay community, the francophone community, and on and on. Even though the location or interests of the members of such communities may be disparate, they are treated as if they are homogeneous. I believe, however, the attempt is to use language to suggest commonality even when there may be little. It also creates an impression of power derived from greater numbers. It is far easier to achieve political goals when you speak in the name of the "Jewish community" than in the name of a few rabbis or agencies who may have particular opinions. So we talk of the Jewish community even though it would be more accurate to speak of Jewish communities. But we retain the idea of community as a vestige of our history. Jews have always organized into communities; communities that created shared institutions that served common needs like soup kitchens, free loan societies, schools, burial societies, and old age homes. When these institutions were in place, the locality earned its Hebrew name: "Kehillat Kodesh," not just a community, but a holy community. Judaism prescribes adding to the world the kinds of institutions that will serve our common needs and transform the world into a holy community.

---

19. David Berreby challenges David Livingstone Smith's thesis in his review of *Less than Human* that appeared in the *New York Times Book Review*, March 6, 2011. Berreby argues that even while operating under the Aristotelian notion that some people are by nature slaves, even the Romans allowed for slaves to be manumitted and, once freed, rise to the highest levels of power. Apparently, "sub-humanity" was not immutable after all. The same is true for enemy soldiers who are demeaned during wartime but rehabilitated when peace is restored.

Prescription for an Ailing World

HOPEFULNESS

One of the most dramatic scenes in the 1995 Academy Award-nominated film *The Shawshank Redemption* featured a philosophical dialogue between the two main characters, Andy, the falsely convicted murderer, and Red, the resourceful veteran prisoner denied parole. They are discussing hope. It was a surreal discussion since it takes place in a prison noted for its stark conditions where inmates are brutalized by each other when they are not being brutalized by sadistic guards. Andy is insistent that hope is both powerful and necessary. But the hardened Red contends that hope is unrealistic and even dangerous. In the end, it is Andy who is vindicated. Hopefulness proves to be both a powerful and sustaining force. It provided Andy with the courage to persevere and overcome his wrongful conviction and escape to freedom. And it ultimately provided Red with the strength to resist the urge of taking his own life and led him to follow Andy to Mexico to start anew.

Helpfulness and holiness, as I have explained them, refer to behavior. Hopefulness is different. Hopefulness refers to attitude. Judaism is not just a system of mechanics, regimented rules to perform. Judaism is also about how we ought to see the world and our place in it. And hopefulness is a useful entry point to that aspect of Judaism.

It was during the halcyon days of the Soviet Jewry movement that a colleague of mine, the late Rabbi Arnold Turetzky, reported on a strange encounter he had in the city of Leningrad, now St. Petersburg again. Rabbi Turetzky had visited the synagogue there and had become curious about an unusual couple: and elderly man and a young woman. The elderly man prayed with observable piety. But the young woman arrived only at the end of the prayer service to escort the elderly gentleman away. Rabbi Turetzky followed the two out the synagogue to a local bus stop. It became clear that the old man was blind and that the young woman, a daughter perhaps, was there to make sure that he arrived home safely. Rabbi Turetzky noticed something else. Although the man was blind, he was wearing a beautiful watch around his wrist. It was not a Braille watch, but a regular one. He excused himself and struck up a conversation with the young woman, whom he presumed would be more likely to speak English. In the course of a short while, he learned that she was indeed his daughter. So he asked: "I noticed that your father has on this beautiful watch. But he is blind. So why does he wear it?" It was a gift, she said; a gift from his son—her brother—who was able to get an exit visa and emigrate to Israel. The poignancy of the gift was not lost on Rabbi Turetzky. But his perceptiveness demanded an answer to one more question: "But the watch is off one hour?" "Yes," she replied. "It is set to time in Israel." Rabbi Turetzky paused to appreciate this delicious anomaly: a blind man wearing a watch he cannot see from a son he cannot see to keep time in a place he may never see. The only explanation for this incongruity is hopefulness. The timepiece wasn't a tool, but a symbol. It was a symbol of hope that old man had that he would one day be free and reunited with his son in Israel.

A similar anecdote is told of Rabbi Levi Isaac of Berditchev, an eighteenth-century Polish rabbi of considerable renown. Reputedly, in his parlor were two clocks: one showed local time and the other showed time in Jerusalem. Rabbi Levi Isaac lived in two worlds. One part of him lived in exile; another part lived in hope. And the hope was just as palpable as the exile. When it came time for Rabbi Levi Isaac's daughter to be married, the invitations read: "The wedding will take place, please God, at this time and on this date in the holy city of Jerusalem. But if, God forbid, the Messiah does not arrive by then, then the wedding will take place in the city of Berditchev." Hopefulness is indeed a powerful and sustaining force.

The national anthem of the Jewish people is called "Hatikvah," meaning, "the Hope." Curiously, "Hatikvah" has never been given official status as Israel's national anthem by the Kenesset, Israel's parliament. It never needed it. Since first written by Naftali Herz Imber in 1878 and first published as "Tikvatenu" ("Our Hope," in Hebrew), the words have plucked at the heartstrings of Jews everywhere. The revised and current version proclaims: "As long as deep in the heart the soul of a Jew yearns, and towards the East an eye looks to Zion, our hope is not yet lost; the hope of two thousand years: to be a free people in our land, the Land of Zion and Jerusalem." When the seventh Zionist Congress ended in Basel, Switzerland, in 1905, it ended with an enormously moving singing of these words by all present. That moment confirmed its semi-official status. But it is the meaning of the words that made it so stirring. Our temple was destroyed. Our people were thrust into exile. We lost our homes and lost our freedom; but we never lost our hope. There may be disappointment in life, but there is no place for despair. As the Jerusalem Talmud says: "So long as a person lives, there is hope."[20]

20. The Jerusalem Talmud was actually completed in Caesaria approximately one hundred years before the Babylonian Talmud. The content of the two varies considerably in some places and the Aramaic dialect is significantly different. The citation on hope appears in *y. Berakhot* 9:1. In the Babylonian Talmud (*b. Berakhot* 10a), the same idea is expressed a little differently. "Even if a sharp sword rests on a man's neck, he should

Prescription for an Ailing World

Think of the story of the woman who was about to go skydiving for the first time. On the ground her instructor gave her a procedural check. "After you jump," he reminded her, "count to ten and then pull the yellow cord. If your main chute fails to open, then pull the red cord. There will be a green pick-up truck waiting for you when you land." Later, she passed through the doorway of the airplane and made her jump. She counts to ten, pulls the yellow cord, and nothing happens. She pulls the red cord . . . and nothing happens. "Great," she says to herself, "Now I suppose the green pick-up truck won't be there either!" Without deconstructing the story it seems that the skydiver is resigned to disappointment, after all, nothing seems to be working as anticipated. However, it is actually a story illustrating hopefulness. If she did not hope to survive, there would be no point in wondering about the truck.

Hopefulness has always been the essence of the Jewish attitude toward life. Of course, faced with many tragedies and catastrophes throughout history, there were only two choices: be hopeful or give up. But surrender and despair was never a real option. The Passover story is familiar to many yet the earlier events leading up to the plagues and the exodus are not so well known. These events are central to understanding how hopefulness has become part of the Jewish outlook. Pharaoh sought to suppress any possible threat against his power by the growing number of Israelites so he commanded that every newborn male be drowned in the Nile and every newborn female enslaved. As simple as the edict sounds, it needed policing. Pharaoh's troops had to monitor all the Israelite households and be present at the time of birth to carry out Pharaoh's orders. Jewish legend tells us that many Israelite mothers tried to hide their newborn babies from the terrible fate that awaited them.[21] The scriptural text, however, records only one instance in which an Israelite mother successfully hid her infant son and protected him from certain death: Moses' mother. Some may question why other Israelite mothers were not as resourceful or successful as Yokheved, Moses' mother. But the more vexing question is why, knowing the fate that awaited their children, Israelite parents continued to have children in the

---

not desist from hope (*rahamim*)." In the popular English translation of the Babylonian Talmud, the word *rahamim*, is rendered "prayer." But the statement is based on a verse in the book of Job (13:15) where the context suggests the word is better translated, as I do here, as hope.

21. For a comprehensive exposition of Jewish legends, see Rabbi Louis Ginzberg, *Legends of the Jews*, originally published in seven volumes. See vol. 2, 257–58, for the legend regarding Israelite mothers hiding their babies from Pharaoh's henchmen.

The Three H's

first place? I believe the answer is clear and illustrates my point. Having children is the ultimate Jewish act of hope. It is based on the expectation that the future will be brighter no matter the current situation. And I further contend that is why having children is the very first commandment in the Torah. Jews are commanded to have children because we are an eternally hopeful people.

The story is told about a duke who called the local rabbi into his palace and informed him that he intended to evict all Jews from the duchy within one year, unless the rabbi could teach the duke's pet monkey to talk. The rabbi brought the sad news back to his congregation. He announced that they all would be exiled in a year at the duke's whim. That is, unless he could teach his pet monkey to talk. The rabbi could see that his listeners were disheartened. "Wait!" he said. "Much can happen in a year. The duke could die. Or all of us could die anyway. Or just maybe I can get that monkey to talk." The Talmud (*b. Ber.* 10a) teaches: "Though the sword may be dangling above your neck, never give up hope."

Among the most well-known stories Jews tell is the Talmudic account of the reasons for lighting the Hanukkah menorah (*b. Shabbat* 21b). When the Jerusalem temple was recovered from the Syrian Greeks who defiled it in the second century BCE, the victors discovered on a small, hidden vial of oil with which to light the golden candelabrum: enough to last but one day. Yet a miracle occurred and the oil lasted for eight days. The part of this story that goes unmentioned is the fact that some anonymous priest during the desperate time of persecution had secretly hidden that vial of oil in the remote hope that one day the temple would be purified and the candelabrum relit. The Hanukkah story is as much a story of hope as it is about miracles.

That Jews—or anyone—should be hopeful in the face of distress is understandable. But Jews express hopefulness in times of joy as well. The year was 1970. Three short years earlier Israel enjoyed a surprising victory. Threatened with being driven into the sea and having to do battle on three fronts, Israel defeated Egypt, Syria, and Jordan in an unbelievable six days. Yet in the aftermath of this unprecedented victory, Israel was not awash with triumphalism but with hopefulness. The most popular Israeli songs were songs expressing a yearning for a time when no war need be fought ever again. "Next year, when peace will come, we shall return to the simple pleasures of life so long denied us. You will see, you will see, of how good it will be—next year!" In another song, "Tomorrow," Israelis hoped for the day when armies would disband, and relaxing with oranges in hand or boating along the placid coast, no thought of war would cross any mind. And in another song, a father promises his young daughter "this will be the last war."

Hopefulness is not the same as optimism. The optimist looks at the world though rose-colored glasses. Judaism puts the world under a magnifying glass. The optimist sees only the good and is certain things will be better. Judaism sees the good and the bad and trusts that things will be better. Adina Schapiro, winner of a 1996 essay contest sponsored by the American Jewish Committee, and published in the *New York Times*, echoes this observation. At the time, she was completing her first undergraduate year at Columbia University. She was diagnosed with brain cancer at age twelve. At the time of the publication of her essay, she celebrated five years of being cancer-free. Her essay, entitled "What Being Jewish Means to Me," read, in part: "We need not search the pages of history to learn that human beings are capable of great inhumanity. Recent events in Rwanda, Oklahoma City, and Tel Aviv, show us time and again how the lives of innocent adults and children are ended in an instant by bullets or bombs. But we have also witnessed human acts of great love, empathy, and healing. These are a reminder of the seeds of compassion and love that God has planted in the human spirit. My own faith in God and my reliance on the power of community have given me strength to face the future with the hope that such seeds will grow and flourish. To me, that is the meaning of being Jewish."

There are two very practical outcomes of hopefulness. First, hopefulness breeds humor, even in the face of adversity. When we trust that things can and will be better, we can afford to laugh at life's incongruities. A classic story that dates back to the Second World War is told of two would-be assassins who observed that Hitler's car goes through a particular intersection every day at two-thirty in the afternoon. These two Jews decided that they would toss a hand-grenade at the vehicle as it passed and, if successful, end the war and save millions of lives. They chose the day, hid in a doorway and waited. Two-thirty came and went but no Hitler. Three o'clock passed and still no sign of him. Then four and five passed: still nothing. So one of the assassins turns to the other and says: "I hope, God forbid, nothing happened to him!" What two Jews would be doing roaming free in Nazi Germany and with access to explosives is immaterial. It is, after all, just a story. But it is a story with a message. The irony of assassins concerned for the well-being of their intended victim should not be lost. Neither should Judaism's concern for the preservation of life be missed. But the more profound message is that even when being victimized and brutalized, Jews could still joke. The ability to joke in the presence of catastrophe is an outcome of hopefulness, in this case, the expectation that as bad as things are, the situation is only temporary. And it is hopefulness that generates courage in confronting catastrophe.

Historically, humor has been a sharp tool in Judaism's shed. When Elijah the prophet challenged the priests of the Canaanite god Ba'al to a contest to determine which God is the more powerful, he sets up an unlit altar and proposes that they pray to their god to ignite the offering placed upon it. The challenge proved impossible for the Ba'al worshippers whose prayers went unanswered. Bible readers get the sense that Elijah must have been laughing out loud when he derided his opponents, imploring them to pray more loudly since perhaps Ba'al was otherwise engaged and couldn't hear them.

> Shout louder! After all he is a god. But he may be in conversation, he may be detained, or he may be on a journey, or perhaps he is asleep and will wake up. (1 Kings 18:27)

The fourth-century teacher known simply as Rabbah is reported to have begun every public lecture with a joke and stand-up comedy was born.[22] But telling jokes was more than a successful strategy in gaining the attention of an audience for the serious message that followed. Laughing at the foibles currently observed is contingent on the hope that something better is deserved.

The expectation that things can and will be better mean that we never have to settle for the status quo. This is the second outcome of hopefulness, what I call the "culture of complaint." Since the future is expected to better, there is no good reason to be satisfied with the present. After the exodus from Egypt and during the next forty years, the Israelites complain about the lack of water, too little meat, too much meat, the leadership of Moses, the obstacles standing in their way and more. Complaining has become part of the Jewish character. When a server in a restaurant in a Jewish neighborhood checks on his patrons, he asks: "Is anything all right with your order?" But complaining is not necessarily a bad thing, even though God is not thrilled with it. Complaints are the engine of change. Rather

---

22. That the Talmudic scholar Rabbah began his discourses with a joke is confirmed by the Talmud in two places: *b. Shabbat* 30b and *b. Pesahim* 117a. His source material unfortunately did not survive.

than accept things as they are, Judaism urges transforming things into what they could be. And that things could be better is the engine of hopefulness.

That idea is expressed in a story told by Al Tapper and Peter Press in their 2000 book entitled *A Minister, a Priest and a Rabbi*. A Jewish grandmother is walking on the beach with her only grandson when a giant wave crashes onshore, sweeping the boy out to sea. The woman looks up to the heavens and says, "Oh, Lord, this is my only grandson, how can you take him away from me like this. My son will not understand. My daughter-in-law will die from grief." Another wave comes by and deposits the boy back at the old woman's feet. The grandmother looks up, points her finger to the heavens, and says, "He had a hat!"[23]

Hopefulness, however, does not mean that we ought to be content to wait for things to get better. Judaism insists that we must not be among those who watch things happen. We must be counted among those who make things happen. To put it in terms of the three "H's," helpfulness trumps hopefulness. The only thing for which Judaism waits is the coming of the Messiah. For all other things, we are guided by the teaching of first-century Rabbi Tarfon who said: "You are not responsible for finishing the task but neither are you free to desist from it."[24]

In his July 16, 1992, acceptance speech for the nomination to be the Democratic candidate for President of the United States, Bill Clinton cited one of his professors, Carol Quigley, who said that America was the greatest nation in history because our people had always believed two things: that tomorrow could be better and that today every one of us has a personal moral responsibility to make it so. That tomorrow could be better is the expression of hopefulness. That each person bears a personal responsibility to make it so is the calling of helpfulness. And both are among the principle values of Judaism.

---

23. The story I cite from Tapper and Press is found on p. 131
24. Pirke Avot 2:21.

Chapter Four

The Two A's

ACTION

AT THE END OF the last chapter I contended that Judaism advocates making things happen. That requires action. And it is action—what we do, more than what we believe—that is at the core of Judaism. The distinction between action and belief is well illustrated by the writings of Moses Mendelssohn.

Moses Mendelssohn is one of the most interesting figures in all of Jewish history.[1] Born in Dessau, Germany, in 1729, with a hunchback and a stammer, he absorbed as much as his community could teach him by the time he was a mere fourteen years of age. At ten he was writing original Hebrew poetry and began to study philosophy independently. Sent to Berlin to expand his Jewish education, he simultaneously immersed himself in general education. He became a master of German language and style. He taught himself literature, philosophy, and Latin, French, and Polish. He studied logic and geometry and aesthetics with anyone who would teach him. Reflecting on this period in his life, he wrote: "I have never been to any university, neither have I ever heard a classroom lecture, and one of the greatest difficulties I had to surmount was that I had to obtain everything by my own effort and industry."[2]

---

1. Kupferberg, *Mendelssohns*, 5ff.
2. Ibid.

Rather than pursuing a rabbinic career for which he was eminently qualified, he became a tutor to the children of a merchant, then a bookkeeper, then manager, and finally partner. At the same time, he launched himself on a career as a critic and writer. He had the temerity to unfavorably review the Prussian King Frederick's volume of French poetry. Facing possible expulsion for his offense, Mendelssohn explained: "Writing poetry is like bowling, and whoever bowls, be he king or peasant, must have the pin boy tell him the score."[3] Apparently, his "explanation" was accepted.

Perhaps one of the most romantic stories of all time is Mendelssohn's brief courtship of the beautiful Fromer Guggenheim of Hamburg. According to the family account, she was taken by his reputation though not with his appearance. Mendelssohn proceeded to tell her a story. "When I was born," he was reputed to have said, "my future wife was also named, but at the same time it was said that she herself would be hump-backed. 'O God,' said I, 'a deformed girl will become embittered and unhappy. Dear Lord, let me have the hump-back, and make the maiden flawless and beautiful.'"[4] They were married shortly thereafter.

While on his honeymoon, he entered an essay contest on the question of whether mathematical proofs could be applied to philosophy. His essay won the prize, beating out, among others, Immanuel Kant, who subsequently became his friend and admirer. Mendelssohn's fame was assured through the publication of his small book entitled *Phaedon, or the Immortality of the Soul*. It was a sensation, becoming the most widely read book in his day, an attempt to bring Plato into modern times. Later in life, he took on the ten-year task of translating the Hebrew Bible into German.

But it was the publication in 1769 of a book by the eccentric Johann Caspar Lavater that thrust Mendelssohn into the uncomfortable position of having to defend his religion in public. In effect, Lavater insulted Mendelssohn's intelligence and challenged him to refute the arguments in his book in favor of Christianity, and, if he were unable, to accept conversion. Mendelssohn responded, in part, by stating that "I have never entered into a dispute about Judaism even if it had been polemically attacked or triumphantly held up to scorn."[5] "I wanted to refute the world's derogatory opinion of the Jew by righteous living, not by pamphleteering."[6] Nevertheless, the

---

3. Ibid.
4. Ibid.
5. Mendelssohn and Jospe, *Jerusalem*, 116.
6. Ibid.

controversy continued and Mendelssohn was compelled to publish a little book with a great message. The book was called *Jerusalem*. Mendelssohn attempted to show that Judaism and Christianity were not rivals but allies under the same God, invoking the bucolic metaphor that "to belong to this omnipresent shepherd, it is not necessary for the entire flock to graze on one pasture or to enter and leave the master's house through just one door."[7] This is probably one of the first defenses of religious pluralism in history.

For my purposes, however, Mendelssohn's important contribution is his claim that Judaism is rooted in action. While others may stress creed, Judaism lays stress on deed. "Judaism has no symbolic books, no articles of faith," writes Mendelssohn. "No one has to swear to creedal symbols or subscribe, by solemn oath, to certain articles of faith."[8] That is because there can be legitimate disagreement on facts and opinions—"what we perceive to be true"—that underlie faith. Instead, Judaism is built on "acts of commission and omission." What we do is a far better barometer of what we hold dear than what we say. To put it somewhat differently, faith is inadequate. A person may hold noble ideas but without acting on them, they remain hollow and vacuous. Un-concretized beliefs are mere lip service. Love of humanity is a grand principle. But without a regimen that puts that principle into action, it remains ethereal. To be sure, actions require mindfulness in Judaism. Religious deeds without conviction, says Mendelssohn in chapter 1, are "empty mechanical motions."[9] But action is the necessary consequence of religious feeling.

Twentieth-century philosopher Leo Baeck, following Mendelssohn, wrote that faith is quite "provisional, it foregoes definite conclusions and binding decisions arrived at once and forever." Pious action, on the other hand, is a definite response to observable needs. Historian Simon Dubnow similarly saw Judaism as a system of ideals "*to be appli*ed directly, day after day, to practical contingencies," rather than merely a series of ideals "*to be yearned for.*"[10]

7. Mendelssohn and Jospe, *Jerusalem*, 107.

8. Ibid., 72.

9. Ibid., 22.

10. Leo Baeck's distinction between faith and action is expressed in *Das Wesen des Judentums* (2nd ed.), 6, and republished in English in Armin H. Kohler's 1929 *Foundation of Jewish Ethics*, 58–59. Eminent Jewish historian Simon Dubnow's opinion on the active demands of Judaism appear in "An Essay in the Philosophy of History" translated from German into English and published in the volume *Jewish History* by the Jewish Publication Society or America in 1903, 54–55.

Prescription for an Ailing World

Deed over creed is repeatedly emphasized in the Bible. Continued life is contingent upon doing that which God commands (Lev 18:5) rather than just believing in God. The psalmist (37:27) encourages us to "depart from evil and do good." It is the *doing* good that secures life. And the prophet Jeremiah (7:3ff.) warns his listeners against putting their faith in the existence of the temple as a guarantor of their security. Instead, what will provide security is doing justice; refraining from oppressing the stranger or the orphan or the widow. The biblical narrative is replete with episodes of action. Upon hearing of the capture of his nephew in battle, Abraham immediately acts to rescue him. Freedom is a noble sentiment but it remains only a sentiment if it is not translated into a cause for action. When Moses sees an Egyptian taskmaster beating an Israelite slave, he immediately intervenes to save him. Protecting the weak is a noble idea but it remains an idea unless it motivates action. Action is the only satisfactory response to what we value. To paraphrase one first-century rabbi: the principle is only as important as the actions that flow from it. And the same early medieval source I cited previously that holds that the divine spirit inheres in all people, ends with the caveat: "All depends on the deeds of the particular individual."[11]

Precisely because actions are paramount, there are very few rules in Judaism that impinge on thinking or feeling in contrast to doing. In fact, there are a mere three. And one in particular, the commandment against coveting a neighbor's wife or property, was understood as precautionary: the worry was that it might lead to adultery or theft. In a famous (infamous?) November 1976 interview with *Playboy* magazine, soon-to-be-president of the United States Jimmy Carter confessed that he had committed the sin of lusting in his heart. Were his thoughts actually covetous, he would indeed have been guilty. But otherwise, thoughts are not punishable offenses—at least not in this plane of existence. Judaism has no "thought police" that arrests people for what is in their minds and then punishes people accordingly. We are held accountable only for what we say and do and not what we think, and not for what we might think or might do.

Philip K. Dick tested this idea in his short story that Steven Spielberg turned into a 2002 film, *Minority Report*. In the not-too-distant future

---

11. It is Rabbi Simon ben Gamaliel who says: what is more essential is not study but action (*Pirke Avot* 1:17). See also Jerusalem Talmud (*y. Pesahim* 3:7): "Doing is more important than learning." That all depends on the deeds of the individual appears in the late medieval anthology *Yalkut Shmoni* on Judges 4:4. See also Rabbi Louis Jacobs, *What Does Judaism Say*, 186.

criminals are caught and punished *before* they commit a crime until an officer in the special "pre-crime" unit is accused of one such future crime and sets out to prove his innocence. But how can you prove what you didn't do? How anyone can be held accountable for a wrong not yet perpetrated is the larger issue the story and the film explore.

The book of Genesis, as read by the expositors of Judaism, includes an illustrative episode of this last point. Unable to father any children with her, Sarah encourages her husband Abraham to use what we would call a surrogate. Sarah encourages Abraham to take her handmaid Hagar and impregnate her in the hopes that a son and heir would continue his line. Hagar gives birth to Yishmael but after Sarah subsequently gives birth to Isaac, the family dynamics change. Abraham, regretfully, was compelled to send Hagar and Yishmael away. When their provisions run out and the two face the possibility of imminent death in the wilderness, God sends and angel to show them where to find life-sustaining water. The two were saved and Yishmael grows up to become a great warrior and progenitor of a nation that later becomes a nemesis to the descendants of Abraham. Knowing that future animosities could have been entirely avoided had Yishmael been left to die in the wilderness, the early interpreters of the biblical text speculate on why God saved the child. They point to an enigmatic phrase as the basis of their answer. The angel sent by God comforted Hagar and Yishmael and informs them that God "has heeded the cry of the boy where he is" (Gen 21:17). The meaning of this phrase and its inclusion is puzzling. The imaginative rabbis, however, envision a kind of heavenly council in which God and his entourage discuss and debate. In this case, the angels all advocate leaving Yishmael to die and thus avert a potential problem later in history. But God insists that the child had to be saved because of "where he is."[12] At that moment, he was in jeopardy. At that moment, he had committed no wrong. So at that moment he merited being saved. What he will do in the future has no bearing upon his current status. Having not acted in any untoward way at present, no punishment is forthcoming.

Action is the necessary response to what we value. Action is also the means by which values are acquired. Maimonides asked rhetorically how might a person first attain and then maintain the cherished values of life. His answer: "He shall always act accordingly, and do so once, twice, and thrice and constantly practice it, until it becomes easy for him to act thus.

---

12. The interpretation of "where he is" appears in RaShI on Gen 21:17.

Then it will become in him a firm disposition."[13] In other words, through training and repetition, people grow accustomed to doing what is noble. Values ethicist Kwame Anthony Appiah correctly notes that folktales, plays, operas, novels, short stories, biographies, histories, ethnographies, fiction and nonfiction painting and music, sculpture and dance all have ways of revealing to us values we had not previously recognized.[14] Indeed, references to many of these techniques appear on these very pages. But Maimonides would remind us that above all else, it is repetitive action that cements value in our lives and Judaism, as a way of life, rests on repetitive action. The very first paragraph of Rabbi Joseph Karo's sixteenth-century code of Jewish law begins with the declamation that we must ready, willing, and able to do God's will; not just to discover God's will, but to act on it.

The Creation story is the locus of many of the concepts of Judaism that are more fully developed later. The same is true with regard to action. Chapter 2 of the book of Genesis begins with a summary. God completed all the works of creation in six days. On the seventh day he abstained from all the kinds of work he had done previously. God then blesses the seventh day, making it holy. And the special nature of the Sabbath day is assured because "on it he ceased from all his work which God created to make." As odd as it reads in English, it reads as oddly in Hebrew. Thus the translating team responsible for a more contemporary English rendition has it: "God ceased from all the work of creation that he had done" (Gen 2:3). The new translation reads better but obscures the real difficulty that exists in the Hebrew text. The verse ends in an infinitive: "to make." Further, the verb "to make" is a transitive verb. That is to say, it requires an object. Something needs to be made. In proper grammar, "to make" cannot stand by itself, unless it is purposely intended to teach a special lesson. The lesson is that though the work of creation is complete to a point, henceforth it requires human action to perfect. It is the task of human beings to make something of this world and of themselves. And that requires action.

AUDACITY

According to the book of Genesis, when God informed Abraham of his plans to destroy the twin cities of evil, Sodom and Amorah (as the Hebrew

---

13. See Mishneh Torah, Laws of Opinions 1:7 for Maimonides's instructions on how to attain the cherished values of life.

14. See Appiah, *Experiment in Ethics*, 158.

text reads), Abraham comes forward immediately and says to God: "Will You sweep away the innocent along with the guilty? What if there should be fifty innocent within the city; will You then wipe out the place and not forgive it for the sake of the innocent fifty who are in it? Far be it from You to do such a thing, to bring death upon the innocent as well as the guilty, so that innocent and guilty fare alike. Far be it from You! Shall not the Judge of all the earth deal justly?" In this remarkable passage, Abraham reprimands God for failing to live up to the standards of justice and fairness. In effect, Abraham challenges God's *bona fides*. Of course Abraham later qualifies his position, acknowledging that he is but "dust and ashes" (Gen 18:27). But that is only after he levels his challenge. That God could be boldly called to account by a mere mortal seems shocking, impudent, almost incomprehensible in its daring. But it is entirely consistent with the way Judaism has traditionally pictured Abraham.

In one of the best known of all ancient legends, a youthful Abraham is remembered as a reluctant salesman in his father's store, selling idols to the general public. Left alone while father tended to business, Abraham shattered all the smaller idols and placed the hammer in the hand of the largest. When his father returned and saw the damage, he was aghast. He demanded an explanation. Abraham said it was obvious: the biggest idol took the hammer and smashed all his inferior rivals. His father, incredulous, pointed out that was impossible. How could a lifeless statue do what Abraham attributed to it. Abraham then asked that his father listen to what he himself admitted. If the idols are powerless, then how could they be worshipped or sold to people who would worship them.[15]

Abraham's iconoclasm was apparently expressed at an early age and continued throughout his life. The Torah (Gen 14:13) describes Abraham as a "Hebrew." The word itself derives from a root meaning "the bank of a river." Applying the meaning to the person, the teachers of Judaism maintained that in his day Abraham stood on one bank of the river, and the rest of the world on the other bank. To be sure, Abraham was an independent thinker. But in his challenge to God regarding the fate of the residents of Sodom, he was audacious. That Judaism considers Abraham to be its founding father is no accident. Abraham is a paradigm of responsibility, saving his nephew from captivity; of helpfulness, welcoming strangers to

---

15. The well-known story of Abraham smashing his father's idols is told by Rabbi Louis Ginzberg, *Legends of the Jews*, vol. 1, 195–98, esp. 97–8. See also *Bereshit Rabbah* 38:13. Abraham's self-identification of an "ivri," meaning an independent thinker, appears in *Bereshit Rabbah* 42:8 and is based on Gen 14:13.

his tent; and of hopefulness, trusting in God that his future will be secured. He is the quintessential man of action. But perhaps more than anything else, Abraham is the model of audacity.

It is that same kind of audacity that enables Moses to stand before the most powerful ruler on earth in his day, Pharaoh, and demand that he let go the slaves he represented. It sounds quite inconceivable that the lowest stratum of society would make any demands on the highest. Yet Moses demands more than just extra rations or a day off. Moses demands an end to the very institution that serves as the source of Pharaoh's power and wealth. And it is that same kind of audacity that enables David to stand up to the giant and heavily armed Philistine Goliath with only his sling and a few stones.

In fact, audacity is associated with the foundational name of the Jewish people, Israel. In anticipation of a stormy reunion with his alienated brother, Jacob, Abraham's grandson, divides his camp and acts to assure their defense. Left alone by the river, he encounters a stranger with whom he wrestles for the entire night. The struggle does not leave Jacob unscathed. He is injured in the hip. Nevertheless, he holds on and refuses to let the stranger go free until he gives him a blessing. The blessing comes in the form of a change of name. No longer will Jacob be called Jacob. Instead, he will be called Israel because "you have wrestled with beings divine and human and have prevailed" (Gen 32:29). Jacob's descendants are the progenitors of the twelve tribes from which the Jewish people are reputed to derive. So Israel, Jacob's new name, becomes synonymous with the people it describes: a people that, like Abraham, wrestles with God. A "God-wrestling people" is an audacious people. For only a people with audacity would dare struggle with the ultimate power of the universe. Judaism thus holds struggling with God—not surrendering to God—as the ideal. Struggle trumps submission. To struggle means to question, and sometimes even to reject.

The Talmud includes an anecdote that seems even more seditious than the scriptural account of Abraham challenging God. Second-century Rabbi Eliezer ben Hyrcanus was recognized as one of the leading scholars of his generation. He also enjoyed a very high approval rating with the audience that matters most: God. When it came to deciding one particular ritual matter, however, his colleagues demurred. In order to support his side, Rabbi Eliezer invoked divine confirmation. "If the law is in accord with my view, let this river reverse its course." Sure enough, the river runs backwards. Visitors to Nova Scotia and New Brunswick will attest to the fact that due to the phenomenon known as the tidal bore, it is possible to see and experience a river running backwards. But this phenomenon was unknown in the Middle East almost two thousand years ago. A reversal of a river's current would have been considered a divine sign. Rabbi Eliezer's colleagues were surely impressed. Yet they insisted that no supernatural phenomenon might be applied to academic debate.[16]

They continued to hold that position even after Rabbi Eliezer invoked and received divine confirmation by having trees relocate and the walls of the school house begin to collapse. Finally, Rabbi Eliezer asks that God himself would support his view. So a heavenly voice proclaims that Rabbi Eliezer is right in this case and in all other disputes with his colleagues. What exactly the nature of this heavenly voice may be is an interesting question but not necessary for appreciating the message of this story. But his colleagues rejected what they heard from the heavenly voice. Their position was simple: since God had given the Torah, it remains the exclusive purview of human experts who received it to determine matters of Jewish practice by majority vote on its correct interpretation.

To apply an analogy, consider three museum-goers reflecting on a work of art. One looks at a painting and concludes that it represents the artist's representation of the regularity of life. The other looks at the same painting and concludes that it represents the artist's worry over the dangers of progress. The third says they are both wrong. It is just a still life with fruit. And he should know because he is the artist. The first two look at him and say: "Well if that's what you intended, you should have been more clear." Once the canvas is completed, the artist's intentions are irrelevant. Each viewer will interpret the work as he or she sees fit based on the strokes and images they see. So it is with the Torah. Once given, each scholar will interpret the work as he sees fit based on the information provided. Different interpretations are possible. But when it comes to standardizing practice, only one view will prevail. And that view will be determined by a vote of the experts. The artist or the author of the work has no subsequent say on the matter. Ignoring the view of the creator is audacious. Ignoring the view of the Creator is even more so.

The Talmud does not end the story here. It goes on to tell of a prominent rabbi who had occasion to meet with Elijah the prophet. Elijah, according to the Bible, did not die. Instead, he was carried off to heaven in

---

16. The story of Rabbi Eliezer ben Hyrcanus is told by the Talmud, *b. Bava Metzia* 59b.

a fiery chariot.[17] According to legend, from time to time Elijah returns to earth to work wonders and provide insight. The rabbi asks Elijah what was God's reaction to the rabbis dismissing Rabbi Eliezer's view that, in effect, meant ignoring divine support. Elijah, according to the Talmud, reports that God was overjoyed, saying: "My children have triumphed!" Now whether the events as described actually occurred is irrelevant. The story in the Talmud reveals more about how Judaism thinks than about what happened. Judaism thinks that God approves of rabbinic audacity.

To be sure, Judaism is founded on the authoritativeness of the Torah. To cavalierly disregard the content of the Torah would be unimaginable. Judaism, however, upholds the authoritativeness of the Torah while also rejecting authoritarianism. Whenever an opinion is rejected or a case decided, a person is entitled to ask: "According to what source have you judged me?" In other words, simply citing superior authority ("Because I said so!") is insufficient.[18] It is as invalid as it is unconvincing.

Eighteenth-century Rabbi Mendl of Kotzk thought there was an inherent contradiction between two biblical passages. In Psalm 89 the author says about God: "You rule the raging of the sea; when its waves rise, You praise them." Yet in the book of Jeremiah (5:22) the prophet states about God: "You have placed the bounds for the sea, a perpetual barrier that it cannot pass, though the waves toss, they cannot prevail; though they roar, they cannot pass over it," a stunning passage about limits and boundaries. But the Kotzker Rebbe, as Rabbi Mendl was called, asked why do the waves rage on and try to exceed their limits? Surely the sea "knows" that it cannot destroy God's established order; that its waves cannot prevail against God who delimited them! Even so, the Kotzker Rebbe concluded, knowing that it cannot exceed its limitations, it rages on passionately as if it could. And—most importantly—God praises it for doing so. Adds the Kotzker, human beings are like the waves of the sea, pushing limits. That is our glory.[19]

Anti-authoritarianism—daring to challenge official conventions and demanding compelling reasons for things rather than caprice—is an aspect of audacity that has proven to be socially and politically constructive. In 1809 Jacob Henry of Beaufort was reelected to the North Carolina

---

17. See 2 Kings 2:11 for the narrative of Elijah the Prophet whisked off to heaven in a fiery chariot.

18. That anyone may ask "From what have you judged me?" is based on the Talmud (*b. Sanhedrin* 31b).

19. The interpretation of Rabbi Mendl of Kotzk is told by Kolitz, *Teacher*, 59–60.

legislature, the first Jew in the state to hold such office. But a provision in the state constitution required elected officials to take an oath of office on a Bible that that included Christian Scriptures. Henry boldly refused, pointing out that "the Language of the Bill of Rights is that all men have a natural and unalienable right to worship Almighty God according to the dictates of his own conscience." Hence, he asked of his fellow legislators: "Will you drive from your shores and from the shelter of your constitutions, all who do not lay their oblations at the same altar, observe the same ritual, and subscribe to the same dogmas?" But his colleagues refused to have him seated and proposed that his seat be vacated. In response he said: "The religion I profess, inculcates every duty which man owes to his fellow men; it enjoins upon its votaries, the practice of every virtue, and the detestation of every vice; it teaches them to hope for the favor of heaven exactly in proportion as their lives are directed by just, honorable, and beneficent maxims—This Gentlemen is my creed; it was impressed upon my infant mind, it has been the director of my youth, the monitor of my manhood, and I will trust be the Consolation of my old age." With his bold and dramatic statement and the support of two prominent Catholics, Henry kept his seat without taking the oath on the Bible in question. It was this Jewish legislator from North Carolina who dared to battle against the entrenched standards of his day, thereby laying the groundwork for later struggles of other minorities.

Henry's grasp of his own tradition was impressive. He saw Judaism as a system of values and duties, including helpfulness and hopefulness. He understood that the values of Judaism were ingrained from an early age and continually practiced throughout life. He appreciated that rewards are directly proportionate to good conduct learned through text. That he calls Judaism a "creed" is misleading. Creed was the nineteenth-century term for religion. Henry was not suggesting that Judaism is a pattern of thinking alone. He explicitly refers to Judaism demanding the "practice" of every virtue, not just their adulation. But it is Henry's audacity that is more impressive.

Similarly, in *The Courage of Their Convictions*, author Peter Irons describes those who have changed society for the better because they refused to be satisfied with the way things were. Seattle college student Gordon Hirabayashi refused to comply with the curfew restricting Japanese-Americans to their homes and defied the relocation orders that sent more than 120,000 Japanese-Americans to internment camps in 1942, claiming that compliance would violate his duty to "maintain the democratic standards for which [the United States] lives."[20] Baltimore high school student Robert Mack Bell challenged the "lunch-counter" segregation laws. Barbara Elfbrandt refused to sign a "loyalty" oath during the "Red Scare" of the early 1960s. Susan Epperson, daughter of a missionary and wife of an Air Force officer, insisted on teaching evolution in her Little Rock, Arkansas, biology class in clear violation of a 1928 law. Her position was aided by State Representative Nathan Schoenfeld, a member of Arkansas's tiny Jewish community, who sought to repeal the law, and by Jewish Supreme Court Justice Abe Fortas of Tennessee who wrote the majority opinion vindicating Epperson. Ishmael Jaffree, who challenged mandatory school prayer in Alabama, reports the personal cost that all these audacious men and women had to endure. "My children have experienced all kinds of abuse from neighbors . . . I have suffered emotionally myself and it has drained me."[21] Many lost their jobs. Some continued to work without pay. But all persisted in fighting for their principles.

The International Military Tribunal held at Nüremberg, Germany, following the end of the Second World War, heard defendants including Wilhelm Keitel, Alfred Jodl and Ernst Kaltenbrunner defend their actions that resulted in mass murder with the now infamous "Befehl ist Befehl," that is, "I was only following orders." They argued that as dutiful military officers they had no choice but to follow their superiors' orders. They claimed that an effective army requires discipline and discipline demands an unquestioning acceptance of authority. Judaism if we recall, asserts that discipline is necessary to attain and then maintain what is moral. The Nürenberg defendants effectively stood the value of discipline on its head, proclaiming that discipline requires doing what is immoral. The tribunal would have none of this. They dismissed the "Orders are orders" defense by citing the principle that "the fact that a person acted pursuant to order of his Government or of a superior does not relieve him of responsibility under international law provided a moral choice was in fact possible to him." The tribunal believed that all the defendants indeed had the possibility of making a moral choice and thus found them guilty. But did they? Christopher R. Browning interviewed members of "Reserve Police Battalion 101," a militia unit sent into Poland in 1942. In the course of a single day in July, this unit composed of clerks and common laborers too old to serve in the military rounded up and shot dead 1500 of the 1800 Jews of Jozefrow. During the next sixteen

20. Irons, *Courage*, 40.
21. Ibid., 375.

months these ordinary men who were not members of the Nazi party and grew up in pre-Hitler Germany never exposed to the relentless propaganda of the Third Reich assisted in the murder of 38,000 more and the deportation of another 45,000 to the death camps.

What Browning discovered was that of the 210 former members of the unit he questioned, all of them pointed to the pressure to conform with what was expected that denied them any choice. Professor Vincent Barry argues that while peer pressure is significant, what really was at work is the desire for personal gain. In this case, the unit members wanted to gain the plaudits of their superiors and show that they were still capable of contributing to the war effort. They perceived that pleasing their superiors was essential to their well-being. So they ceded personal responsibility in favor of personal gain. Hence, they followed orders uncritically and persuaded themselves that they could not help but do so. From the perspective of Judaism, what they sorely lacked is the audacity to challenge authority in the name of maintaining the values of respect for all, responsibility for others and helpfulness. Judaism advocates the kind of audacity that calls leaders to account, that demands that justice prevail, and insists that innocent lives be protected.[22]

According to the Torah, farmers must leave the "corners" of their fields unharvested so that the poor could take the crops.[23] It is one of the many laws of the Torah aimed at assisting the indigent. The Mishnah states that the landowner may not gather up the crops and leave them for the poor. Instead, he must leave the crops in the corners in place and allow the poor to take it for themselves.[24] The reasoning behind this law is concern for the dignity of the poor.[25] It is bad enough that people must rely on assistance, but to make them line up for handouts is worse. Allowing the poor to participate in some meaningful way in gathering the crops reduces the indignity. But suppose the poor decide that rather than each one gathering their own crops from the "corner," they would make a pile of all that was collected and then divide the total amongst themselves. And suppose everyone was in agreement except for one. Says the Talmud: "Even if ninety

---

22. I am grateful to, Vincent Barry, author of *The Dog Ate My Homework*, 97, for bringing to my attention the research on Reserve Police Battalion.

23. Lev 19:9 and 23:22.

24. *m. Pe'ah* 4:1.

25. Although some commentators say that it is intended to prevent the danger associated with the climbing of trees to access the fruit.

nine say divide and one says gather, we listen to the one since the law is in agreement with him."

The rationale of the law is less relevant than the idea of one person standing up to a vast majority. That the Talmud could even imagine that one person would stand in the way of popular will assumes that a person must have considerable audacity. But that is precisely what Judaism advocates. The popular will may be popular by definition but that does not make it right. Standing up for what is right even if unpopular is the Jewish way.

Chapter Five

The Big "I"

THE "I" STANDS FOR integrity. I call it the Big "I" because of its importance: it shapes—or should shape—the entirety of our acting and thinking. Integrity means transfusing every action and thought with the highest standards of noble living. It is very much linked with the value of holiness. When the Greek sculptor Phidias was at work on the incomparable statue of Athena that once graced the Parthenon, we are told, he took great pains to realistically render every hair on the back of her head. The statue stood at the rear of the temple facing forward so onlookers would see her face only. An apprentice wondered why Phidias would take so much time and put so much effort into a part of his creation that will not be seen by visitors. He asked his master: "If the goddess' hair was not perfect who will know?" Phidias is said to reply: "I will." Integrity means doing things properly even when no one else will know.

Whenever a friend of mine would hang pictures on the wall he wouldn't measure. He would estimate the position by sight alone. If he bought furniture that came in a kit, as long as the pieces fit together when assembled, he really didn't care that the sides were flush or all the pieces were aligned. When he would cook a meal, he would not take the time to measure; he would approximate the amount of each ingredient. His attitude was reflected by his oft-repeated phrase: "Close enough for government work." Aside from being an insult to government employees who are assumed to do shoddy work with a lackadaisical attitude, my friend reflected a lack of integrity. He wanted to "get away with" as little as possible. He wanted to spend the least of amount of time requiring the least bother in order to complete the task. Many companies have gone bankrupt when their employees operated with the same absence of integrity.

On November 20, 2012, a basketball player from tiny Grinnell College set the record for most points scored in a single game: a phenomenal 138! As accomplished a professional star as LeBron James took note of this tremendous feat. Yet *Sports Illustrated* columnist Phil Taylor was not only unimpressed, he was practically offended. He called Jack Taylor's performance "distorted" because his teammates consistently passed up their own shots and fed Jack the ball "as if they're under hypnosis."[1] In other words, the legitimacy of any record must be called into question when the record is set through contrivance, like the case of Nykesha Sales.

In 1998, Sales was so close to breaking the University of Connecticut's career scoring mark in women's basketball until a knee-injury foreclosed that possibility. To allow her the glory of ending her college career with the record in hand, Villanova colluded with UConn to allow Sales to hobble out on the court at the start of their game and take an uncontested lay-up (which she made) to "earn" the record. UConn returned the favor, and with the score now tied 2-2, the real competition began. Columnist Taylor calls all such records "inauthentic" because these are achievements that lack integrity in their accomplishment. To be sure, Villanova may be applauded for their charitableness toward an outstanding player. But they, along with the University of Connecticut, diminished the value of the record and the integrity of the game.

Judaism insists that integrity must never be compromised. That lesson is derived from the Bible. The book of Exodus includes detailed instructions for the construction of the portable sanctuary used by the Israelites following the exodus from Egypt and until the building of the temple in Jerusalem. Moses is given "blueprints" for the outer structure and all the components: the ark that housed both sets of tablets, the two altars, the golden candelabrum, the table, and all the implements needed. In the penultimate chapter of the book, all of the same things are mentioned again, this time reporting that each and every one of them was made according the specifications and instructions. And each report ends with the recurrent phrase: " . . . as the Lord commanded Moses." No less than eight times do we read that phrase. But this is not an idle repetition included in a trivial list. It serves a crucial purpose, namely, to indicate that not even the

---

1. Phil Taylor's article "It's Time to Scratch a Few Records" appeared in *Sports Illustrated*, December 3, 2012, 72.

slightest detail escaped attention. Every piece of the tabernacle, no matter how insignificant it may have seemed, was completed precisely as required. It is a matter of integrity.[2]

Integrity is not easy to define. Bruce B. Roberts, Craig D. Rice, and Joe E. Smith, in their book *Where in the World Is Integrity?* put it simply: "integrity happens." Integrity is easier illustrated than defined. The American Film Institute lists Atticus Finch as the number one hero of all movies in one hundred years of film. Atticus Finch is the protagonist in Harper Lee's 1960 book *To Kill a Mockingbird*, played extraordinarily well by Gregory Peck in the film of the same name. Attticus Finch became a paradigm for a generation of lawyers who saw his devotion to justice and willingness to challenge the scourge of discrimination while risking his standing in the community in order to defend a man accused of a heinous crime. Finch's integrity resided in the fact that what mattered to him most was the fairness of the system, rather than the innocence of the accused. It was only later on, in his vigorous pursuit of the truth that Finch finds evidence that could clear the defendant.

In the Bible we have the example of Abraham who refused to accept any personal reward for rescuing the king of Sodom. Abraham, always looking after the welfare of others, only asked compensation for his retainers (Gen 14:3). Joseph, who refused to surrender to the seductive appeals of Pharaoh's wife, is another example of integrity (Gen 39:8–9). When Jacob made peace with his brother-in-law, he reminded him of his twenty years of service. As shepherd of Laban's flock's Jacob reports of his diligence: "Your ewes and she-goats never miscarried, nor did I feast on the rams from your flock. That which was torn by beasts I never brought to you; I myself made good the loss . . . often scorching heat ravaged me by day and frost by night, and sleep fled from my eyes . . ." (Gen 31:38ff.). Jacob was a model of integrity.

Integrity applies to a wide area of life. Integrity applies to how we responsibly deal with communal funds. The twelfth-century Talmudic commentators known as "Tosafists" ask a pertinent question related to the end of the book of Exodus. A record of all the donations—gold, silver, copper— were "drawn up at Moses' bidding" (Exod 38:21). Was Moses so unreliable and his character so suspect that he had to allay the fears of the people that he might be "skimming" some of the funds and enriching himself? That, in their opinion, could not be. Rather, Moses drew up the list in order to

---

2. See the book of Exodus, ch. 40, for the details of the construction of the tabernacle.

demonstrate that all collections in the name of the community must be beyond reproach. Integrity demanded that even Moses give a full and accurate count.

Similarly, the Second Book of Kings (12:7ff.) tells how a collection chest was invented so deposits could be made without having donations pass through the hands of the priests. Likewise, the tunics worn by the priests, according to the Talmud, were sewn without pockets so that no one would have grounds to suspect anything untoward in the handling of communal funds. That is what integrity demands.[3]

Integrity is essential in business. The Talmud (*b. Eruvin* 65b) tells of Rabbi Shimon ben Shetah who bought a mule from an Arab. His students discovered a precious gem hanging around the neck of the animal and celebrated his good fortune. But Rabbi Shimon promptly returned the jewel to the Arab, insisting that his purchase was for the animal only. The jewel belonged to the seller. The Arab is reputed to have proclaimed: "Praised be the God of Shimon ben Shetah!"

The Talmud (*b. B. Metzia* 44a) also considers what constitutes a lawful sale such that neither party may renege. Two essential acts are characteristic of a sale. The first is the payment of the agreed sum by the buyer to the seller. The second is the seller taking the object sold into his or her possession. Ordinarily, both acts follow one after the other. But the rabbis were aware of the fact that sometimes either the buyer or seller may have a change of mind. Suppose the buyer took the object into his possession but had not yet paid the agreed upon sum and then wished to abrogate the deal. The Talmud rules that once that buyer took ownership of the goods, the sale is final, even though the money did not yet change hands. Suppose, however, that the money was paid but the purchaser did not yet take the goods. The Talmud rules that the purchaser can still change his mind. The deal is not final. It is the actual transfer of ownership that effects the transaction. While this addresses the legal requirements for sale, it opens the possibility that a party to fair negotiations, in this case, the purchaser, may opt out at the last moment, after the other party had every reason to believe that the deal was concluded in good faith. Thus the Talmud condemns the purchaser in the strongest terms, invoking God's displeasure:

---

3. See *Da'at Zekenim l'Ba-alei haTosafot* on Exod 38:21 for their view on how Moses' remained above reproach. The Talmud reports that the priests had no pockets in their tunics. And those delegated to collect public funds were appointed in pairs, never allowed to separate, and not allowed to exchange personal funds for money collected (*b. Bava Batra* 8b).

The Big "I"

"He Who punished the generation of the Flood, and the generation of the Tower of Babel, and the men of Sodom and Amorrah, and the Egyptians who drowned in the sea, shall exact punishment from whoever does not stand by his word." Rabbi Joseph Karo restates the Talmudic discussion and frames it in context of the expectation of integrity:

> When one has paid a purchase price, but not pulled the moveable goods (in order to effect acquisition), even though acquisition of the goods has not been effected, as has been explained, whoever withdraws from the transaction, whether buyer or seller, has not behaves as a Jew should and is obliged to take upon himself the formal rabbinic condemnation of "He who punished." This holds even if only part of the price was paid.[4]

Standing by one's word is a matter of integrity.

And the paradigm for standing by one's word is located in the Bible. According to the ninth chapter of the book of Joshua, the Gibeonites, a native Canaanite tribe, were much fearful that Joshua would destroy them as he had destroyed the neighboring city-states of Jericho and Ai. So they hatched a cunning plan. They sent a delegation posed as a tribe from a distant land and proposed a "non-aggression" pact with Joshua. Joshua and the Israelites were wary, even skeptical. But the Gibeonites produced evidence to support their claim. They pointed to their threadbare clothes, worn and patched sandals, drained water skins, and crumbly food as proof of the great distance they had traveled. Of course, all these things were cleverly designed to make it appear so. Joshua made the pact. No less then three days later, the strategy was exposed. Much to the Israelites' dismay, they discovered that they were fooled. In reality, the Gibeonites were locals who were to have been destroyed. Nevertheless, they were neither destroyed nor attacked. The Israelites were not happy. In fact, in reading the text we get the distinct notion that what the people argued was that a deal made under false pretenses was no deal at all. But the leaders of Israel responded (v. 9): "We swore to them by the Lord, the God of Israel; therefore we cannot touch them." A deal is a deal. Fooled they were; but that is not grounds for reneging. Integrity demands that even a bad deal be honored.

Investing in the monetary instruments of the State of Israel is not a bad deal at all. In fact, it is a great deal. The rates are better than many other bonds. Moreover, the return on investment is guaranteed. Israel is

---

4. *Shulhan Arukh*, Hoshen Mishpat 204:1 translation by Steven M. Passamaneck, *Traditional Jewish Law of Sale*.

only one of three countries in the world (the other two being Switzerland and Luxembourg) that has never failed to repay all loans on time, no matter the circumstances. At war or in peace, Israel has never deferred, delayed, or reneged on any loan. That is because the State of Israel is a Jewish state and Judaism demands integrity.

The psalmist reflects on the qualities of a worthy man. He lives without blame, does what is right, acknowledges the truth in his heart, never speaks evil, does no harm to a fellow human being, and more. But added to this list (Ps 15:4) is the special mention of he "who stands by his oath even to his own harm." Such a man is a man of integrity.

Integrity is often, and correctly, associated with honesty.[5] One of the most influential twentieth-century philosophers was Bertrand Russell.[6] In his autobiography he speaks about the honesty of his colleague G. E. Moore: "I have never but once succeeded in making him tell a lie, and that was by subterfuge. 'Moore,' I said, 'do you always speak the truth?' 'No,' he replied. I believe this to be the only lie he ever told." For the Talmud, while lying was permitted under very limited—but understandable—circumstances, like saving a life or protecting someone's feelings, the general rule was that honesty is essential.[7] Hence the Torah prohibits deceit, fraud, rendering unfair decisions, or showing deference to the rich or to one's kin. The Talmud includes truth as one of the pillars upon which the world stands, meaning that civilized society would be impossible without it. As Rabbi Menahem Mendl of Kotzk (1787–1859) framed it, truth is the beginning, the end, and the heart.[8]

---

5. It is noteworthy that the Torah (Exod 23:7) does not prohibit lying outright, as it does with murder, theft, and adultery. Rather, it uses a more circumspect expression, namely, "stay away from deceitful things," implying that lying might be justified in certain circumstances. It is on this basis that the Academy of Hillel, cited in the Talmud (b. Ketubot 17a) allowed telling a bride she was beautiful and pious even though the facts might be otherwise. And the sages of the Talmud permitted lying to evade a murderer or robber (m. Nedarim 2:4). Otherwise, lying would violate the fundamental principles of Judaism, or, as the Talmud (b. Sanhedrin 92a) puts it, lying is tantamount to idolatry. (See also Prov 12:29; Ps 99:104, 128, 163.) See Exod 23:3, 6, and Deut 16:19 for the laws against perverting justice, and Deut 16:20 for pursuing justice. See also Exod 23:8 and Deut 16:19 for the law against taking bribes. Deuteronomy 19:14 prohibits moving landmarks and Deut 25:13–16 requires fair weights and measures. According to Rabbi Simon ben Gamaliel in Pirke Avot (1:18), the world stands on three things: truth, justice, and peace.

6. Bertrand Russell's autobiography was published in three volumes from 1967–69.

7. For an excellent, comprehensive, and readable presentation of the centrality of truthfulness along with the exceptions to the principle, see Rabbi Joseph Telushkin, Book of Jewish Values and Code of Jewish Ethics, vol. 1.

8. Rabbi Abraham Joshua Heschel's stirring paean to the Kotzker Rebbe, as he was

The Big "I"

One of my heroes is Rabbi Moses J. Feldman. He was not only a great scholar and author of an encyclopedic dictionary of Jewish prayer, he was also a man of unparalleled integrity. I visited him the day he was to be released from a Los Angeles hospital in the early 1980s. But a problem with his bill delayed matters. He refused to pay for a box of tissues that he did not request and did not use. The itemized bill was lengthy and detailed. And the cost of a single box of tissues was infinitesimally small compared to others procedures listed. But, he explained, the bill was going to be paid by insurance. If everyone paid inflated bills it would result in an increase in all premiums. He wanted no part in being responsible—even marginally—for the increase in health care costs. The bill was adjusted. And I witnessed a firsthand lesson in integrity.

But it is especially in the realm of intellectual matters that Judaism demonstrates and advocates integrity. The Talmud reports on a debate that goes back about two thousand years ago. The question at the root of the debate is the relative importance of study and action. This differs from the question of the relative importance of action and faith, or deed versus creed, that I addressed in the previous chapter. All authorities in Judaism agree that deed trumps creed. Study, however, is a kind of action. It is sedentary and could be solitary but it is an action nonetheless. Two views are articulated. One rabbi insisted that action is more important than study. Another argued that study is more important than actions. After considering both sides, the consensus of opinion is that study is more important than action since study inevitably leads to action. The rabbis simply could not imagine that anyone would learn what ought to be done and then would fail to do it. The rabbis, of course, operated under a Jewish bias that to be fully human requires doing what is right, not simply knowing what is right. But without knowing what is right, it is impossible to do what is right. Hence, study becomes paramount in Judaism.[9]

---

known, is called *A Passion for Truth*. Interestingly, the Hebrew word for truth, *emet*, is composed of the first, middle, and last letters of the Hebrew alphabet.

9. The Talmud (*b. Kiddushin* 40b) tells the following story:

> One day Rabbi Tarfon and the elders were sitting together on the upper floor of the house Nitza in Lod and there the question was put before them: "Is studying or doing more important?" Rabbi Tarfon was of the opinion that doing was more important. But Rabbi Akiva thought that learning was more important. They finally agreed that studying was more important by reason of the fact that it leads to doing.

Prescription for an Ailing World

In *The Jewish Mystique*, a study of the disproportionate success Jews have enjoyed in the professions, arts, and sciences, Ernst van der Haag makes the point that is has been the historical dedication to learning that mainly contributed to high achievement. Jewish illiteracy is virtually unknown. And Jewish scholarship was propagated uninterrupted over successive generations.[10]

But it is the *way* of studying, not just the *act* of studying, that is of particular note. Judaism promotes intellectual integrity. For instance, the Talmud teaches that anyone who cites by name the author of the statement made brings redemption to the world.[11] It seems like hyperbole: linking universal redemption with giving credit of authorship. Yet it is based on a deduction from the biblical book of Esther (2:2). It is Esther who informs the king in the name of her guardian Mordechai of the imminent assassination plot. It is Mordechai who is rewarded with special place in the king's service. And that in turn led to foiling the plan that would have meant genocide. Hence, the chain of events that began with reporting information in the name of the person who came to it resulted in saving many lives. But aside from the textual proof, what the Talmud affirms is that taking credit for someone else's ideas is tantamount to intellectual theft. And if depriving someone else of his or her rightful property is the norm, then society itself is untenable. The relatively trivial act of proper citation has cosmic consequences. Accordingly, not a page of the Talmud is turned without reading of an opinion transmitted in the name of a chain of scholars leading back to the originator. Maimonides was recognized as great thinker, arguably the greatest thinker in Jewish history. In the introduction to his commentary to a tractate of *First Principles*[12] (better known as *Pirke Avot*), he writes:

> Know . . . that the ideas presented in these chapters and in the following commentary are not of my own invention; neither did I think out the explanations contained therein, but I have gleaned them from the words of the wise occurring in the legends, the Talmud, and other rabbinic works, as well as from the words of

---

10. See Haag, *Jewish Mystique*, ch. 1, "Are Jews Smarter than Other People?"

11. Authors must be cited by name according to the Talmud (*b. Megilah* 7a, 15a). See also *Pirke Avot* 6:6.

12. Lerner, *Literature of the Sages*, 263f. contends that *Pirke Avot* should better be rendered as First Principles, based on the commentary of Rabbi Menahem HaMeiri (Introduction to Avot) and the general usage in the Mishnah (see, e.g., *m. Bava Kamma* 1:1; *Shabbat* 7:2). The popular English rendition of Pirke Avot is "Chapters of the Fathers," not without its defenders. See *Philologos*, at mosaicmagazine.com, January 25, 2017.

the philosophers, ancient and recent, and also from the works of various authors.

But when Maimonides wrote his code of Jewish law he failed to cite the authorities from whom he digested the law and was criticized roundly for the omission.

Interestingly, the statement in the Talmud requiring proper citation of sources is repeated in *First Principles* (6:6) and studied by Jews weekly during the spring and summer seasons. This means that the average person who may not be too familiar with the Talmud would still have access to this important principle. The frequency with which the principle of intellectual integrity is studied attests to its importance.[13]

Moreover, scholars like to distinguish between two types of interpretation of text. One type, called *eisegesis*, works by starting with the view you endorse and then impose that view on the text in such a way that your predetermined position is justified. The second type, called *exegesis*, works by analyzing the text and deducing from it some fact or truth. Eisegesis reads into the text; exegesis reads out of the text. To give an example, consider the folk song *Puff, the Magic Dragon*, popularized by Peter, Paul and Mary in the 1960s. The eisegetical approach begins by asserting that it is clearly a song promoting the drug culture of its day, "puff" and Jackie "Paper" being an obvious reference to marijuana smoking and the word "sea" in the phrase "land by the sea" (where *Puff* frolicked) should be read as the letter "C" for cocaine. The exegetical approach, however, starts with the words of the song, and after careful analysis concludes that it is a sentimental reflection on growing up and growing old and the consequent loss of imagination. Judaism rejects as manipulative and thus worthless the eisegetical approach as a retrojection of a predetermined view.

Judaism has always taken the biblical text too seriously to allow its self-serving manipulation. And Judaism has always taken the biblical text to be a living guide for good conduct. Consequently, the first interpreters of the Bible saw themselves neither as curators determined to preserve the Bible as a museum piece nor as propagandists intent on promoting a particular ideology. Instead, they saw themselves as detectives dedicated to searching out the meaning of the text and the actions that necessarily flow from it. Interpretation of Scripture must be based on sound philological method

---

13. Telushkin, *Book of Jewish Values*, 94, explains that citing another's work is an affirmation that the speaker or writer seeks only to advance knowledge rather than self-aggrandizement. Thus it is a redemptive act.

Prescription for an Ailing World

and establishing the meaning of difficult words or concepts from parallels with other places in Scripture where the meaning is clear contextually. All Scripture was treated as a cohesive unit. Consequently, apparent contradictions had to be reconciled by way of precise comparisons and analysis. But once a rather complicated system of interpretation was put in place, it was followed rigorously. At times when rabbinic practice was not supportable by the objective outcome of the interpretive system, Judaism did not force its justification into the text. Rather, the rabbis acknowledged that the actual derivation could not be borne out by the text and chose instead to find scriptural allusions that admittedly carried less weight. The integrity of the method, the integrity of the text, and the integrity of the text's interpreters had to be maintained.

Intellectual integrity is also the hallmark of the scholars revered in Judaism. The most respected and popular commentator in Jewish history was RaShI, acronym for Rabbi Shlomo Itzhaqi of Troyes, France, who lived in the eleventh century.[14] It was his commentary that made both the Torah and the Talmud comprehensible to the masses. The respected and popular twentieth-century Bible teacher, scholar, and author Nehama Lebowitz once told me that she has no less than 127 super-commentaries on RaShI. These were books written to explain or qualify what RaShI had to say, rather than on what the text upon which RaShI was commenting had to say. Given RaShI's preeminence, his approach to textual study is highly influential.

As well trained and as knowledgeable as he was, RaShI was not infallible. Having admitted that he had misinterpreted a passage in the Talmud, hid students report that he declared: "I have been in error here . . . I therefore retract my statement and thank my colleagues for the correction." Again, regarding an admitted mistake in his reading of a verse in the book of Ezekiel he writes: "My thanks to my colleague from whose arguments I have learned. I have been in error in this explanation . . . and now I am reviewing it with our colleague." It is not to call into question the reliability of RaShI's commentary that I mention these admissions but to demonstrate

---

14. For an excellent biography of Rabbi Isaac of Troyes, see Esra Shereshevsky's *Rashi: The Man and His World*. Shereshevsky gives an even longer list of places where RaShI admits he does not know the correct explanation or interpretation. His admitted error in understanding Ezekiel appears in *Mahzor Vitry*, ed. Hurwitz, para. 182, 444. That he will review it with his colleague is mentioned by Shereshevsky, *Rashi*, 50. Some of the places in Talmud where RaShI admits to be unclear are *b. Betzah* 25b, *b. Yoma* 85a, and *b. Niddah* 67a.

his willingness to admit error, his graciousness in retracting his opinion, and his gratefulness to those who pointed out the mistake.

And consider the number of passages where RaShI confesses to not knowing the correct meaning or interpretation. Genesis 28:5 narrates that Isaac sent Jacob to Aram where he could reside with his mother's brother, to which RaShI says: "I don't know what this comes to teach us," since it is information readily deducible from earlier verses. Regarding the meaning of Genesis 35:13 that states, "God parted from him from the spot where He had spoken to him," RaShI says the same thing. Regarding a grammatical difficulty in Exodus 15:1, RaShI says: "I am unable to reconcile this language." In Exodus 22:28 RaShI admits he does not know what the Hebrew root of the word translated as "the first yield of your vats" really means. RaShI admits he cannot explain the meaning of a white discoloration that "appears deeper than the skin" in Leviticus 13:4. He admits that he cannot account for the doubling of a particular Hebrew letter in Leviticus 27:3. In Deuteronomy 33:24 RaShI indicates that of all the tribes only Asher is given a blessing through his children and he cannot explain how. In the Talmud, RaShI will admit that he doesn't understand what the text describes or that he is unsure what a particular expression means. Collectively, these admissions convey RaShI's honesty or better, intellectual integrity. RaShI epitomizes the Talmudic teaching that instructs each person to "Teach your tongue to say 'I don't know.'"[15]

Almost five hundred years after RaShI, Don Isaac Abarbanel stretches the bounds of intellectual integrity by dismissing the often-fanciful rabbinical accounts in favor of a stricter, plain sense, contextual approach to interpreting the Torah. Sometimes laudatory, sometimes perfunctorily deferential, occasionally circumspectly critical, Abarbanel cites rabbinic legends before proceeding to discount them. In a manner that a contemporary biblical scholar Eric Lawee calls uncharacteristically blunt, Abarbanel brands the legendary material often held as true to be unlikely, insufficient, dubious, weak, or strange.[16] Even his esteemed predecessor RaShI is not spared. While RaShI cites a legend that the absence of the healing north wind accounted for the postponement of circumcision until reaching the borders of the land of Canaan, Abarbanel notes that common experience is such that male infants are circumcised "north wind or no." Dispatching RaShI's interpretation, Abarbanel opts for another. While Abarbanel wrote

15. *b. Berakhot* 4a.
16. See Eric Lawee's *Abarbanel's Stance towards Tradition*, 94–103.

no treatise of his method of interpretation, what seems to have directed him was an unremitting dedication to truth. He was not interested in propagating the fanciful views held by some earlier rabbis merely because they are part of tradition. He was interested in explicating the text. Knowing what the text means is different from knowing what meaning has been given to the text. Intellectual integrity demanded that he unlink the two.

Intellectual integrity also meant adopting knowledge and practice outside of Judaism when it was necessary. Knowing the precise times for the celebration of the holidays was essential to Judaism. In ancient days, the Jewish calendar was fixed by observation. That required witnesses to report on the position of the moon before a new month could be declared. Since the fourth century, however, the Jewish calendar was fixed by astronomical calculations rather than observation. Maimonides readily admits that this expertise was not indigenously Jewish but it does not matter.

> With respect to the principle which governs all these calculations, why we have to add or deduct certain figures, how all these matters became known and the proof of each of them—this is the science of astronomy and mathematics about which the Greek philosophers composed many books which are still today in the possession of contemporary philosophers and scientists . . . Since all these matters have been established by clear demonstrations in which there are no fallacies, demonstrations which no one can refute, we have no concern with who the author of them was, or whether he was a prophet [of Israel] or a Gentile. For in the case of any claim whose principles have been exposed [to our scrutiny] and whose truth has been established by sound proofs in which there is no fallacy, we rely on the person who has set it forth or taught it only to the extent that his claim has been unequivocally demonstrated and its principles stand up to our scrutiny.[17]

17. For Maimonides's view on the acceptability of Greek astronomy, see his *Mishneh Torah*, Laws of Sanctifying the New Moon 17:24. For the English translation, see the very fine Yale Judaica Series 17:25. Fox also provides an English translation, 327. Isadore Twersky was among the preeminent modern explicators of Maimonides. See his *Introduction to the Code of Maimonides*, esp. 498–99, for his discussion on Maimonides's use of external sources. Marvin Fox, like Twersky, spent a good part of his academic career in Maimonidean studies. See his *Interpreting Maimonides*, especially p. 34 on reason. See Maimonides, *Treatise on Resurrection* in *Iggerot Ha-Rambam*, ed. Y. Kafih (1972) on the two theories on the existence of the world and his preference. See Fox, *Interpreting Maimonides*, 34, for an English translation. Another translation appears in A. Halkin and D. Hartman's *Crisis and Leadership: Epistles of Maimonides* published in 1985. Maimonides expresses the view that truth should be accepted from any sources in *Eight Chapters of Maimonides on Ethics*, translated by Joseph Gorfinkle, 36, and Fox,

To Maimonides, what counts is truth. Incontrovertible truths must be accepted from whatever source they come. That Judaism relies on external knowledge is not a weakness of Judaism but is a strength. It speaks of Judaism's openness to all ideas, testing them to determine their usefulness, yet never excluding them merely on the grounds that Judaism did not have them first or at all. Isadore Twersky explains that to Maimonides, external sources are not "foreign" at all since any source that helps explicate the Torah is complementary to it. What makes any idea worthwhile is its utility and reasonableness.

Maimonides, says Marvin Fox, "was committed to the principle that we must follow reason wherever it takes us, because intellectual honesty demands that we accept conclusions that reason has demonstrated to be true."[18] Maimonides makes this view explicit in an essay written later in his life.

> Our effort and similarly the effort of the small number of the philosophically sophisticated people is exactly the opposite of the masses. The unreflective masses of the various religious communities find nothing, in their foolishness, which is more attractive and more satisfying than to conceive religion and reason as polar opposites which stand in contradiction to each other. They account for all phenomena in a way that goes contrary to reason, and affirm that whatever occurs is a miracle. In this way they move us far away as possible from conceiving events as occurring within the order of nature, whether they be past events, about which we have been told, or events that are predicted to take place in the future. We, on the other hand, make every effort to unite religious teaching and reason. To the fullest extent possible we account for all events in the context of the order of nature.[19]

And Maimonides also makes this view explicit in the concluding phrase of a passage I cited earlier in which he acknowledges that others are the source of most of his insights. He mentions that he will advance the view of any thinker whose words would help explain the work in question since "one should accept the truth from whatever source it proceeds."

Interpreting Maimonides, 28. Maimonides admission that both theories of the existence of the world are possible in his *Guide of the Perplexed*, bk. 2, ch. 25, see the excellent translation into English by Shlomo Pines, vol. 2, 327.

18. Fox, *Interpreting Maimonides*, 34.

19. *Treatise on Resurrection* in *Iggerot Ha-Rambam*, ed. Y. Kafih, 87–88, translated by Fox, *Interpreting Maimonides*, 34.

Intellectual integrity further demanded that Maimonides admit that when it comes to the two regnant theories on the existence of the world, the theory that held the world was eternal and the theory that proposed the world was created, neither one could be demonstrated with certainty. In principle, Maimonides believed that the matter was incapable of a philosophical solution. In the end, Maimonides opts for the theory of creation. But he does not pretend that his choice incontrovertible. Admitting that other opinions may be valid is a consequence of intellectual integrity.

No doubt Maimonides's son, Rabbi Abraham—an authority in his own right—was influenced by his father when he wrote:

> We, and every intelligent and wise person, are obligated to evaluate each idea and each statement, to find the way in which to understand it; to prove the truth and establish which is worthy to be established, and to annul that which is worthy of being annulled.[20]

Blind obedience to authority—even religious authority—is not the Jewish way. No one is expected to suspend reason in favor of supporting tendentious religious doctrine or the homiletical interpretations of a single individual no matter how well placed or revered. As Rabbi Samuel ben Hofni, one of the giants of Babylonian Jewry after the Talmudic period, put it: "If the words of the ancients contradict reason, we are not obligated to accept them."[21]

Less than a century after Maimonides, the sons-in-law and grandsons of RaShI, known collectively as the Tosafists, took the Talmudic concept of "changing times" and elevated it to a principle for determining Jewish law. For instance, the Tosafists rules that liquids left overnight are no longer forbidden on the grounds that poisonous snakes that might secrete venom into such liquids are not common nowadays. And since the average person now lacks the expertise to repair musical instruments, the rule prohibiting handclapping on Shabbat lest it lead to repairing musical instruments no longer applies. The Tosafists recognized that the prescribed Talmudic medical remedies that were once thought to be effective but have proven by

---

20. Rabbi Abraham ben Moses' statement appears in his essay entitled *Odot Derashot Hazal* (On the History of Rabbinic Interpretation) printed in the introductory section of the compendium of Talmudic legends entitle *Ein Ya'akov*. The translation I cite is that of Rabbi Marc Angel appearing in his article "Reflections on Torah Education and Mis-Education," 11.

21. Rabbi Samuel ben Hofni's support of reason over ancient opinions appears in B. M. Levin, *Otzar HaGeonim*, vol. 4, 4–5.

experience not to be are no longer applied. Even rules based on Talmudic statements about animal physiology could no longer be maintained in light of a more sophisticated knowledge of veterinary medicine.[22]

Judaism does not reject advances in the biological sciences on the basis of a preconceived notion of scriptural requirements. That would be imposing an idea on the text that the text itself does not warrant. When anesthetics were first administered to women in childbirth in the middle of the nineteenth century, it evoked a firestorm of protest from those who thought it contravened a biblical requirement that women given birth in pain, the penalty imposed on the first woman who sinned. Judaism, however, welcomed the medical advance. That women give birth in pain was deemed a curse, not a requirement. And relieving pain was a physician's responsibility.[23] Further, the acceptance of advances in medical science speaks to the intellectual integrity of Judaism. When medical science progresses to the point that earlier assumptions are unequivocally disproven, retaining those assumptions would be irrational. Thus while bloodletting was once considered efficacious for many symptoms, medical science now recognizes it as largely useless. Hence, retaining bloodletting as a proper treatment since it is recommended in the Talmud would be a mistake. Intellectual integrity demands surrendering bad information for good.

It is enlightening to see how Judaism looks at the controversial issue of evolution. Intellectual integrity demands that the scientific data accumulated over the last two hundred years of human history must be evaluated and, if held to be compelling, accepted—even if the data contradicts Scripture. That does not mean that Scripture need be abandoned. Scripture, in Judaism, is considerably plastic; it's narrative portions allow for broad interpretation. But facts cannot be interpreted away.

Thus, seventeen years before the publication of Darwin's *Origin of the Species*, Rabbi Israel Lipschitz of Danzig addressed his congregation during the Passover holiday.[24] He reviews for his listeners the most recent scientific

---

22. I discuss the Tosafists' views on changing facts in an essay entitled "Jewish Law and Changing Times" that appeared in *Halakhah and the Modern Jew*, published by the Union for Traditional Judaism in 1989, 1–8. The Union for Traditional Judaism, founded in 1984, made intellectual integrity one of its two foundational principles.

23. I owe this insight to Rabbi David M. Feldman, *Health and Medicine in the Jewish Tradition*, 62.

24. Rabbi Israel Lipschitz's sermon appended to his commentary to the *Mishnah Sanhedrin*, in the standard edition called *Yakhin u'Boaz*. It was published in English in 1976 as part of an anthology called *Challenge: Torah Views on Science and Its Problems*,

discoveries in the Pyrenees, the Carpathians, the Himalayas, and the Rocky Mountains. Geologists found them to be formed "of mighty layers of rock lying one upon the another in amazing and chaotic formations, explicable only in terms of revolutionary transformations of the earth's surface." Geologists also noticed stratification and "fossilized remains of creatures; those in the lower layers being of monstrous size and structure, while those in the upper and more recent layers being progressively smaller in size but incomparably more refined in structure and form." Note how Rabbi Lipschitz suggests to his listeners that the fossilized creatures that succeeded the dinosaurs were more complex, indicating an undeniable advancement.

He goes on to describe "a monstrous species of elephant" discovered under the Siberian ice in 1807 that was three to four times the size of any of its contemporary kin. He deduces: "Since that icy region is incapable of supporting any species of elephant, we must conclude either that the creature was swept there as a result of some cosmic upheaval, or that in some previous epoch the climate of Siberia had been warm enough to support elephants." He adds that fossilized sea creatures have been discovered in the recesses of high mountains, that scientists have calculated that of every seventy-eight species found in the earth, forty-eight have gone extinct. He specifically identifies the mammoth discovered near Baltimore and an iguanadon over ninety feet long from whose internal structures scientists have concluded that it was herbivorous. Rabbi Lipschitz grasped the idea that the paleontological and geological record dispute the contention that there was a single act of creation in which all species were created. Different strata of rock and different fossils in different strata prove it. That no fossils of large mammals have ever been found in the same layers as dinosaurs conclusively demonstrates that they lived in different periods. The question he faced was what to make of all this; information that suggests that the earth and its creatures have changed over time, a seeming challenge to the Genesis account.

Of course, he could have chosen to challenge any or all these scientific discoveries. He could have deemed them elaborate hoaxes. He could insist that the scientists have erred in the analyses. Instead, he accepts all the data as valid and chooses to interpret the Torah in a way that conforms to science! He explains that the first verse of the Torah refers to the original act of creation while the phrase "the earth was null and void" refers to epochs

---

edited by Aryeh Carmell and Cyril Domb under the auspices of the Association of Orthodox Jewish Scientists. The sermon appears on pp. 132–34.

of "upheaval and destruction" that came after. In other words, God created a world in which change ensues. That the details of this process are lacking in the text is attributed to the fact that these details "have no immediate relevance to us." That the creation account, however, begins with the simplest and proceeds to the most complex, is a hint of the evolutionary theme. One of the most authoritative scholars of this same period, Rabbi Sholom Mordechai Schwadron of Berzhan, Poland, approved of Rabbi Lipschitz's analysis, lending it even greater validity. Other rabbis followed suit. For instance, Rabbi Tzvi Hirsch Chajes (d. 1855) pointed to a passage in the Jerusalem Talmud that states the mountains were not included in the original creation of the world but were formed later over the course of time.[25]

By 1873, when even more evidence of evolution came to public attention, Rabbi Samson Raphael Hirsch, the founder of the Neo-Orthodox movement in Judaism, wrote:

> Even if this notion were ever to gain complete acceptance by the scientific world, Jewish thought, unlike the reasoning of the high priest of that notion [i.e., Darwin], would nonetheless never summon us to revere a still extant representative of this primal form [i.e., apes] as the supposed ancestor of us all. Rather, Judaism in that case would call upon its adherents to give even greater reverence than ever before to the one, sole God Who, in His boundless creative wisdom and eternal omnipotence, needed to bring into existence no more than one single, amorphous nucleus and one single law of "adaptation and heredity" in order to bring forth, from what seemed chaos but was in fact a very definite order, the infinite variety of species we know today, each with its unique characteristics that sets it apart from all other creatures.[26]

Hirsch argues that the theory of evolution is no threat to Judaism. Even if Darwin were entirely correct, it would only lead to greater admiration for the Creator's remarkable design. Hirsch vigorously affirms that Judaism "does not fear of the advances of science."[27]

---

25. Rabbi Schwadron's approval of Rabbi Lipschitz's view was published in the former's *Tekhelet Mordechai*, Bereshit 2 and appears as a translator's note in *Challenge*, 135. Rabbi Zvi Chajes's cites the Jerusalem Talmud *Niddah* 3:2. It appears in English in *Challenge*, 135.

26. Rabbi Samson Raphael Hirsch's remarks on evolution appear in his *Collected Writings* (1984), vol. 7, 264, in the essay entitled "The Educational Value of Judaism."

27. *Collected Writings of Samson Raphael Hirsch*, vol. 7, 257.

Accepting a nonliteral reading of the Torah in order to reconcile Scripture with science was supported by Rabbi David Tzvi Hoffman (d. 1921), who reminded his readers that

> one should remember that even with the legal portions of the Torah, there is an accepted tradition in our hands that sometimes the literal meaning is changed. All the more so, it is permitted to do so with the account of creation, an account in which the Sages found many things that cannot be identified from the words of Scripture, but which can be derived by means of deeper methods of investigation.[28]

From a more mystical approach, Rabbi Abraham Isaac Kook (d. 1935), first chief rabbi of what was then called Palestine, reasoned by analogy that just as there is a spiritual evolution in humanity, there is a physical evolution in the universe.[29] In finding the scientific evidence compelling, these scholars and those who follow after have not, to use Rabbi Natan Slifkin's words, "removed God from the picture" but have discovered a new picture for God to have drawn.[30]

Rabbi Gedaliah Nadel (d. 2004) of Israel explains why Judaism is at pains to reconcile with science. He writes:

> One should realize that with intellectual knowledge of that which must be so, that which is impossible and that which is possible, one could fall into error. Human knowledge is developing, and there are things that were once considered true, and were later overturned . . . In general, no person has *definitive* knowledge regarding anything the physical world . . . Even regarding certain things that Maimonides thought to be correct from a scientific perspective, these are known today as mistaken, and (were he alive

---

28. Rabbi David Tzvi Hoffman was one of the leading German authorities of the early twentieth century. While he was generally skeptical about the applicability of science in all areas, he leaves room for the possibility that the scientific view of creation can be consistent with the Jewish view when literalism is surrendered, which appears in his commentary to Genesis, 48.

29. Rabbi Kook's view is expressed in his *Igrot HaRe'iyah*, Letter 91 where he goes on to say that the only reason the Torah does not reveal that the world is billions of years old is to give preeminence to humanity; making human beings the culmination of a six-day creation.

30. See Rabbi Natan Slifkin, *Challenge of Creation*, for a thorough discussion of Judaism's encounter with science, cosmology, and evolution. See also p. 279 where he sums up "a natural, scientific explanation of things in no way contradicts the concept of God as a Designer. Instead, it provides a new tapestry for Him to have drawn."

today) he would have certainly admit this to us . . . [But] that which convinces the intellect, according to the knowledge and givens of a person in his respective situation, force a person.[31]

Knowledge is tendentious. Nevertheless, we are compelled to accept what our reason holds to be true. That is the essence of intellectual integrity.

Giving credit to those whose ideas have shaped your own, proper citation of sources, objective analyses devoid of preconceived ideas, a vigorous pursuit of truth, a willingness to be swayed by the facts wherever they may lead and from whomever they come are the hallmarks of intellectual integrity. These elements are what operate in Judaism and what Judaism recommends. It is a recommendation that could only help the world of academic, social, and political discourse if it were consistently adopted.

---

31. Rabbi Nadel's views appear in the Hebrew *B'Torato Shel Rav Gedaliah*, 79–80.

Chapter Six

Unfinished Business—
How to Read the Bible

IN THE PREVIOUS CHAPTERS I have referred to passages in the Bible for illustration or support. As such, they "work" regardless of whether or not one believes the Bible is the actual word of God. Like any reference to the classics, Shakespeare, popular culture, songs and anecdotes they serve to make a point. But unlike Shakespeare, for example, the Bible carries considerably more weight. When Polonius tells his son Laertes in act 1, scene 3 of *Hamlet* not to "dull his palm with entertainment," warns him of "entrance into a quarrel," advises him to give every man his ear but few his voice, counsels him "neither a borrower nor lender be," and emphatically bids him to be true to himself above all, we read it as useful fatherly advice to a son returning to college. But when the Bible says, "Do not murder," "Do not steal," "Do not commit adultery," we read it differently. It is no longer in the realm of good advice. We call them commandments, not suggestions. There is an authoritativeness ascribed to the Bible not given to other texts. And its very authoritativeness implies some demand on our conduct. Rabbi Abraham Joshua Heschel once imagined that if archaeologists ever discovered the tablets upon which were inscribed the Ten Commandments he would ask: "Now that you found them, will you observe them?" implying that there is some expectation of performance attached.

But when the Bible specifically demands that we behave in a way that seems contrary to the very principles we hold dear in modern, Western democracies, it challenges the esteem in which we hold it. Thus Richard Dawkins, for example, says that whether through the actual laws in the

Bible or through the example of its characters, they "encourage a system of morals which any civilized modern person, whether religious or not, would find... obnoxious."[1] In other passages he claims the Bible promotes indecency, deception, misogyny, violence and more. Sam Harris claims that the Bible fosters totalitarianism, advocates inquisitions, and murder.[2] These are serious charges that demand serious answers. Whether or not the evidence supports these charges depends on how one reads the Bible. Yet before I address how to read the Bible, I need to first explain what the Bible is.

When Maimonides was challenged to define what God is, he found it much easier to begin with what God is not. After eliminating all those things he considered in error, God was discovered to be in the remainder. Similarly, I begin with eliminating what the Bible is not, before analyzing the remainder and coming to a conclusion on what the Bible is.

First, and not in order of importance, the Bible is not a cookbook, even though it contains recipes. For example, in the book of Exodus (30:22f.), God gives Moses the recipe for anointing oil: "Take choice spices: five hundred weight of solidified myrrh, half as much—two hundred and fifty—of fragrant cinnamon, two hundred and fifty of aromatic cane, five hundred—by the sanctuary weight—of cassia, and a measure of olive oil." Then "blend together" and "serve as a sacred anointing oil." And a few verses later, God gives Moses the recipe for incense: equals parts of stacte, onycha, galbanum, and pure frankincense mixed together and pulverized. But the fact that the Bible includes recipes does not make it a cookbook.

Second, the Bible is not a phone directory or a census record. Accordingly, it does not include the names of every person since creation. There is a marvelous scene in the 1960 film *Inherit the Wind* (based on the 1955 Jerome Lawrence and Robert E. Lee play by the same name) that dramatizes the 1925 "Scopes Monkey Trial." In real life Henry Scopes was a Tennessee high school teacher who was co-opted into bringing a test case against the state law forbidding the teaching of evolution. He was convicted of violating the law and fined. In this scene, Spencer Tracy, in the role of Clarence Darrow, the greatest criminal defense attorney in his day, calls to the stand Frederick March in the role of William Jennings Bryan, nicknamed "The Silver Tongued Orator," three-time Democratic presidential nominee, former secretary of state, and Bible expert. It is in this last capacity that he is

---

1. See Dawkins, *God Delusion*, 237.
2. Sam Harris, *End of Faith* (2004), 82ff. For an entirely perspective on religion, see Houston Smith's *Why Religion Matters*.

questioned. Tracy asks him if he believes the Bible is true and infallible; a complete record of human history. March replies with a resounding "Yes" to all. If that is the case, since the Bible describes how all creatures are created by God at the same time, the gradual development of one form of life into another would be impossible. Taking aim at the assumption that the biblical record was complete, Tracy asks March to explicate Genesis 4:17. Here is the problem: Cain kills his brother Abel. At that point, readers are aware only of four human beings on earth: the original couple and their two children, Cain and Abel. Cain kills Abel, leaving a total of three. Cain is punished for his crime by being banished "from the presence of the Lord" and settles in the land of Nod. The next verse reads: "Cain knew his wife, and she conceived and bore Enoch." The question Tracy puts to March is "Where did Mrs. Cain come from?" Since there is no record of her being "begotten" by anyone, her existence is inexplicable. March is dumbfounded and resorts to a pious declamation of the truth of the Bible despite this annoyance.

Actually, the same sort of question could have been raised by the earlier passage in which a fearful, almost remorseful Cain asks God for protection from others he may meet in his wanderings who wish to kill him (Gen 4:14). On its face, the worry is absurd. Since there is no mention of anyone else in the area he would travel, exactly of whom should he be afraid? But in either case, the questions raise a serious challenge to anyone who wants to hold that biblical record is true and complete. Here, holding that position implies that the text must include the names of every person ever born, at least in the formative years of humanity. In other words, the Bible is expected to be a phone directory or census record. What the dramatic scene in *Inherit the Wind* points out is that such a position is untenable. There were many other people around in early human history but the Bible was under no compunction to name them. Only those important to the story of the moral development of humanity receive mention.

The Bible includes the story of the birth, early years, maturation, and career of Moses but it would be mistaken to call the Bible a biography. The Bible contains many chapters devoted to building construction: Noah is given plans on how to construct an ark and Moses is given extensive and detailed plans on how to build the tabernacle. Yet no one would claim that the Bible is a construction manual. The Bible includes many significant historical events, but it would be misleading to call the Bible a history book. And, even though the Bible includes a narrative of the origins of the universe and classifications of wide variety of animals, it would be inaccurate to call the Bible a science book. Likewise, the Bible includes, on the traditional Jewish count, 613 commandments, but it would be inaccurate to label the Bible a law book. There is no law book that I have seen or read that includes the narrative, prophetic, didactic, and poetic sections we find in the Bible. Recipes, genealogies, biographies, building plans, historical events, facts of nature, and laws are all *elements* in the Bible but it would be fallacious to define the Bible by any one of its elements. So if the Bible is not a cookbook or census record or biography or construction manual or history book or science book or law book, then what precisely is it?

Rabbi Samson Raphael Hirsch answers:

> As Jews we will read this book, as a book tendered to us by God in order that we learn from it about, what we are and what we should be during our earthly existence. We will read it as Torah—literally, "instruction"—directing and guiding us within God's world and among humanity, making our inner self come alive.[3]

The Torah is an instruction manual, but for a very specific kind of instruction. The Torah provides direction and guidance. It provides moral instruction.

As the story goes, one day after an interschool athletic event, Father Henri Martine Didon ended his inspirational talk to the participants with the Latin "Citius, Altius, Fortius" (Faster, Higher, Stronger) as an encouragement to even greater achievement. A friend, and founder of the modern Olympics, Baron Pierre de Coubertin, was present to hear the charge to the students and thought it would be the perfect motto for the renewed Olympic games. Judaism does not have a motto, and it would be presumptuous of me to offer one. But if ever one were to be contemplated, it surely would not be "Faster, Higher, Stronger." More likely, it would closer to "Better, Kinder, Wiser," since the moral improvement of humanity is the aim of Judaism and it begins with the Torah. Through law and through narrative examples the Torah guides us toward becoming better people. It exposes readers to the highs and lows of human behavior. It is, as Dr. Leon Kass puts it, "an anthropology in the original meaning of the term: a *logos* (account) of *anthropos* (the human being)."[4] As such, the Torah conveys universal teachings about human nature.

---

3. Rabbi Samson Raphael Hirsch's take on Torah appears in his *Nineteen Letters*, Letter 2.

4. Kass, *Beginning of Wisdom: Reading Genesis*, 10.

Interestingly, the word "Torah" itself comes from the same Hebrew root that means "to shoot an arrow at a target." The arrow's direction must be straight and true to hit the bull's-eye. Human conduct must be straight and true to be "on target." It is through following the Torah that we learn two things: what the target is and how to take proper aim.

Understanding what the Torah is gives us a handle on how to read it. That God is depicted in human terms—what scholars call anthropomorphism—has never been a worry for Jews who vigorously maintain that God takes no human form. Maimonides gives a number of reasons why this is so. For my purposes, one will suffice. Says Maimonides: "If the Creator were a physical body, He would have bounds and limits, for it is impossible for a physical body to be without limits."[5] Physical bodies, like all material things in the universe, take up space and are restricted to a specific location. Consider the story of the philosophy major who returns home to New York and is questioned by his immigrant father on what philosophy is. Rather than trying to explain it, the son decides to offer an example. By using philosophy, he says, he can prove that he is not here. The father is intrigued and asks how. So the son asks: "Am I in Europe?" "No," says the father. "Am I in Asia?" "No," says the father. "Am I in Africa?" Again the father answers "No." "So," argues the son, "if I am not in Europe or Asia or Africa I must be someplace else." "That's right," the father agrees. With a contented smile on his face the son concludes, "If I am someplace else, I can't be here!" The father hesitates for a minute and then slaps his son's face with the back of his hand. "Why did you slap me, Dad?" the son asks indignantly. "How could I have slapped you," asks the father, "when you are not here?" The father in this story makes the point that physical bodies are indeed rooted in a specific space no matter how we might argue otherwise. If God had a body, then God would be limited to a specific place at a specific time. That would contravene the idea that God is everywhere. And it would be impossible, to Judaism, to believe that God was not everywhere. Besides, material things are also of limited duration. Even the sturdiest mountains

---

5. For Maimonides's view on the non-corporeality of God see *Mishneh Torah*, Laws of the Fundamentals of Torah 1:8. A useful abridged version of this code was published in pointed Hebrew with English on the facing pages by Philip Birnbaum in 1967. See p. 7 for his translation of this passage. See also Rabbi Louis Jacob's explication of Maimonides's thirteen principles of faith in *Principles of the Jewish Faith*. Chapter 4, 118ff., focuses on the third principle, the incorporeality of God. See also book 1, chs. 5, 46, and 47, based on b. Ber. 31a. Maimonides's contention that Scripture is not intended to be read literally appears in his *Guide of the Perplexed*, bk. 1, chs. 5, 46, and 47, and especially bk. 2, ch. 29.

will crumble over time. As George Gershwin wrote: "In time the Rockies may crumble, Gibraltar may tumble, they're only made of clay." Animated bodies age; they can take ill and die. That would contravene the idea that God is eternal. Since God is held to be without limits, omnipresent, and eternal, God could have no body.

However, when the text states that human beings were created in the image of God, it would seem more than likely that the average reader would—at least initially—understand the verse to refer to some kind of physical form. After all, if human beings have physical bodies and we are created in God's image, it seems like a simple deduction that God must have a physical body, as well. Moreover, there are many references in the Bible to some part of God's anatomy. For example, Moses and the elders are said to have seen a pavement of sapphire beneath God's "feet" (Exod 24:10). The "hand" of God brings the plague against Egyptian livestock (Exod 9:3). Judah's son, Er, did not find favor in God's "eyes" (Gen 38:7). And the people's complaints reached God's "ears" (Num 11:1). To these passages and all other similar ones, Maimonides explains:

> All these expressions are adapted to the mental capacity of the majority of mankind who have a clear perception of physical bodies only. The Torah speaks in the language of men. All these phrases are metaphorical.[6]

In other words, the problem of God seemingly taking a physical form—what scholars call corporeality—is essentially a problem with language and communication. On Maimonides's account there is simply no other way for the Torah to say anything about God that would be understandable to human beings. So anthropomorphism is an unfortunate but inevitable outcome. The goal, however, is not to be mislead by such passages but to navigate through them.

Maimonides does more than solve a theological problem, as important as that is. Maimonides affirms that *the Torah cannot be read literally*. To one of his students he writes that when the Torah describes God's anger, using such expressions as "My wrath shall wax hot, and I will kill . . ." it does not mean that God actually has a temper but that God holds wrongdoers accountable for their actions. And when the Torah suggests that God instantaneously "hears" the prayers of the oppressed and hastens to their aid

---

6. Maimonides, in his *Guide of the Perplexed*, bk. 2, ch. 29, writes that "the account of creation given in Scripture is not, as generally believed, intended to be literal in all its parts."

it really means that petitionary prayer has value. In fact, he explicitly writes: "The account of creation given in Scripture is not, as generally believed, intended to be literal in all its parts."[7]

A recurrent character on the classic 1960s television comedy *Get Smart* was Hymie, the robot. Hymie worked with Maxwell Smart and Agent 99 to eliminate KAOS, the international organization of evildoers. Hymie was virtually indestructible but, unfortunately, entirely literal. He had no understanding of the nuances of language, like idioms. So, at the end of a meal, when Smart would ask him to "Grab a waiter," rather than just get the waiter's attention, Hymie would physically take hold of the waiter. Before bedtime, when Smart asked Hymie to "Kill the light," rather than switching the lights off, Hymie took out his revolver and shot the light bulb. Hymie suffered from severe literalism, which for television viewers made great comedy. For readers of the Bible, however, literalism could result in theological problems. Hence, the only available course was to reject it.

Maimonides was not the first or the last to suggest a nonliteral approach to reading the narrative portions of the Bible. Philo of Alexandria applied the allegorical method to all of Scripture. The Talmud includes the opinion that Job never existed and that the entire book was a parable.[8] The ninth-century scholar Sa'adia ben Joseph Gaon writes that when the senses contradict the text, or when reason demands it, the literal meaning of the text may be rejected.[9] It is a position with which Maimonides concurs. And thirteenth-century Rabbi Levi ben Gershon states: "We must believe what reason has determined to be true. If the literal sense of the Torah differs from reason, it is necessary to interpret those passages in accordance with

---

7. His *Guide of the Perplexed* is, in fact, a lengthy letter to a former student, Rabbi Joseph ibn Aknin, who questioned how it is possible to hold fast to the Jewish tradition yet retain a modern outlook. That question was paramount in the twelfth century no less our own.

8. That the book of Job ought to be read as a parable is suggested by the Talmud, *b. Bava Batra* 15a.

9. Sa'adiah Gaon, in his *Beliefs and Opinions*, bk. 7, sect. 1, writes:

> And I so declare . . . that it is a well-known fact that every statement in the Bible is to be understood in its literal sense except for those that cannot be so construed for one of the following four reasons: It may . . . be rejected by the observation of the senses . . . or else the literal sense may be negated by reason . . . or by an explicit text of a contradictory nature . . . or any Biblical statement to which the rabbis gave a particular meaning is to be read in accordance with that authentic tradition.

the demands of reason."[10] His contemporary, Rabbi Solomon ibn Adret, adds: "Indeed we are forced to admit that in many places Scripture spoke by way of allegory."[11]

Thus far I have tried to show that, to Judaism, the Bible is a kind of instruction manual that cannot be read literally though must be read seriously. Accordingly, Judaism need not be concerned with whether or not the contents are factual. The story is told of a Jewish father who asked his child what he learned in religious school that day. The child said that he learned that when the Israelites were being pursued by the Egyptians, Moses sent out his tanks, and then his fighter planes and bombers, and finally wiped them all out with a nuclear bomb. The father asked, "Is that exactly what the teacher told you?" "No," said the child, "but if I told you what she really said you'd never believe it." Judaism finds no need to defend the view that everything described in the Bible happened exactly that way. Although the default position endorsed by all authorities is that we accept the narrative as presented unless we have sufficient reason to conclude otherwise. What is essential are the moral lessons we derive from the text.

Accordingly, Judaism distinguishes between fact and truth. Aesop's fables, for example, convey truths even though we dismiss the facts. No one believes that hares and tortoises talk or that the animal kingdom occasionally arranges races between different species for their entertainment. But we accept as true the lesson that "slow but steady wins the race."[12] Similarly, no one believes that goats and foxes express themselves through human speech. That would be counterfactual. But we accept as true the wisdom that is generated from the fable of the fox that tricks a goat into jumping into the well into which the fox had fallen and then using the goat as a ladder escapes to leave the goat behind, namely, "look before you leap."[13] Truth exists independent of facts. Thus Judaism can assert the "truth" of the Bible regardless of whether all the details are factual.

When Plato first conceived of a kingdom of Atlantis in his dialogue called *Timaeus*, he was not claiming that such a kingdom ever existed.[14] He

10. *The Book of Wars of God* is Gersonides's, that is, Rabbi Levi son of Gerson's, masterpiece. The citation appears on p. 98.

11. Rabbi Solomon ibn Adret's opinion is expressed in his collection of responsa (*Responsa RaShBA* 1:9). Rseponsa are learned answers to specific religious questions.

12. *Aesop's Fables*, 50.

13. Ibid., 58.

14. For the entirety of Plato's writings in contemporary English, see John M. Cooper's 1997 *Complete Works of Plato*. His myth of Atlantis appears in his dialogue *Timaeus*,

was merely using it as a vehicle for speculating on how a society comes into being and how it governs itself. (That later speculators, fortune-hunters, and would-be-archaeologists have misspent their time and resources trying to "discover" the "lost" continent of Atlantis shows the silly result of reading literally a text that was never intended to be read that way.) Plato called his description of Atlantis a "myth," actually, *eikos muthos*, meaning, "a likely story," in Greek. Plato did not defend the story of Atlantis as true, meaning factual, but he did argue that his thinking about Atlantis contained valuable truths that applied to civic life. Likewise, the Bible is read as "a likely story," not because all events transpired exactly as described, though they might have, but because the Bible contains eternal truths that are indispensable to raising our ethical standards and improving the world. As Mircea Eliade explains in his groundbreaking study *Myth and Reality*, myths are not "fiction" or "fairy tales" but that which "supplies models for human behavior and, by that very fact, gives meaning and value to life."[15] Myths are true because they deal with ultimate realities, those values that impact most on what it means to be human. Accordingly, as I tried to show in the previous chapter, Judaism is not determined to uphold the Creation story as a factual account of the beginning of the universe where each and every detail must be defended against the regnant scientific theory. Instead, the creation story comes to teach the "truths" that the world did not come into being by accident, that there is a cause for everything, that there is an order to the universe, that the world is fundamentally "good," that there is purpose to human existence, that all human beings come from the same family and that together we must take responsibility for maintaining the world. Thus David Ariel calls the Creation story a "sacred myth" in Judaism.[16]

Having explained what the Bible is, it is necessary to address what the Bible says. By understanding that the Bible is an instruction manual or guide to conduct, and by applying the method of reading the text seriously though not literally and by approaching the text with intellectual integrity, the passages that have been cited by Dawkins and others as incompatible with modern sensibilities and morality will be shown to be the opposite.

24e–25d. Similar myths of the origin of Sparta appear in bk. 3 of his *Laws*, 680f.

15. Mircea Eliade has written extensively on myth. *Myth and Reality* was published in 1963. The passage cited appears on p.2 but the entirety of ch. 1, "The Structure of Myths," is worth careful reading.

16. David Ariel applies the concept of myth to the Torah in his book *What Do Jews Believe?*, 15–16.

Unfinished Business—How to Read the Bible

The story of Noah and the flood does not conclude with the "appalling" moral that God takes a "dim view of humans," as Dawkins claims.[17] Rather, the story emphasizes that humanity is held accountable for its violence and cruelty, a message that still finds resonance today. Dawkins goes on to question why Lot would offer up his daughters rather than his houseguests to the marauding residents of Sodom. The lesson Dawkins wants to derive is that the Bible has no respect for women. One lesson Judaism derives, in contrast, is that life is often punctuated with difficult choices. Lot was conflicted about whether hospitality to strangers and the protection a host must extend to his guests—especially in the depraved city of Sodom—outweighs the concern and care a father must give to his children. Another lesson is that such is what happens when an otherwise good man takes up residence in an undesirable city: he becomes affected by the culture around him. Hence, the story comes as a warning against living among evil people. But in any case, the need to compromise his daughters' dignity was averted by divine intervention. Of course Dawkins could have interpreted this intervention to be the Bible's way of showing that *women's virtue must be respected*, rather than considering it some fortuitous event. But Dawkins approaches the text with the preconceived idea that it is inherently loathsome.

Not done with Lot's daughters, Dawkins points to the passage telling how they got their father drunk and then committed incest as an example of family dysfunction and biblical immorality. But he misses the point. The Bible is often stark and brutally honest in revealing the failings of human beings. Scripture is not *endorsing* their behavior, but *condemning* it. As Dr. J. H. Hertz writes in his widely read commentary: "Their conduct does not admit of any extenuation; they were true children of Sodom."[18]

I cannot tell whether Dawkins is more offended by the gang rape or the subsequent dismemberment of the concubine at Gibeah (Judges 19). But again, he misses the point. The host, living in this frontier town, was just as conflicted as Lot in Sodom. And the concubine's body was dismembered by her partner and sent to the different tribes of Israel in order to marshal their support against the lawlessness and immorality that resulted in her rape. In other words, it is a story that asserts that unless civil society is prepared to enforce the law, acts of violence and brutality are inevitable.

---

17. Dawkins's reading of Noah and the flood appears on p. 238.
18. Hertz, *Pentateuch and Haftorahs*, 69.

Prescription for an Ailing World

The Bible is not condoning a "misogynistic ethos,"[19] as Dawkins maintains, but condemning violence and lawlessness.

Dawkins is disturbed by Abraham passing off his beautiful wife, Sarah, as his sister in order to avoid danger to his life. Presumably, he is concerned about the immorality of lying rather than a lack of chivalry. Here Dawkins simply fails to read the text. Sarah is, in fact, Abraham's half-sister (Gen 20:12). So Abraham is, at worst, guilty of a half-truth. But let's not quibble. It is not this episode in Abraham's life that qualifies him to be an exemplar. This episode only qualifies him to be human: he thought his life was at risk, that he would be killed so his beautiful wife could be "available," and he did what he thought was necessary. What qualifies Abraham as an exemplar is his defense of the inhabitants of Sodom, arguing that if there were ten righteous men among them the city should be spared. What qualifies Abraham as an exemplar is his willingness, against great odds and at personal risk, to save his captured nephew Lot. Dawkins makes the unwarranted assumption that a role model must be perfect. Surely that is not the case in athletics or politics or any other area of human endeavor. And it is not the case in the Bible either. It is the sum of a person's actions and the totality of a person's character that makes him or her an exemplar, along with the direction a person's life is taking. A Hasidic rabbi once asked his disciples: "One man is on the second rung of a ladder, another on the sixth. Who is higher?" The disciples looked at each other and at their master in disbelief. How could their esteemed teacher ask such a ridiculous question? "Obviously, the person on the sixth rung," they answered. "Have I taught you nothing?" the rabbi said in disappointment. "It all depends which way they are going." Joseph starts out in life as a tattletale but grows to become a pillar of moral strength and benefactor to all. Joseph is an exemplar not because he is consistently perfect but because he grows morally.

That Abraham would take his beloved son Isaac as a sacrifice and that God would actually command Abraham to do so is further evidence of the Bible's failing as a moral text, according to Dawkins. What kind of God would make such a horrible demand? And what kind of hero would follow it? In fact, the lesson of the story is less to glorify Abraham as a model of obedience or as the focus of the Kierkegardian "leap of faith," but to forever repudiate the ancient practice of child sacrifice. As Hertz points out, in its day what would be surprising is not that Abraham was asked to sacrifice his son but that he was prevented from doing so! In this historical context, the

---

19. Dawkins, *God Delusion*, 241.

binding of Isaac is intended to demonstrate, according to Hertz, that "unlike the cruel heathen deities, *it was the spiritual surrender alone that God required.*"[20] Hence, far from being evidence of the Bible's immorality, the episode of the binding of Isaac is testimony to the Bible's progressive view on the sanctity of life and its preservation. Far from being, in Dawkins's words, "appalling" and "deplorable," this biblical episode serves as the underpinning for modern, civilized thought.

The banning of human sacrifice seems to be contravened by a later biblical story. When Jephthah returns from his victory over the Ammonites, he pledges to make an offering the first thing that comes out of his door to greet him, which was unfortunate for his daughter who emerged first. To claim that this story should not be read literally just raises the question, for Dawkins, "How do we know?" Dawkins insists that without any criteria for determining which texts are read literally and which not, interpreting the Bible becomes an exercise in subjectivity. And even if the story is read allegorically, we would be hard pressed to determine what it comes to teach. That last worry certainly does not apply in this case. Were this passage to be read allegorically that lesson would be the wise admonition: "Watch what you say." But Judaism's traditional interpreters did not have to dismiss this story as an allegory. Armed with the Abraham and Isaac story, we see this as a contradiction that must be resolved. The earlier text shows that human sacrifice was wrong; the latter text showed that it apparently happened. So the rabbis had two choices. One choice would be to concede that the Jephthah story was true and serves to show that in those lawless times, terrible things took place. The Bible is not endorsing human sacrifice or the cavalier treatment of women. It is merely reporting on the events that occurred. Dawkins seems to hold that any event that is recorded in the Bible is mentioned with approbation. That is simply wrong. The second choice would be to use the interpretive techniques at hand—what Dawkins calls "criteria"—and apply them to the text as forensic specialists. Accordingly, they understood Jephthah to have sequestered his daughter, not sacrificed her. And the Hebrew lends itself to that reading.

There are a number of biblical passages that seem outright barbaric. That the seven nations that heretofore populated the promised land had to be entirely destroyed by God's command smacks of genocide to Dawkins. And that the Midianites had to be thoroughly dispatched, including all male children and sexually active females, seems strikingly barbaric. It is

---

20. Hertz, *Pentateuch and Haftorahs*, 201, italics original.

unclear whether Dawkins objects to all war or whether he objects only to the nature of these wars. I am going to assume the latter because I would hardly imagine that anyone would want to defend the absolute pacifist position that all war is wrong, no matter the circumstances.

In 1938 Mohandas K. Gandhi wrote an essay in which he braved to give advice to Jews on what to do under Hitler. He began by recognizing that the persecution of Jews under Hitler seems to have no parallel in history. To Gandhi, Hitler's program was nothing other than "a new religion of exclusive and militant nationalism in the name of which any inhumanity becomes an act of humanity to be rewarded here and hereafter." Recognizing the uniqueness of the situation and the ferocity with which Hitler has unleashed his fury, Gandhi reasoned that if any war could be justifiable, a war against Hitler would qualify. Yet, on his pacifist principle he nevertheless concluded that "war is not the answer." Instead, he advocates nonviolent resistance.

> If I were a Jew . . . I would claim Germany my home even as the tallest gentile German may, and challenge him to shoot me or cast me in the dungeon; I would refuse to be expelled or to submit to discriminating treatment. And for doing this, I should not wait for the fellow Jews to join me in civil resistance but would have confidence that in the end the rest are bound to follow my example. If one Jew or all the Jews were to accept the prescription here offered, he or they cannot be worse off than now. And suffering voluntarily undergone will bring them an inner joy which no number of resolutions of sympathy passed in the world outside Germany can.[21]

Gandhi recognized that this plan might result in enormous casualties, adding: "The calculated violence of Hitler may even result in a general massacre of the Jews." Even so, he counseled, "if the Jewish mind could be prepared for voluntary suffering, even the massacre I have imagined could be turned into a day of thanksgiving and joy that Jehovah had wrought deliverance of the race even at the hands of the tyrant. For the god-fearing death has no terror. It is a joyful sleep to be followed by a waking that would be all the more refreshing for the long sleep."

Gandhi's wish for the eternal rest of the Jewish people is quaint, but that is not the kind of deliverance that the Jewish people—in fact, any people—would welcome. Gandhi's pacifism entailed voluntary suffering.

---

21. Mohandas Gandhi's essay on how Jews should confront Hitler was published in his newspaper *Harijan* under the title "The Jews" on November 26, 1938.

Judaism stands for the elimination of suffering. Gandhi's plan would have played into Hitler's. History has proven that if the idea here is that "Hitler's willing executioners,"[22] to use Daniel Goldhagen's phrase, would somehow be shamed into remorse and abandon their genocidal plans, it is clearly wrong. Surrendering to what Immanuel Kant called "radical evil," even in the name of a higher purpose, will not defeat it. It will only encourage it. Such evil can only be defeated through force.

Hence, I presume that Dawkins will concede that some wars are indeed justifiable. Were it not for the military service of Dawkins's father and other like him, Dawkins would have grown up speaking German and saluting Hitler. Assuming this to be the case, what needs to be addressed is why Dawkins sees biblical wars as particularly immoral. Perhaps it is the fact that these wars are sometimes preceded with terms that strike the modern ear as harsh. For example, in the war against the seven nations that inhabited the promised land, Moses says God demands that when they are defeated "you must doom them to destruction: grant them no terms and give them no quarter" (Deut 7:2). Dawkins reads "doom them to destruction" as complete annihilation. That is precisely what the text says later on (Deut 20:16). In his restatement of this command, Maimonides writes: "You shall not let a soul remain alive," meaning women and children are to be killed as well as men. In modern terms, it sounds like ethnic cleansing. But what Dawkins breezily overlooks is the scope and context of this command. It applied only to those nations and at that time. It is not considered a precedent for any future wars. That is evident from a later passage in the same biblical book (Deut 20:10) that commands: "When you approach a town to attack it, you shall offer it terms of peace." If the city surrenders, no one at all is to be killed. If it does not, then only the males—presumably soldiers—are put to the sword. All others are spared. Besides, warfare, though sometimes necessary, is never welcome. That is why the prophets Isaiah and Micah envision a time when "nation shall not lift up sword against nation neither shall they learn war anymore."[23]

Further, the use of metal implements in building the sacrificial altar (Exod 20:22) was prohibited on the grounds that "by wielding your tool [literally, "your sword"] upon them you have profaned them." In other words,

---

22. Daniel Goldhagen's controversial book *Hitler's Willing Executioners* was published in 1996.

23. Both Isaiah (2:4) and his younger contemporary Micah (4:3-4) prophesy the cessation of war.

Prescription for an Ailing World

using instruments of war would violate the altar upon which peace offerings are presented. God prevented King David from building his hoped-for temple because he had "shed much blood and fought great battles." A warrior was not the appropriate person to build the House of God. This is hardly the stuff of a blood-lusting culture.[24]

Paradoxically, as Rabbi Abraham Bloch notes, it was the desire to eradicate bloodshed that accounts for the biblical tolerance of the institution of the blood-avenger.[25] As kin to the victim of a murder, the blood-avenger felt it his duty to seek out and kill the perpetrator (Num 35:19). Avenging the death of a relative was part of the ancient code of honor. But if every death were to be avenged, the cycle of retribution would be unending. Indeed, blood feuds lasting for generations are not unknown in human history, like the long-lasting battle of the Hatfields and McCoys in the American Ozark Mountains. The Bible, in contrast, imposed limits on the avenger's perceived duty to make good the death of his kin. The avenger was permitted to catch the killer, but he could not execute him until such time that the suspected culprit was convicted by a duly established court (Num 35:12). If the court ruled the death accidental or unintentional, the killer was granted sanctuary in designated cities of refuge (Num 35:11). Given the climate of the ancient world, it would have been impossible to outlaw vengeance altogether. Therefore the Bible wisely acts to control it. But a superficial reading of the text would not yield this appreciation. It requires a careful comparison with other ancient cultures and text to realize how revolutionarily compassionate the Bible is.

In context, the seven nations doomed to utter destruction were not simply killed because they were an inconvenience or because they were different. They were an existential threat to the people Israel. These nations engaged in the most abhorrent practices, including child sacrifice and sexual perversions that would have inevitably involved the Israelites among whom they would live. That is precisely what happened with the Midianites at Ba'al Pe'or (Num 25:6) and serves as the justification for total war against them (Num 31). And as we saw with Lot and his daughters, even good people can become degenerate when living among immoral ones. The Israelites would, citing the words of the fourteenth-century *Sefer*

---

24. King David's desire to build a permanent temple for God was stifled by God who could not tolerate a center for peace built by a man of war (1 Chr 22:8).

25. See Rabbi Abraham Bloch, *Book of Jewish Ethical Concepts*, 65, for his explanation of the blood-avenger.

Ha-hinukh, "learn from their actions." The classical interpreters of the Torah draw the same conclusions with regard to Israelites. Careful reading of the text shows that those who joined with Korah in the rebellion against Moses and Aaron (Num 16:1) were encamped in the same area—the clan of Kohat was positioned at the south side of the camp along with the tribe of Reuben (Num 3:29; 2:10)—leading the commentators to proclaim: "Woe to the wicked, woe to his neighbor!"[26]

Of course one might argue that it could be the other way around: the wicked could learn from the righteous and the Canaanites and Midianites should be spared. That is the way things ought to happen, and that is the way we want things to happen but experience shows that is not the way things actually happen. Values ethicist at Princeton Kwame Anthony Appiah recalls the Rwandan genocide of 1994 when many thousands of Hutus took machetes to their Tutsi neighbors, and says: "If you and I had been planted on this earth as Hutus at that time and place, we too would probably have been participants."[27] His is not just a dim view of human nature but the recognition of how, in certain situations, people act as badly as those around them. Judaism would qualify that those situations about which Appiah speaks are those in which immorality is rampant. In a way, the closest parallel is the case of the wayward, disobedient son who is stoned to death (Deut 21:18f.). The Torah makes no allowance for his reform because the son is deemed incorrigible. The same can be said of the Canaanites and Midianites. Also in this regard it would be appropriate to cite the view of David Hume in his *Enquiry concerning the Principles of Morals*. In pt. 1 of sect. 3 he writes:

> And were a civilized nation engaged with barbarians, who observed no rules even of war, the former must also suspend their observance of them, when they no longer serve to any purpose; and must render every action or recounter as bloody and pernicious as possible to the first aggressors.

Since the Canaanites and the Midianites were indeed engaged in war against Israel, a war in which they engaged in the most insidious of tactics, the expected laws of warfare were suspended and replaced with a "bloody

---

26. That one's neighbors may have a deleterious effect on conduct is expressed in the end of the Talmudic tractate of *Sukkah* and in the Mishnah *Nega'im* 14:6. It is cited by RaShI on Num 16:1.

27. Princeton professor and noted ethicist Kwameh Anthony Appiah makes his bold claim in his *Experiments in Ethics*, 71.

and pernicious" response that Hume legitimates. Since the Canaanites and Midianites were incorrigible and since their tactics were despicable, the only possible solution was their elimination.

Besides, there is the example in the Bible of King Saul who, rather than carry out the command to eradicate Amalekites and their king, Agag, decided to spare him. The result was that descended from the Amalekite king, before he was summarily executed by the prophet Samuel, was a line of Agagites ending with Haman who then plotted to murder all the Jews in the Persian empire. Saul tried to be too merciful, unaware of the consequences and subsequently lost his own kingdom. In concert with the lesson from King Saul, the unknown fifteenth-century author of the ethical tract *Orhot Tzadikkim* or *The Ways of the Righteous*, asserts that "a man should be cruel in his battle against the wicked and have no mercy upon them."[28] The very same author reminds us that while love and compassion are noble virtues they can be vices when a person lets love become stronger than wisdom. For example, out of great love for his children a father may not correct and guide them and if they become delinquent, it is to no one's benefit.

That the Bible includes the well-known passage "an eye for an eye" is true (Exod 21:24). But there is absolutely no such record in the Bible or Talmud that any such punishment was ever applied. That is because it is evident, from a comparison with other biblical passages, that the meaning was never assumed to be physical mutilation. The stipulated punishment of the owner of a habitually violent ox that gored a human being to death is death (Exod 21:29). But the owner is permitted to redeem himself through monetary payment. According to the verse in the book of Numbers (35:31), monetary payment for damages applies to all cases except for murder. So in the case of causing another to lose an eye—or for any other civil tort—we must deduce that monetary payment was the rule. Thus the Talmud insists with good cause that "an eye for an eye"—what scholars call *lex talionis*, the law of retaliation—was never intended to be taken literally. Hence, adducing this phrase as evidence of biblical barbarity only reveals an absence of familiarity with text.[29]

---

28. See Rabbi Seymour J. Cohen's exceptionally good translation of *Orhot Tzaddikim*, published in 1969 under the title *The Ways of the Righteous*. It has remained an influential ethical tract since it first appeared. The two passages I cite appear in the chapter "On Cruelty," 153, and in the chapter "On Love," 101, respectively. See also Midrash Rabbah Ecclesiastes 7:28, Soncino ed., 199 that condemns King Saul for being "overly righteous," that is, letting his impulse for compassion cloud his moral and political judgment.

29. That the *lex talionis* should not be taken literally is the position the Talmud

The various laws that restrict the worship of one God or demand sexual fidelity and punish violations of both severely also trouble Dawkins. But that Dawkins disagrees with these laws does not mean that itself renders them cruel. And that the Israelites with some regularity tend to violate the first does not necessarily mean that the law is ridiculous. Some could argue quite the opposite: precisely because Israelites are drawn to idolatrous practices that include sexual perversions is the law needed. And that the Bible advocates sexual fidelity, I have argued in an earlier chapter, is to the benefit of women in particular and to society as a whole. That the Bible does not conform to Dawkins's libertarian views is obvious. But that in and of itself does not make the Bible wrong or worse.

It seems to me that Dawkins et al. are contemptuous of the Bible because they are not prepared to read it with even a modicum of critical understanding. To paraphrase F. Scott Fitzgerald: they "dismiss it with the contempt we reserve for what we don't understand."[30]

The Bible, I contend, is indeed a source of great insight and guidance, provided that it is read seriously. Hence, throughout the earlier chapters I have invoked biblical examples and cited biblical passages as evidence of the values that can be teased out of the text, whatever its origin. I need not defend the proposition that the Bible is the unerring word of God in order to rely on the contents of the Bible as support for the values of Judaism that is based upon it.

---

defends in *b. Bava Kamma* 83b. Jews would be universally appalled to hear that the Iranian judiciary had scheduled the blinding with acid of Maji Mohadevi for blinding with acid of Ameneh Bahrami in 2009. It is not that his crime should go unpunished. All Bahrami did was complain about Mohadevi's unwanted touching in a university classroom. His threats to kill her were followed by the acid attack. The unjustified assault is deserving of severe punishment. But the literal application of the *lex talionis* has been long repudiated. (The literal application of the law implies, incidentally, that a blind perpetrator could blind other victims at will and go unpunished. Or a childless murderer would go unpunished for taking the life of someone's child.)

30. See F. Scott Fitzgerald's opening page to *The Last Tycoon*.

Chapter Seven

The Prescription

> A town was suffering from famine and had only a pile of grain to alleviate its hunger. But the grain was suspected of being poisoned. The townspeople believed that eating from the grain might drive them mad. So the town council in its collective wisdom decided to distribute the grain to everyone except one man. His function was to refrain from eating and maintain civil order by standing on watch. Should the need arise, he would warn those who had eaten: "Gentlemen, you are mad!"
>
> —A TALE OF RABBI NAHMAN OF BRATSLAV,
> AS TOLD BY RABBI MORDECHAI WAXMAN

I BEGAN BY SAYING that human beings have always killed. But that does not mean that human beings are killers. We must not confuse our history with our nature. Human beings are neither born saintly nor sinful but with the capacity to be either. Judaism holds that it is just as possible for human beings to rise to the heights, as history has shown that we have fallen to the depths. Reviewing the current state of affairs in his 1999 book *Humanity: A Moral History of the Twentieth Century*, Jonathan Glover concludes that "to avoid further disasters, we need political restraints on a world scale."[1] Experience has taught us, however, that would be highly unlikely, if at all feasible. Instead, Judaism would argue that what we need are moral restraints on a personal scale. Political restraints are subject to what Glover himself identifies as a "gentle slide," the gradual change from developing the atomic

---

1. Glover, *Humanity*, 414.

The Prescription

bomb as a deterrent against Germany to actually using it against Japan. It is the same "gentle slide" that has allowed governments to justify torture in the name of national security or for terrorists to rationalize the killing of innocent civilians. The world will not be transformed by politics but by people. And people can only be transformed with new ways of thinking and acting. As Glover puts it: "The means for expressing cruelty and carrying out mass killing have been fully developed. It is too late to stop the technology. It is to the psychology that we should now turn."[2]

In his 1984 book *Inside the Criminal Mind*, Dr. Stanton E. Samenow describes the pioneering work of Dr. Samuel Yochelson in changing criminal behavior. Working with convicts at the Saint Elizabeth's Hospital in Washington, DC, Yochelson was able to test his theory of rehabilitation that required demolishing old thinking patterns and replacing them new ones. One particular convict was named Leroy. Samenow writes:

> All his life, Leroy heard the word "responsibility" bandied about, a word used so promiscuously that it means everything and nothing. Leroy was used to parroting the word even though he knew nothing about being responsible. To him, to be responsible meant to erect a façade and appear respectable. He commented, "Once a person is responsible, he can get away with a hell of a lot."[3]

Leroy's misimpression of responsibility is reminiscent of Monica's trenchant observation on the television comedy series *Friends* that honesty is the most important quality in a relationship, and if you can fake that, you're home free. For Leroy, "responsibility" was a vacuous term, just as "honesty" was to Monica. In order to make the term practically meaningful, Yochelson needed to get Leroy to put into practice those patterns that would make the term meaningful. That is what the world today needs. It does not need more preaching. It does not need articulation of high-minded principles as if by simply invoking the word it magically transforms the world like a sorcerer's spell. For the world to improve, new patterns must be put in place. Judaism provides precisely those patterns.

Consider the unique requirement of affixing a *mezuzah*. Literally, *mezuzah* refers to the doorpost. In practice, *mezuzah* consists of a thin, oblong case into which a parchment scroll is placed and then attached to the doorposts as commanded in Deuteronomy 6:9 and 11:20. Some insist that the purpose of the *mezuzah* is one of identification: indicating that a

---

2. Ibid., 403.
3. Samenow, *Inside the Criminal Mind*, 216.

Jew lives inside. Others see a prophylactic function of the *mezuzah*: providing protection for those who live inside.[4] But the most compelling reason for affixing a mezuzah is that it serves as an ever-present reminder to live a principled life in fulfillment of divine service.[5] This purpose takes on considerable value in light of the research of Dan Ariely.

Ariely's considerable testing leads him to the conclusion that dishonesty in woven into the fabric of the human psyche. But this does not mean that all people lie all the time. Most people want to think of themselves as honest even though they will lie on occasion. What allows for this apparent contradiction is an elaborate system of rationalization whereby lies can be justified on the basis of what the liar perceives to be reasonable grounds such as avoiding hurting the feelings of a loved one. A remarkable feature of Ariely's extensive research is that inducing test subjects to consider their higher or nobler selves can reduce the frequency of lying significantly. In one experiment, five hundred UCLA undergraduates were given a task of solving simple math problems for a dollar reward for each self-reported correct answer. Most students exaggerated their performance by at least two answers. But when students were first asked to list the Ten Commandments before proceeding to the math problems, cheating declined to zero.[6] Similar experiments on undergraduates at other universities yielded the same results. What Ariely deduced from the experiments is that just getting people to think about virtue leads to virtue. Hence the seemingly odd commandment of affixing a mezuzah is rooted in human psychology. Each time a Jew leaves his home s/he sees the mezuzah and is induced to think about the divine. In so doing, it would be more difficult to lie or cheat and dishonor God. In effect, the Jewish tradition long ago anticipated what researchers have come to realize. Goodness can be habituated with the right pattern of behavior.

Once the new patterns are in place, rather than surrender to the impulses that lead to a life of crime, self-gratification by any means, and absence of respect for other people and their property, human beings can overcome those impulses through restraint.

---

4. Exodus 12:22–23 support both these explanations. See also Rabbi Jacob ben Asher, *Tur, Shulhan Arukh,* Yoreh De'ah 285.

5. Cf. Rabbi David HaLevy, *Shulhan Aruk*h, Yoreh De'ah 285:1 and Rabbi Samson Raphael Hirsch, *Horeb*, ch. 40, sect. 287.

6. Interestingly, the listing of the Ten Commandments had the same effect on self-declared atheists.

The Prescription

Returning to the Vancouver Riot of 2011 is instructive. In its aftermath, a number of those participating in looting came forward publicly to admit their complicity. Many apologies were broadcast through social networking. A part of one apology was published by the *National Post* (June 22, 2011). Camille Cacnio confessed that she did indeed take two pair of men's pants for fun—as a souvenir—but insisted she was a good person. Her misdeed was the result of the potent mix of alcohol and adrenaline. Yet at the same time she succumbed to the pressure of the mob and stole the clothing, she prevented vandals from uprooting trees. She pleaded with the mob to leave the trees in place. Rather than moralizing about the fact that she put her concern for trees above that of people (the store owners deprived of their rightful property), we ought to note that she managed to overcome the alcohol and adrenaline in her system to take a stand on principle. This is a valuable reminder that when people have principles for which they are willing to fight, they are able to withstand any other pressure or effect in their application. It is toward this end—the development and strengthening of principle—that we ought to be striving and for which Judaism has much to contribute.

I am not suggesting that the entire world is criminal. But I am saying that human beings by nature or by habituation have lapsed into ways of thinking and acting that have not served us well as a species. Consider the description of the American student offered by professor Allan Bloom in his 1987 book *The Closing of the American Mind*:

> The great majority of students, although they as much as anyone want to think well of themselves, are aware that they are busy with their own careers and relationships . . . Survivalism has taken the place of heroism as the admired quality . . . The things that almost naturally elicit attention to broader concerns are simply not present . . . The affairs of daily life rarely involve concern for a larger community in such a way as to make the public and private merge in one's thought . . . The modern economic principle that private vice makes public virtue has penetrated all aspects of daily life in such a way that there seems to be no reason to be a conscious part of civic existence. As Saul Bellow has put it, public virtue is a kind of ghost town into which anyone can move and declare himself sheriff.[7]

I would venture to say that what Bloom says about college students is equally applicable to society at large. Most people today are not criminal.

---

7. Bloom, *Closing*, 84–85.

But most people are prisoners of their own solitude, unable to look beyond themselves. What the world needs, however, is not for someone to move into this ghost town and declare himself sheriff. What the world needs is the transformation of the ghost town into caring community. And Judaism stands ready and able to lead the transformation.

The Canadian band *Rush* released its twentieth studio album in June 2012. Interviewed in *Maclean's* magazine (August 20, 2012), drummer and lyricist Neil Peart reflected on the enduring anger he has harbored over the years; anger that inspired his song-writing. He acknowledged: "There's still a lot I'm angry about, a lot of behaviour that's appalling and despicable, but you choose what you can fight against." Like Peart, people need to be angry at despicable human behavior and choose to fight against it. People need to be judicious in their choices but, Judaism would say, not free to opt out of the struggle.

"Every society has its own problems," said Professor Schwartz to his former student Mitch Albom in the 1997 best-selling *Tuesdays with Morrie*.[8] But the way to solve them is not to evade them but to "work at creating your own culture." "The biggest defect we human beings have is our shortsightedness," said Morrie. "We don't see what we could be."[9] Judaism sees that human beings are created a little lower than the angels even though we do not always listen to what Abraham Lincoln called "the better angels of our nature."[10] We are endowed with possibility of doing great good, even though we have the capability of doing great evil. The choice is before us and Judaism urges us to "Choose life" and to opt for good.

"We should be looking at our potential, stretching ourselves into everything we can become," said Morrie.[11] That translates into rejecting the attitude that says "I want mine now." Western democracies, as blessed as they are, are focused on rights. Judaism is built on duties. The difference is important. Rights speak to what you demand for yourself; duties speak to what you owe others. It is only natural for people to want to look after themselves. But it is necessary for people to look after others.

Caring for others is contingent on the respect generated by the acknowledgment that we are all part of the same human family, the lesson

---

8. Albom, *Tuesdays*, 156.

9. Ibid., 50.

10. Abraham Lincoln's famous phrase ends his first inaugural address. It is published in William Safire, *Lend Me Your Ears: Great Speeches in History*, 828.

11. Albom, *Tuesdays*, 156.

that Judaism derives from the Bible and applies to behavior. As Morrie put it: "The problem, Mitch, is that we don't believe we are as much alike as we are. Whites and Blacks, Catholics and Protestants, men and women. If we saw each other as more alike, we might be very eager to join in one big human family in this world, and to care about that family the way we care about our own."[12] Once we see each other in this light, then empathy inevitably follows. Suffering from a degenerative disease, Morrie confesses: "But it's hard to explain, Mitch. Now that I'm suffering, I feel closer to people who suffer than I ever did before. The other night on TV, I saw people in Bosnia running across the street, getting fired upon, killed, innocent victims . . . and I just started to cry. I feel their anguish as if it were my own. I don't know any of these people. But . . . I'm almost drawn to them."[13] That is why Jews fast on the Day of Atonement: to feel the anguish of the hungry. Empathy leads to helpfulness and helpfulness is linked to holiness.

The starship *Enterprise* was launched on a mission to "boldly go where no man has gone before." Judaism's mission is not a five-year one; it is an eternal one. But it does require the audacity to do things that are neither popular nor comfortable. Yet that is the small price to pay to live with integrity. Judaism does not offer instant solutions to all the problems I have mentioned both here and in the introduction. It is not simply a matter of taking Two Tablets and seeing how we feel in the morning. Judaism is a way of life that must be practiced and practiced and practiced, not because we haven't got it quite right but because there is no substitute for doing. The old joke has it that a tourist once asked a jaded New Yorker how to get to Carnegie Hall. The curt answer was: "Practice!" If human beings want to get to the Carnegie Hall of moral living, it requires practice. Practice is not a substitute for giving directions (what makes the joke work); "Practice!" is the directions. It requires taking the values of respect, restraint, responsibility, reverence for life and adding to them helpfulness, and holiness, and hopefulness, acting on them with audacity and being guided by integrity. It is precisely these things that characterize Judaism that, if adopted by all human beings, could transform the world. The world does not need the world to be Jewish for the world to be better. But the world needs the values and principles that inhere in Judaism to be practiced. And, with a tip of the hat to Louis Armstrong, if practiced, what a wonderful world it could be.

---

12. Ibid.
13. Ibid., 50.

Bibliography

Aesop. *Aesop's Fables*. Translated by George F. Townsend. Garden City, NY: International Collectors Library, 1968.
The Age. "Is the World Getting Better?" *The Age* (Melbourne), November 22, 1924. www.newspapers.com/newspage/123105972.
Albom, Mitch. *Tuesdays with Morrie: An Old Man, a Young Man, and Life's Greatest Lesson*. New York: Doubleday, 1997.
Allen, Aviva. *The Organic Kosher Cookbook*. Toronto: Aviva Allen, 2007.
Allen, Wayne. "Jewish Law and Changing Times." In *Halakhah and the Modern Jew: Essays in Honor of Horace Bier*, edited by J. Leonard Romm and Leonard Levy, 1–8. Mt. Vernon, NY: Union for Traditional Conservative Judaism, 1989.
Anderson, Ronald E. *Human Suffering and Quality of Life: Conceptualizing Stories and Statistics*. Dordrecht: Springer, 2014.
Angel, Marc. "Reflections on Torah Education and Mis-Education." *Tradition* 41 (2008) 10–23.
Appiah, Kwame Anthony. *Experiment in Ethics*. Cambridge: Harvard University Press, 2008.
Ariel, David S. *What Do Jews Believe? The Jewish Faith Examined*. London: Rider, 1996.
Ariely, Dan. *The (Honest) Truth about Dishonesty: How We Lie to Everyone—Especially Ourselves*. London: HarperCollins, 2013.
Aristotle. *The Nicomachean Ethics*. Translated by David Ross. New York: Oxford, 1980.
Barry, Vincent. *The Dog Ate My Homework*. Kansas City: Andrews McMeal, 1998.
Baumeister, Roy F. *Evil: Inside Human Violence and Cruelty*. New York: Freeman, 2013.
Bayard, Pierre. *How to Talk about Books You Haven't Read*. New York: Bloomsbury, 2009.
Beauchamp, Tom L., and David Hume. *David Hume, An Enquiry concerning the Principles of Morals: A Critical Edition*. Oxford: Clarendon, 1998.
Berman, Louis A. *Vegetarianism and the Jewish Tradition*. New York: Ktav, 1982.
Bernfeld, Simon. *The Foundations of Jewish Ethics: Being Volume One of the Teachings of Judaism from the Sources*. New York: Ktav, 1968.
Bier, Horace. *Halakhah and the Modern Jew: Essays in Honor of Horace Bier*. Edited by Romm et al. Mount Vernon, NY: Union for Traditional Conservative Judaism, 1989.
Bloch, Abraham P. *A Book of Jewish Ethical Concepts: Biblical and Postbiblical*. New York: Ktav, 1984.

Bibliography

Bloom, Allan David. *The Closing of the American Mind*. New York: Simon and Schuster Paperbacks, 2012.
Bok, Sissela. *Lying: Moral Choice in Public and Private Life*. New York: Vintage, 1989.
Boon, Marcus. *In Praise of Copying*. Cambridge: Harvard University Press, 2010.
Bradley, Bill. *Values of the Game*. New York: Broadway, 2000.
Cahill, Thomas. *The Gift of the Jews*. New York: Nan A Talese, 1998.
Campbell, Jeremy. *The Liar's Tale: A History of Falsehood*. New York: Norton, 2002.
Carmell, Aryeh, and Cyril Domb. *Challenge: Torah Views on Science and Its Problems*. Jerusalem: Association of Orthodox Jewish Scientists, 2000.
Chamberlain, Wilt. *A View from Above*. New York: Penguin, 1991.
Cherry, Robert Allen. *Wilt: Larger than Life*. Chicago: Triumph, 2006.
Clifford, John. "Is the World Getting Better?" *Mercury Supplement*, June 12, 1897. http:www.trove.nla.gov.au/newspaper/article/9399054.
Cohen, Seymour J., trans. *Orchot Tzaddikim; The Ways of the Righteous*. Introduction by Seymour J. Cohen. Jerusalem: Feldheim, 1969.
Cohen, Shaye J. D. *From the Maccabees to the Mishnah*. Louisville: Westminster John Knox, 2014.
Cohn, Jacob. *The Royal Table: An Outline of the Dietary Laws of Israel*. Jerusalem: Feldheim, 1981.
Dawkins, Richard. *The God Delusion*. New York: Houghton Mifflin, 2006.
Diamond, Jared. "The Worst Mistake in the Human Race." *Discover*, May, 1987, 64–66.
Dresner, Samuel H., and Seymour Siegel. *The Jewish Dietary Laws: Their Meaning for Our Time; A Guide to Observance*. New York: Burning Bush, 1966.
Dubnow, Simon. *Jewish History: An Essay in the Philosophy of History*. English translation from German by J. Friedlander. German translation from original Russian by H. Szold. Philadelphia: JPS, 1903.
Eichhorn, David Max. *Conversion to Judaism*. New York: Ktav, 1966.
Eliade, Mircea. *Myth and Reality*. Translated from French by Willard R. Trask. New York: Harper & Row, 1963.
Elias, Norbert. *The Civilizing Process*. Oxford: Blackwell, 1978.
Ellis, Lee. "Religiosity and Criminality." *Journal of Research in Crime and Delinquency* 24 (1985) 215–32.
Ember, Carol R., and Melvin Ember. *Cultural Anthropology*. Boston: Pearson, 2015.
Feldman, Daniel Z. *The Right and the Good: Halakhah and Human Relations*. New York: Yashar, 2005.
Feldman, David M. *Health and Medicine in the Jewish Tradition: L'hayyim—to Life*. New York: Crossroad, 1986.
Feldman, Robert S. *The Liar in Your Life: The Way to Truthful Relationships*. New York: Twelve, 2010.
Fisher, Helen E. *Anatomy of Love: A Natural History of Mating, Marriage, and Why We Stray*. New York: Norton, 1993.
Fitzgerald, Francis Scott. *The Last Tycoon: An Unfinished Novel; The Great Gatsby*. Two books in one volume. New York: Scribner, 1951.
Fleg, Edmond, et al. *Why I Am a Jew*. Translated from French by Louise Waterman Wise. N.p.: Read, 2007.
Fox, Marvin. *Interpreting Maimonides: Studies in Methodology, Metaphysics, and Moral Philosophy*. Chicago: University of Chicago Press, 1990.
Frankfurt, Harry G. *On Truth*. New York: Knopf, 2013.

Bibliography

Freeman, Derek. *Margaret Mead and Samoa: The Making and Unmaking of an Anthropological Myth*. Ann Arbor: UMI Books on Demand, 2004.
Friedman, Susan Harris, et al. "Child Murder by Mothers: A Critical Analysis of the Current State of Knowledge and a Research Agenda." *American Journal of Psychiatry* 162 (2005) 1578–87.
Ganzfried, Solomon, ed. *Code of Jewish Law: A Compilation of Jewish Laws and Customs*. Translated by Hyman Goldin. New York: Hebrew Publishing, 1961.
Garrett, Neil, et al. "The Brain Adapts to Dishonesty." *Nature Neuroscience* 19 (2016) 1727–32.
Gersonides. *The Wars of the Lord*. Translated by Seymour Feldman. Philadelphia: Jewish Publication Society of America, 1984.
Gilbert, Martin. *In Ishmael's House: A History of Jews in Muslim Lands*. New Haven: Yale University Press, 2011.
———. *The Jews of Arab Lands: Their History in Maps*. Oxford: Merton College, 1975.
Ginzberg, Louis. *The Legends of the Jews*. Philadelphia: Jewish Publication Society of America, 1942.
———. *An Unknown Jewish Sect*. New York: Jewish Theological Seminary of America, 1976.
Girard, Rene, and Patrick Gregory. *Violence and the Sacred*. London: Bloomsbury, 2013.
Glover, Jonathan. *Humanity: A Moral History of the Twentieth Century*. New Haven: Yale University Press, 2012.
Goldhagen, Daniel Jonah. *Hitler's Willing Executioners*. London: Abacus, 1996.
Grunfeld, Dayan I. *The Jewish Dietary Laws*. London: Soncino, 1972.
Gurr, Ted Robert. "Historical Trends in Violent Crime: A Critical Review of the Evidence." *Crime and Justice* 3 (1981) 295–353.
Haag, Ernest Van den. *The Jewish Mystique*. New York: Stein and Day, 1977.
Harari, Yuval Noah. *Homo Deus*. N.p.: Vintage, 2017.
Harris, Robert A., and Vic Lockman. *The Plagiarism Handbook: Strategies for Preventing, Detecting, and Dealing with Plagiarism*. Los Angeles: Pyrczaj, 2001.
Harris, Sam. *The End of Faith: Religion, Terror and the Future of Reason*. London: Simon & Schuster, 2006.
Hertz, Joseph H. *The Pentateuch and Haftorahs: Hebrew Text, English Translation and Commentary*. London: Soncino, 1975.
Heschel, Abraham Joshua. *A Passion for Truth*. Woodstock, VT: Jewish Lights, 1995.
Heyn, Dalma. *The Erotic Silence of the American Wife*. New York: Plume, 1997.
Hirsch, Samson Raphael. *The Collected Writings*. New York: Feldheim, 1984.
———. *Horeb: A Philosophy of Jewish Laws and Observances*. Translated by I. Grunfeld. London: Soncino, 1981.
———. *The Nineteen Letters*. Edited and translated by Joseph Elias. Jerusalem: Feldheim, 1996.
Hobbes, Thomas, and C. B. Macpherson. *Leviathan*. London: Penguin, 2003.
Hoffman, David Tzvi. *Commentary of the Book of Genesis*. Translated from German to Hebrew and edited by Asher Wiesertiel. Bnei Brak, Israel: Nezach, 1969.
Howe, Irving. *A Treasury of Yiddish Stories*. Drawings by Ben Shahn. New York: Schocken, 1977.
Irons, Peter H. *The Courage of Their Convictions: Sixteen Americans Who Fought Their Way to the Supreme Court*. New York: Penguin, 1990.
Jacobs, Louis. *Principles of the Jewish Faith: An Analytical Study*. New York: Basic, 1964.

Bibliography

———. *What Does Judaism Say About . . . ?* New York: Quadrangle, 1973.
Josephus, Flavius. *The Works of Josephus.* Translated by William Whiston. Peabody: Hendrickson, 1993.
Karsh, Efraim. "The War against the Jews." *Israel Affairs* 18 (2012) 319–43.
Kass, Leon. *The Beginning of Wisdom: Reading Genesis.* Chicago: University of Chicago Press, 2006.
———. *The Hungry Soul: Eating and the Perfecting of Our Nature.* Chicago: University of Chicago Press, 1999.
Keeley, Lawrence H. *War Before Civilization.* New York: Oxford, 1996.
Keneally, Thomas. *Three Famines Starvation and Politics.* New York: Public Affairs, 2011.
Klein, Isaac. *A Guide to Jewish Religious Practice.* New York: Jewish Theological Seminary of America, 1979.
Kolitz, Zvi. *The Teacher: An Existential Approach to the Bible.* Northvale, NJ: Aronson, 1995.
Kook, Abraham Isaac. *Rav A. Y. Kook: Selected Letters.* Translated by Tzvi Feldman. Jerusalem: HaMakor, 1986.
Kupferberg, Herbert. *The Mendelssohns: Three Generations of Genius.* New York: Scribner, 1972.
Lackmann, Thomas. *Jewrassic Park: Wie Baut Man (k)ein Jüdisches Museum in Berlin.* Berlin: Philo, 2000.
Lawee, Eric Jay. *"Inheritance of the Fathers": Aspects of Isaac Abarbanel's Stance towards Tradition.* Ann Arbor, MI: U Microfilms International, 1998.
LeBlanc, Steven A., and Katherine E. Register. *Constant Battles: The Myth of the Peaceful, Noble Savage.* New York: St. Martin's Griffin, 2004.
Lewis, Bernard, and Mark R. Cohen. *The Jews of Islam.* Princeton: Princeton University Press, 2014.
Lieberman, Saul. *Hellenism and Jewish Palestine.* New York: Jewish Theological Seminary of America, 1962.
Lomborg, Bjørn. *Cool It: The Skeptical Environmentalist's Guide to Global Warming.* London: Marshall Cavendish, 2010.
Lubetski, Meir. *Saul Lieberman (1898–1983): Talmudic Scholar and Classicist.* Lewiston: Mellen, 2002.
Luzzatto, Moshe Hayyim. *The Way of God = Derech Hashem.* Edited by Aryeh Kaplan. Jerusalem: Feldheim, 1997.
Magee, Bryan. *Confessions of a Philosopher.* London: Phoenix, 2000.
Maimonides, Moses, et al. *Crisis and Leadership: Epistles.* Philadelphia: Jewish Publication Society of America, 1985.
———. *The Eight Chapters of Maimonides on Ethics.* Edited by Joseph I. Gorfinkle. New York: Ams, 1966.
———. *The Guide of the Perplexed.* Edited and translated by Shlomo Pines and Leo Strauss. Chicago: University of Chicago Press, 1963.
Marcus, Jacob Rader. *The Jew in the Medieval World.* New York: Atheneum, 1969.
Masson, Jeffrey Moussaieff. *Beasts: What Animals Can Teach Us Aabout the Origins of Good and Evil.* London: Bloomsbury, 2014.
Mendelssohn, Moses, and Alfred Jospe. *Jerusalem: And Other Writings.* New York: Schocken, 1969.
Midrash Rabbah. Translated and edited by H. Freedman and Maurice Simon. 10 vols. London: Soncino, 1983.

Milgram, Stanley, and Philip G. Zimbardo. *Obedience to Authority: An Experimental View*. London: Printer & Martin, 2013.
Milgrom, Jacob. *Leviticus*. New York: Doubleday, 1991.
Morinis, E. Alan. *Everyday Holiness: The Jewish Spiritual Path of Mussar*. Boston: Trumpeter, 2009.
Morris, Ian. *War! What Is It Good For? Conflict and the Progress of Civilization from Primates to Robots*. New York: Farrar, Straus and Giroux, 2014.
Mueller, John. *The Remnants of War*. Ithaca, NY: Cornell University Press, 2004.
Nance, John. *The Gentle Tasaday: A Stone Age People in the Philippine Rain Forest*. New York: Harcourt Brace Jovanovich, 1977.
Nelson, Maggie. *The Art of Cruelty: A Reckoning*. New York: Norton, 2011.
Novak, David. *Law and Theology in Judaism*. New York: Ktav, 1974.
Orwell, George. *1984*. Harlow, UK: Pearson Education, 2008.
Parker-Pope, Tara. *For Better: The Science of a Good Marriage*. New York: Dutton, 2010.
Passamaneck, Stephen M. *The Traditional Jewish Law of Sale: Shulhan Arukh, Hoshen Mishpat Chapters 189–240*. Cincinnati: Hebrew Union College Press, 1983.
Peck, M. Scott. *The Road Less Traveled*. New York: Simon & Schuster, 1978.
Peretz, Isaac Leib. *Three Gifts and Other Stories*. Translated by Henry Goodman. New York: Book League, 1947.
Philo. *The Essential Philo*. New York: Schocken, 1972.
Pinker, Steven. *The Better Angels of Our Nature: Why Violence Has Declined*. NY: Penguin, 2012.
Plato. *Complete Works*. Edited with intro and notes by John M. Cooper. Indianapolis: Hackett, 2009.
Potok, Chaim, et al. *The JPS Torah Commentary: The Traditional Hebrew Text with the New JPS Translation*. Philadelphia: Jewish Publication Society, 1989.
Roberts, Bruce B., et al. *Where in the World Is Integrity? The Challenge of Doing What Is Right*. Minneapolis: Augsburg, 2005.
Rousseau, Jean-Jacques. *Discourse on Inequality*. Rookhope, UK: Aziloth, 2013.
———. *The Social Contract*. Edited by Maurice Cranston. London: Penguin, 2004.
Rummel, Rudolph Joseph. *Death by Government*. New Brunswick: Transaction, 2008.
Rushkoff, Douglas. *Nothing Sacred: The Truth about Judaism*. New York: Three Rivers, 2004.
Russell, Bertrand. *Bertrand Russell: Autobiography*. New York: Routledge, 2000.
Safire, William. *Lend Me Your Ears: Great Speeches in History*. New York: Norton, 2004.
Safrai, Shemuel, ed. *The Literature of the Sages*. Assen, Netherlands: Van Gorcum, 1987.
Samenow, Stanton. *Inside the Criminal Mind*. N.p.: Random House USA, 2014.
Schochet, Elijah Judah, and Solomon Spiro. *Saul Lieberman: The Man and His Work*. New York: Jewish Theological Seminary of America, 2005.
Schoeck, Helmut. *Envy: A Theory of Social Behavior*. New York: Harcourt, Brace & World, 1970.
Schwartz, Richard H. *Judaism and Global Survival*. New York: Lantern, 2002.
Shereshevsky, Esra. *Rashi: The Man and His World*. Northvale, NJ: Aronson, 1996.
Shermer, Michael. "The Ignoble Savage." *Scientific American*, August 2003.
———. "Paradigms in Collison: Margaret Mead's Mistake and What It Has Done to Anthropology." *Skeptic* 5 (1997) 66–73.
———. *The Science of Good and Evil: Why People Cheat, Gossip, Care, Share, and Follow the Golden Rule*. New York: Times / Henry Holt, 2005.

Bibliography

Slifkin, Natan. *The Challenge of Creation*. Jerusalem: Gefen, 2012.
Smith, David Livingstone. *Less than Human: Why We Demean, Enslave, and Exterminate Others*. New York: St. Martin's Griffin, 2012.
Smith, Huston. *Why Religion Matters: The Fate of the Human Spirit in an Age of Disbelief*. San Francisco: Harper San Francisco, 2002.
Solzhenitsyn, Aleksandr, and Thomas P. Whitney. *The Gulag Archipelago*. New York: Harper & Row, 1975.
Stark, Rodney. *The Victory of Reason: How Christianity Led to Freedom, Capitalism, and Western Success*. New York: Random House Trade Paperbacks, 2006.
Steinberg, Milton. *As a Driven Leaf*. Springfield, NJ: Behrman House, 2015.
Stern, Lisë. *How to Keep Kosher: A Comprehensive Guide to Understanding Jewish Dietary Laws*. New York: William Morrow, 2004.
Stewart, James B. *Tangled Webs: How False Statements Are Undermining America: From Martha Stewart to Bernie Madoff*. New York: Penguin, 2012.
Stewart, Jon. *Naked Pictures of Famous People*. New York: Harper, 2001.
Stillman, Norman. *The Jews of Arab Lands*, Philadephia: JPS, 1979.
Tapper, Al, and Peter Robert Press. *A Minister, a Priest, and a Rabbi*. Kansas City: McMeel, 2000.
Telushkin, Joseph. *The Book of Jewish Values: A Day-by-Day Guide to Ethical Living*. New York: Bell Tower, 2000.
———. *A Code of Jewish Ethics*. New York: Bell Tower, 2006.
———. *Jewish Humor: What the Best Jewish Jokes Say about the Jews*. New York: Harper Collins, 2002.
Thomas, Elizabeth Marshall. *The Harmless People*. New York: Vintage, 1989.
Trivers, Robert. *The Folly of Fools: The Logic of Deceit and Self-Deception in Human Life*. New York: Basic, 2013.
Twenge, Jean M., and W. Keith Campbell. *The Narcissism Epidemic: Living in the Age of Entitlement*. New York: Atria Paperback, 2013.
Twersky, Isadore. *Introduction to the Code of Maimonides: Mishneh Torah*. New Haven: Yale University Press, 1980.
Vaillant, Maryse. *Men, Love, Fidelity*. Paris: Albin Michel, 2009.
Visser, Margaret. *The Gift of Thanks: The Roots, Persistence, and Paradoxical Meaning of a Social Ritual*. Toronto: HarperCollins Canada, 2009.
Wade, Nicholas. *Before the Dawn: Recovering the Lost History of Our Ancestors*. London: Duckworth, 2007.
White, Matthew. *Historical Atlas of the Twentieth Century*. N.p.: Matthew White, 2001.
Whitehead, Neil L. *Violence*. Oxford: James Currey, 2005.
Wiesel, Elie. *Sages and Dreamers: Biblical, Talmudic, and Hasidic Portraits and Legends*. New York: Simon & Schuster, 1993.
Williams, Jessica. *50 Facts That Should Change the World*. Thriplow, UK: Icon, 2007.
Wise, Michael Owen, et al. *The Dead Sea Scrolls: A New Translation*. San Francisco: HarperSanFrancisco, 2005.
Wright, Robert. *The Moral Animal: Why We Are, the Way We Are; The New Science of Evolutionary Psychology*. New York: Vintage, 1995.
Zevin, Shelomoh Yosef. *A Treasury of Chassidic Tales*. New York: Mesorah, 2003.
Zimbardo, Philip G., and Michael R. Leippe. *The Psychology of Attitude Change and Social Influence*. New York: McGraw-Hill, 1991.

Author Index

Abells, Dr. Yoel, 97
Aesop, 153
Albom, Mitch, 51–52, 168
Allen, Aviva, 55n24
Allen, Wayne, 141n22
Anderson, Dr. Ronald E., 3
Andresen, Trond, 8
Angel, Marc, 140n20
Appiah, Kwame Anthony, 161
Ariel, David, 154
Ariely, Dan, 166
Aristotle, 4, 5

Baeck, Leo, 115
Barry, Vincent, 125
Barondes, Samuel, 39n37
Bassonni, M. Cherif, 13
Baumeister, Roy F., 15
Bayard, Pierre, 29
Bell, Robert Mack, 124
Ben Hofni, Rabbi Samuel, 140
Ben Moses, Rabbi Abraham, 140
Berman, Louis A., 55n24
Berreby, David, 105n19
Bloch, Abraham, 46n10, 160
Bloom, Allan, 67n40, 167
Bok, Sisela, 21n17
Boon, Marcus, 37
Bradley, Bill, 55n25
Browning, Christopher R., 124, 125
Brzezinski, Zbigniew, 13

Cahill, Thomas, 8n10
Campbell, W. Keith, 20
Carmell, Aryeh, 142n24
Chamberlain, Wilt, 62
Cherry, Robert, 63n26
Clifford, John, Reverend 1
Cohen, Seymour J., 162n28
Cohen, Shaye J. D., 48n15
Cohn, Jacob, 55n24

Dawkins, Richard, 146, 154–58
Diamond, Jared, 11n3
Dick, Philip K., 116
Dresner, Samuel, 55n24
Drori, Amir, 74n56
Dubnow, Simon, 115n10

Eichhorn, David Max, 49n15
Eliade, Mircea, 154
Elias, Norbert, 18n10
Ellis, Lee, 7n6
Ember, Carol, 11
Emden, Rabbi Jacob, 49

Feldman, David M., 82n70, 85n75
Feldman, Daniel Z., 44n7
Fisher, Helen, 102
Fitzgerald, F. Scott, 163n30
Flavius, Josephus, 45
Fleg, Edmund, 75, 75n58
Fox, Marvin, 138n17

Author Index

Frankfurt, Harry G., 25
Freeman, Derek, 12
Friedman, Susan Hatters, et al, 18n11
Fulford, Robert, 37n35

Gandhi, Mohandas K., 158–59
Ganzfried, Solomon, 70n44
Garret, N., 25
Gilbert, Martin, 80n65
Ginzberg, Louis, 64n38, 73n56, 108n21, 119n15
Girard, Rene, 15n8
Glover, Jonathan, 164–65
Goldhagen, Daniel, 159
Goldin, Hyman, 70n44
Gorfinkle, Joseph, 138n17
Grundfeld, I., 55n24
Gurr, Ted Robert, 17n10

Haag, Ernst van den, 134
Halevi, Rabbi David, 55n24, 166n5
Halkin, A., 138n7
Harari, Yuval, 13n7
Harris, Sam, 147
Haynes, Reverend Carlyle B., 4
Healey, David, 38n37
Heschel, Rabbi Abraham Joshua, 132n8, 146
Hertz, J. H., Rabbi Dr., 155
Heyn, Dalma, 102
Hircsh, Samson Raphael, 143, 149, 166n5
Hobbes, Thomas, 5, 11n3
Hoffman, David Tzvi, 144
Howe, Irving, 99
Hume, David, 100, 161

Irons, Peter, 123n13

Jacobs, Louis, 50n17, 67n39, 71n51, 116n11, 150n5
Jaffree, Ishmael, 124
Jerusalem, Wilhelm, 76
Josephus. *See* Flavius, Josephus.

Kafih, Y., 138n17
Karsh, Efraim, 8n9

Kass, Leon, 54, 149
Keeley, 11n3
Keneally, Thomas, 19n13
Klein, Isaac, 85n75
Kolitz, Zvi, 122n19
Kook, Abraham Isaac, 144
Koss, Mary, 62
Kotzk, Rabbi Mendel of, 122, 132
Kupferberg, Herbert, 113–15

Lackmann, Thomas, 7
Landau, Rabbi Ezekiel, 81n78
Lawee, Eric, 137n16
Leblanc, Steven A., 11
Lerner, M. B., 134n12
Levin, M., 140n21
Lewis, Bernard, 80n65
Lieberman, Saul, 60n33
Lipschitz, Israel, 141–43
Lomborg, Bjorn, 35
Lubetski, Meir, 60n33
Luzzatto, Moses Chaim, 72, 73n53

Magee, Brian, 7
Maimonides, 51, 59n33, 69, 70n46, 94, 94n6, 97, 98, 104, 104n18, 117, 118, 134, 138–40, 147, 150, 151, 152
Marcus, Jacob R., 85n76
Masson, Jeffrey Moussaieff, 11n3
Milgram, Stanley, 14, 15n8
Milgrom, Jacob, 47n12
Morinis, Alan, 42n3, 44
Morris, Ian, 13n7
Moses ben Maimon, Rabbi. *See* Maimonides
Mueller, John, 2

Nadel, Gedaliah, 144
Nance, John, 12n6
Nelson, Maggie, 15n8
Novak, David, 81n68

Orwell, George, 25n22

Parker-Pope, Tara, 104
Peck, M. Scott, 53, 56

Author Index

Peretz, I. L., 82n71, 99
Phillips, J., 38n37
Philo, 77–78, 152
Pines, Shlomo, 139n17
Pinker, Steven, 18n10
Prager, Dennis, 45

Roberts, Bruce B. *et al*, 129
Rousseau, Jean-Jacques, 11n2
Rummel, Rudolph, 13
Rushkoff, Douglas, 8

Sa'adiah Gaon, 152n9
Safire, William, 168n10
Safrai, Shmuel. *See* Lerner, M. B.
Samenow, Stanton E., 165
Savage, Dan, 102–3
Schochet, Elijah J., 60n33
Schoeck, Helmut, 18n10
Schwartz, Richard H., 78n64
Shereshevsky, Esra 136n14
Shermer, Michael, 11n3, 12n5
Slifkin, Natan, 144
Smith, David Livingstone, 104
Smith, Huston, 147n2
Solzhenitsyn, Alexander, 15
Spiro, Solomon, 60n33
Stark, Freya, 8n9
Stark, Rodney, 7
Steinberg, Milton, 51n18
Stern, Lisë, 55n24

Stewart, James B., 21n17
Stewart, John, 7
Stillman, Norman, 80n65

Tapper, Al, 112
Taylor, Phil, 128
Telushkin, Joseph, 74n57, 132n7, 135n13
Thomas, Elizabeth, 12n6
Trivers, Robert, 22
Twain, Mark, 39
Twenge, Jean M., 20
Twersky, Isadore, 138n17

Vaillant, Maryse, 28
Visser, Margaret, 47n10

Wade, Nicholas, 12
White, Matthew, 13
Whitehead, Neil, 18n10
Wiesel, Elie, 77
Williams, Jessica, 39
Wise, Michael, *et al*, 74n56
Wright, Robert, 103
Wolfe, Alan, 8n10
Wurtzel, Elizabeth, 38n37

Yochelson, Dr. Samuel, 165

Zevin, Shelomoh Yosef, 76n59
Zimbardo, Philip G., 14, 15n8

Subject Index

Aaron, 77n62
Abarbanel, Don Isaac, 137
Abbott and Costello, 45
Abraham, 70, 71n47, 76, 88, 116, 117, 118–20, 129, 156
Abramoff, Jack, 6
accepting blame, 66
action, 113–18
Adam and Eve, 64, 88
adermatoglyphia, 61
Albo, Rabbi Joseph, 18n10
Amalekites, 90
Ammonites and Moabites, 90
Anthropomorphism, 150
apathy, 95
Apocrypha, 68
aravot, 48
arete, ix
Armstrong, Louis, 169
art, interpretation of, 121
Ashley-Madison, 27
astrology, 67
atheists, 166n6
Atlantis, 153–54
atrocitologists, 13
audacity, 118–26, 169

basketball, 51–52, 55n25, 62–63
Bellow, Saul, 167

Ben Asher, Rabbi Jacob, 166n4
Ben Hyrcanus, Rabbi Eliezer, 120–21
Ben Meir, Rabbi Samuel, 49
Ben Nahman, Rabbi Moses. *See* Nahmanides
Ben Porat, Eliyahu, 95
Ben Sira, 51
Berditchev, Rabbi Levi Isaac of, 107
Bergman, Rabbi Bernard, 6
Bernheim, Rabbi Gilles, 6
Bible
    as a kind of instruction manual, 153–54
    as unerring word of God, 163
    how to read, 146–63
    read non-literally, 144, 151, 153
    what it is not, 147
Birnbaum, Philip, 150n5
"blackening the mice", 35
Blacks, 169
blood avenger, 160
blood feud, 160
bloodletting, 141
Boesky, Ivan, 6
Bonfils, Rabbi Jacob ben Eliezer, 50n17
Bratzlav, Rabbi Nahman of, 164
Brecht, Bertolt, 32n31
Brown, General George S., 8n9
Bryan, William Jennings, 147–48

Subject Index

Cacnio, Camille, 167
Cain, 148
capital punishment, 86
Carnegie Hall, 169
Carter, Jimmy, 116
Castro, Fidel, 66
Catholics, 123, 169
censorship, 49, 50n17
Chamberlain, Wilt, 62–63
changing times, concept of, 140
Chajes, Rabbi Tzvi Hirsch, 143
character, standards for determining, 61
charitableness, 72, 94
Chelm, Wise Men of, ix
Cheating, 27–31
    on exams, 33–34, 38
    in chess, 29
Chelbat, Chakir, 66
child labor, 16–17, 39n38
Christianity, 49, 49n16, 100, 114, 115
Circumcision, 73
Clinton, Bill, 112
Clinton, Hillary, 66
coarse language, 104
commandments, 43
    traditional number of 613, 149
community, overuse of term, 105
complaining, 111–12
confirmation bias, 3
conflict, how to avoid, 53
conversion to Judaism, 48
creation, story of, implications, 52, 84, 118
crime, 17–18
cruelty, sometimes an asset, 162
culture of complaint, 111

David, 65–66, 96, 120, 160
Darwin, Charles, 141, 143
Day of Atonement, 69, 74, 77, 82, 83, 169
deception, 31–32, 36–38
    has become justifiable and acceptable, 38
de Coubertin, Pierre, Baron, 149
deflecting blame, 66–68
de Gaulle, Charles, 8n9

democracy
    not expanding, 2
Didon, Henri Martine, Father, 149
dietary laws. *See* Kashrut
dinosaurs, 142
divorce, 1, 102, 104n17
doctors, Jews becoming, 85
"dogging", 20
drives, human, 53–54
Dryden, John, 11n2
duties, 168

ecology, Jewish concern for, 41
Eight Degrees of Charity, 94n6
eisegesis, 135
Eliezer, 88–89
Elijah the Prophet, 121–22
Elisha ben Abuya, 51
empathy, 74–75, 169
Enterpise, 169
environmental protection, 78
Epperson, Susan, 124
Essenes and *Qumran*, 73
Esther, 134
ethnic cleansing, 159
Etrog, 48
evolution, 141–45
exegesis, 135

fallacy of equivocation, 4
"false memoirs", 31
Feldman, Moses J., 133
fidelity, marital, 103, 163
Finch, Atticus, 129
Fortas, Abe, 124
four species, 48
Friends, 165
funeral procession, yields to wedding procession, 80

Garden of Eden, 58, 64–65, 78, 83
genocide, 157, 159
Genovese, Kitty, 91
Gershwin, George, 151
Gersonides (Rabbi Levi ben Gershon), 152
Get Smart, 152

ghetto, 80
Gibeonites, 131
gladiatorial combat, 81, 90–91
God
    image of, 151
    morality of, 156–57
    non-corporeality of, 150
Goliath, 120
goodness, 6, 166
    for citizens, 94
Good Samaritan Laws, 93
Gordis, Robert, 69n43
gratification, delayed, 55–56, 57
gratitude, 46
Green, A. C., 63–64
Guggenheim, Fromer, 114

habit, habituation, 5, 55n24
    good habits secured through proper eating, 54
hadas, 48
halakhah, origin and meaning of term, 60n33
Hanukkah, 109
happiness, more elusive than ever, 38–39
Hatfields and McCoys, 160
Hatikvah, 107
Hazik, Mohn Asyraf, 87
Hebrew, meaning of word, 119
helpfulness, 87–101, 169
hermeneutics, 89
Henry, Jacob, 122
heroes, not perfect, 60–61
Hippocratic Oath, 97–98
Hirabayashi, Gordon, 123
Hitler, Adolf, 110, 125, 158
holiness, 101–5, 169
    holy community, 105
honesty, 132, 137
Honi, 56
hopefulness, 106–12, 169
    not equivalent to optimism, 110
House of Avtinas, 94n7
human beings, purpose from creation, 97
humane care, 97

humor, 110–11
hunger, 2
hunting, 81

Ibn Adret, Rabbi Solomon, 153
Ibn Ezra, Rabbi Abraham, 50
image of God, 43
Imber, Naftali Herz, 107
infant mortality, 1
infidelity, 27–28, 102–3, 116
    ascribed to a biological cause, 28
Inherit the Wind, 147–48
integrity, 127–45, 169
intellectual integrity, 136, 137, 138, 141, 145
Isaac, binding of, 157
Israel, State of, 79, 131, 132

Jacob, 129
Jephthah, 157
Jewish Star (Shield of David), 99
Jews
    becoming doctors, 85
    not all are ethical, 6
Jonah, 76
Joseph, 60–61
Joshua, 131
Judaism, 6
    as a prescription for an ailing world, 5–6
    critics of, 7–8
    does not fear advances in science, 143
    ecology, view on, 41
    evolution, position on, 141–45
    medical advances, position on, 140–41
    predicated on duties, not rights, 167
    uniqueness of, 9
    values of, 112, 169
justice, 132n5

Kant, Immanuel 98, 114, 159
Karo, Rabbi Joseph, 70n46, 93n5, 97n11, 131
Kashrut, 53–55
kavod ha-briyot, 42

Subject Index

Kierkegaard, Søren, 156
kindness, 100
Knight Jr., Rodney, 26

Laban, 129
Lavater, Johann Casper, 114
leap of faith, 156
lex talionis, 162
lies and lying, 21–25, 166
    tolerance of, 24
    when permitted, 132n5
life
    preservation of, 82
    sanctity of, 83
    takes precedence over death, 80
life expectancy, 1
limits, 57–60, 150
Lincoln, Abraham, 168
Lot, 155
Lulav, 48

Madoff, Bernie, 6
martyrdom, 85
Matos, Angel, 66
Mazal Tov, meaning, 67
medical advances, Jewish position on, 140–41
mellah, 80
Mendelssohn, Moses, 113–15
Merkavah tank, 79–80
Messiah, 84
mezuzah, purpose of, 165–66
Midianites, 157, 160, 161
    and Canaanites, 161
Moore, G. E., 132
Mordechai, 134
Morsadegh, Ciamak, 98
Moses, 116, 120, 128, 129, 130n3, 147, 148, 151, 159
    and Aaron, 161
Mozart, 102
Mugabe, Robert, 66
murder
    declining homicide rates, 2
myth, meaning of, 154

Nader, Ralph, 66
Nahmanides, 101
Nathan, 65–66
neutron bomb, 79–80
Nineveh, 96, 97
Noah, 148, 155
Nürenberg Trials, 124

Olympic games, 66, 149
organ transplants, 8

Parrot, Andrea, 61
Passover, 141
    Seder, 96–97, 108
peace, 132n5
Peart, Neil, 167
Peck, Gregory, 129
people, four kinds of, 59
Phidias, 127
Physician's Prayer, 97
plagiarism, 32–33, 34, 35
Plato, 10n2, 153
Playboy, 116
Pope Gregory XIII, 14
pornography, 101
Poverty, 2, 19
    poor man's offering, 47
Prager, Dennis, 45
Prayer and prayers, 45, 71, 93
    petitionary prayer has value, 152
prescription, 5, 6
primogeniture, 72n52
Protestants, 169
Puff the Magic Dragon, 135

Quigley, Carol, 112

rationality, 79
    at work in Maimonides, 138n17
RaShI, 101, 117n12, 136–37, 140, 161n26
Rebecca, 89–90
religions
    worthiness of, 8
remission of debts, 71n49
respect, 41–53, 72

Subject Index

responsibility, 64–79, 141, 169
    differs from rights 78
restraint, 53–64, 166, 169
reverence for life, 79–86, 169
Rich, Mark, 6
ritual,
    as a way of developing good habits, 55n24
    matters of health more important, 82n70
Russell, Bertrand, 132
Rwandan genocide, 161

Sabata, Hannah, 26
Sabbath, 81–82, 118
Salanter, Rabbi Israel, 42
sale, Jewish law of, 130–31
Sales, Nykesha, 128
Saramago, Jose, 7
Satan, 68
Saul, 162
Schapiro, Adina, 110
Schoenfeld, Nathan, 124
Schwadron, Sholom Mordechai, 143
Scopes Trial, 147
Sefer Ha-hinukh, 73, 160
self-control, 61, 63
sexual relations, non-consensual, 61–6
Shakespeare, William, 67, 146
Shawshank Redemption, 106
Shimon ben Shetah, 129
Simpsons, Homer and Bart, 66
slavery, 16
sock-puppeting, 33
Sodom, 129, 155
Spielberg, Steven, 116
Sports Illustrated, 128
Sprecher, Eli, 61
Statue of Liberty, 97
"Storekeeper's Law", 45
study, paramount in Judaism, 133
suffering
    in decline, 3
    increasing, 3
suicide, 39
suicide bombing, 86
Sukkot, 47

survivalism, 167
Swift, Jonathan, 39

tabernacle, 47, 129n2
Tabernacles, 47
Taylor, Jack, 128
Ten Commandments, 43, 166n6
theft, 25–27
Timaeus, 153–54
To Kill a Mockingbird, 129
Todd, Amanda, 21
Torah
    cannot be read literally, 151
    origin of word, 150
torture, 16
Tosafists, 129, 140, 141n22
Tree of Knowledge, 83
Trump, Donald, 24–25
truth, 132n5, 132n7, 153
Turetzsky, Arnold, 106–7
Twinkies Defense, 66
tzedakah, not charity, 94

unburdening an overloaded animal, 94
Urdangen, Jeffrey, 92
Uzzah, 96

value, ix
Vancouver, riot of 2011, 20
vegetarianism, 83–84
violence, 12, 13n7, 15, 21, 155, 156
    can be redirected, 18n10
    not attributable to poverty alone, 21
    still pervasive, 18n10
volunteerism, 96

warfare
    current, 12
    in 20th century, 12–13
    not in decline, 2
    only days without war, 14
    prophesied to end, 159n23
    universal among primitives, 11–12
wedding procession, precedence over funeral procession, 80
White, Dan, 66
will power, 55

Subject Index

Wilson, Flip, 68
windows, in synagogues, 70
Woods, Tiger 28
Word, Deletha, 91–92
worth over birth, 72n52

Yokheved, 108

Ancient Documents Index

SCRIPTURE

Genesis

1:4	58n30
1:5	50
1:11–12	58n30
1:16	58n30
1:25	58n30
2:3	118
2:10	58n31
2:15	78
2:16	41n1
2:18	93
3:8–13	65
4:7	68
4:14	148
4:17	148
5:1	43
9:3	84n73, 151
9:6	70n44
14	71n47
14:3	129
14:13	119
18:27	119
19:36–38	90n3
20:12	156
21:17	117
24	88
24:55	90n2
24:59	90n2
24:64	90n2
25:20	89n1
25:34	54
28:5	137
31:38	129
32:29	120
35:13	137
38:7	151
39:7	60n34
39:8–9	129

Exodus

2:11–14	71n48
6:12	76n59
9:3	151
12:22–23	166n4
15:1	137
16:29	59n33
17:8	90n3
21:29	162
20:22	159
22:8	137
23:3	132n5
23:5	45, n7
23:6	132n5

Exodus (continued)

23:7	132n5
23:8	132n5
24:10	151
30:22	147
31:13	82n70
31:16	82n70
36:6	96n9
38:21	129
40	129n2

Leviticus

1:17	47
13:4	137
16:6	77n62
16:17	77n62
18:4	82
18:5	82n70, 116
19:2	101
19:9	125n23
19:16	92
19:18	43
23:22	125n23
27:3	137

Numbers

2:10	161
3:29	161
9:14	72n52
11:1	151
15:15	72n52
15:37–41	72n51
16:1	161
25:6	160
31	160
35:5	59n33
35:11	160
35:12	160
35:19	160
35:31	162

Deuteronomy

1:2	50n17
5:16	41n2
6:4–9	71n51
6:9	165
7:2	159
11:13–21	71n51
11:15	78
11:20	165
15:1	71n49
16:19	132n5
19:14	132n5
20:10	159
20:16	159
20:19	41
21:7	95
21:15	72n52
21:18	161
21:23	45n7
22:1	94
22:2	95
22:7	41n2
22:8	83
23:4–5	90, 90n3
25:13–16	132n5
25:18	90n3
30:9	85
33:24	137

Joshua

9	131

Judges

19	155

2 Samuel

6	96n10
12:1–4	65
12:13	66

1 Kings

18:27	111

2 Kings

2:11	122n17
12:7	130

Isaiah

2:4	159n23
9:16	104n18
11:6–10	84n73

Jeremiah

5:22	122
7:3	116

Micah

4:34	159n23

Malachi

2:10	43

Psalms

8:5–6	10
15:4	132
37:27	116
89	122
99:104	132n5
99:128	132n5
99:163	132n5

Proverbs

12:10	83
12:29	132n5
14:10	82

Esther

2:2	134

Job

1:7	68
13:13, 15	43, 108n20

Ezra

4:13	60n33

1 Chronicles

28:8	160n24

RABBINIC WRITINGS

Mishnah

Pe'ah

4:1	125n24

Shabbat

7:2	134n12

Yoma

8:7	83n72

Mo'ed Katan

1:6	48n14

Ancient Documents Index

Bava Kama

1:1	134n12
8:7	69n44

Bava Metzia

4:10	44n7

Sanhedrin

4:5	84n74

Makkot

1:10	86n77

Avot

1:14	70n44
1:17	116n11
1:18	132n5
2:21	112n4
4:10	49n16
4:23	44n7
6:6	135

Babylonian Talmud

Berakhot

4a	137n15
10a	107n20; 109

Shabbat

21b	109
146a	67n41

Eruvin

65b	59n33; 130

Pesahim

3a–b	104n18

Sheqalim

14a	94n7

Yoma

83a	82
85a–b	82n70; 136n14

Betzah

25b	134n14

Ta'anit

7a	xi
23a	56n28

Megilah

7a	134n11
15a	134n11

Ketubot

8b	104n18
17a	132n5

Nedarim

56b	59n33

Sotah

32b	45n8
45b	96n8

Ancient Documents Index

Gitin

60a	50n17
61a	97n12

Kiddushin

30b	68n42
40a	68n42
40b	133n9

Bava Kama

15a	83
83b	163n29
91b	69n44

Bava Metzia

44a	130
58b	44n7; 45n9
59b	121n16

Bava Batra

8b	130n3
15a	152n8
16a	68n42

Jerusalem Talmud

Berakhot

45a	73n55

Midrash

Ecclesiastes Rabbah

7:28	41n1, 162n28

Leviticus Rabbah

30:12	48n13

Sanhedrin

27b	71n50
31b	122n18
32b	45n8
40a	53n20
73a	92n4
92a	132n5

Makkot

23b	43n4

Shevu'ot

39a	71n50

Avodah Zarah

17a	69
18b	81n67

Hullin

10a	82n70

Niddah

67a	136n14

Nedarim

9:4	43n4

Sifre Deuteronomy

3:25	47n10
76	43n4

Yalkut Shimoni, Judges

4:4	43n5, 44n6

www.ingramcontent.com/pod-product-compliance
Lightning Source LLC
Chambersburg PA
CBHW050759160426
43192CB00010B/1577